D0769002

DATE DUE

DEMCO 38-296

Bukharin's Theory of Equilibrium

Bukharin's Theory of Equilibrium

A DEFENCE OF *HISTORICAL MATERIALISM*

Kenneth J. Tarbuck

Riverside Community College PLUTO ▲▲ PRESS

First published 1989 by Pluto Press
11–21 Northdown Street
London N1 9BN

Distributed in the USA by Unwin Hyman Inc.
8 Winchester Place, Winchester
MA 01890, USA

Typesetting: Ransom Electronic Publishing,
Woburn Sands, Bucks

Printed in Hungary by Interpress

British Library Cataloguing in Publication Data

Tarbuck, Kenneth J.
  Bukharin's theory of equilibrium
  1. Soviet Union. Socialism. Role of
  Bukharin, N. (Nikolai), 1911 – ca. 1930
  I. Title
  335'.0092'4

  ISBN 0–7453–0292–0

Contents

Preface   vii
Introduction   1

1 Historical Materialism and the Theory of
   Equilibrium   6
2 The Legend and Reality: Bukharin's Critics   34
3 Equilibrium and Economic Growth   54
4 Equilibrium and Crisis Theory   72
5 War Communism and the New Economic Policy   84
6 Unproductive Consumption and Expanded Negative
   Reproduction   113
7 The Laws of the Transition Period: Bukharin
   versus Preobrazhensky   126
8 The Notes of An Economist: Optimum versus
   Maximum Investment   145
9 Conclusions   161

Appendix: Bukharin and the Acceleration of Capital   171
Notes and References   177
Bibliography   189
Name Index   195
Subject Index   196

To the memory of Sam Gordon (1910--82),
a steadfast friend whose evergreen spirit lives on.
He helped keep alive critical Marxism
during the dark days of Stalinism, Fascism and McCarthyism.

Preface

On the night of 15 March 1938 Nikolai Bukharin was taken to the cellars of the Lubyanka prison in Moscow and shot in the base of the skull. Officially it was an execution, in reality it was a murder. Thus died, a few months before his fiftieth birthday, one of Lenin's most devoted companions. Bukharin, who had led the Bolshevik uprising in Moscow in 1917, was a brilliant orator and writer and a gifted Marxist theorist. He was also a man of great personal charm, warm hearted and a protector of the oppressed before he too was swept up to become a victim of the madness that Stalin unleashed with the murder of Kirov in 1936.

Why was such a man shot? The official reason given at the time was that he was the co-author of a gigantic and monstrous plot – along with most of those who had led the revolution, including Trotsky – to overthrow the very regime he had helped to create. Moreover, this plot was allegedly to restore capitalism, something that Bukharin and all the defendants at the obscene Moscow 'trials' had fought against all their adult lives. The enormity of the accusations, the clearly ludicrous charges that were piled up in the court, should have been met with derision. The nightmarish farce played out in the courtroom, with all the accused confessing with varying degrees of alacrity to all the preposterous charges should have alerted the world to the fantasies being enacted in Moscow at that time. Instead most of the world accepted these charades at face value. Yet no independent witnesses were ever produced at Bukharin's, or any other of the Moscow trials. All the evidence rested upon the confessions of the accused. Bukharin himself pointed to this when he drew the parallel with the medieval judicial practices of the Holy Office! Yet for many, many years these proceedings were accepted as true trials.

Now, 50 years after his murder, Bukharin and all those who actually stood in the dock with him, have been declared innocent of all the charges by the Supreme Court of the Soviet Union. The filth of history is beginning to be swept from Bukharin's head as he pleaded for in a letter given to his wife a few days before his death.

Why now? After all it is over 25 years since Khrushchev declared that Bukharin had not been a spy. The truth of the matter is that the forces of inertia and reaction have been too strong until now. It has taken the policies of Glasnost and Perestroika of Gorbachev to reveal some of the most murky corners of Soviet history inside that country to the Soviet peoples themselves; information that has been common currency elsewhere for decades. With the judicial rehabilitation of Bukharin and his co-defendants one of the last ties with the old Stalinist past has been broken and it will never again be possible to return to the lies and slander that passed for history about these people for so long. That is not to say that Gorbachev's policies are assured of success, but like all sea-changes on a social scale reaction can never wholly return to the status-quo even if it gains the upper hand.

But what is the particular significance of Bukharin? Even allowing for the wave of openness that is rolling over Soviet society, why should Gorbachev and his allies take time out to go over 50-year-old history? The truth of the matter is that the Soviet economy is in a profound crisis, one that has rumbled on for many years and has now become acute. The old Stalinist model of a centrally directed command system has obviously run out of steam and is in danger of bringing the whole economy to a grinding halt. The system that produces more defective goods than saleable ones cannot go on for much longer. As will be shown in this book, Bukharin was the theoretician of the New Economic Policy of the Soviet 1920s. And once more a new economic policy is being formulated in the Soviet Union. Since Bukharin was quite clearly seen in the 1920s as being a possible successor to Lenin it is obvious that Gorbachev needs to cloak his own campaign for revitalising the economy with an aura of Leninist respectability via the ideas of Bukharin. The NEP period in the Soviet Union can be truly said to be one of a mixed economy, i.e., one of planning and ownership of the commanding heights by the state but running in tandem with large areas of private enterprise, in agriculture, industry and trade. And there can be little doubt that something along these lines is being planned now. Just what form it will take it is not possible to say at present, but the rehabilitation of some of the basic ideas of Bukharin can be seen as a prelude to a return of the market and private enterprise to some degree in the Soviet Union, possibly with the introduction of foreign capital once more to help modernise the Soviet economy. As to whether Bukharin's ideas will be implemented in reality or merely used to cover some quite different policies remains to be seen. No one should expect the Soviet Union to return to 1920s – they are long since gone along with the millions of peasants who died during the forced collectivisation of Stalinism. What we may expect, however, is that Bukharin will be given pride of place in any rewriting of Soviet economic history if Gorbachev wins his battles against the entrenched bureaucracy. Bukharin will be used to legitimise the final dismantling of Stalin's structures that lingered on until well after the death of Brezhnev, but it will require great determination and tenacity to overcome the institutionalised inertia that pervades Soviet life. Bukharin may or may not prove to be a salutary remedy in the field of ideas; it depends who uses them and how. But of one thing we may be sure, Bukharin's ideas on equilibrium and proportionality will find many supporters in the Soviet Union as the struggle for restructuring economic and political life is engaged in in earnest.

To understand fully the significance of certain aspects of the struggles going on inside the Soviet Union it is necessary to come to terms with Bukharin's basic ideas. I hope this book enables readers to make up their own minds on these issues. Although this book deals, in the main, with abstract theories, the reader would do well to remember that all such are born of struggle in the real world. Behind the rejection of Bukharin's apparently mild prescriptions on economic and political issues in 1928–9 lay waiting hunger and death for millions of Soviet citizens. The contemptuous dismissal of Bukharin by Stalin meant the demise of hope for many years to come for the whole of Soviet society, even though the worst was not yet then revealed. The traumas of Stalin's rule are only now beginning to be overcome as his heirs die or are pushed aside. The rehabilitation of Bukharin is a part of that process.

Introduction

People die, fade from the memory and in time even those small traces they leave are expunged from the records to make room for those that follow. Ideas, however, are much harder to remove from history; they seem to acquire a life of their own, and no matter how hard they are stamped upon somehow leave their seed scattered in hidden corners to bloom again when the time is propitious. Theories and ideas are generated by people and one such person is Nikolai Bukharin. His creativity in the field of ideas has meant that he has not been forgotten, since despite all attempts his ideas have lingered on, to once more excite speculation. But of all his ideas which are the most enduring? To some extent that is still a matter of debate, but what is certain is that unless the enquirer comes to grips with his theory of equilibrium they will be floundering. This is why a study of Bukharin's theory of equilibrium is both necessary and rewarding.

The purpose of this work, then, is to examine N.I. Bukharin's theory of equilibrium and to arrive at some conclusions regarding its consistency and compatibility with Marxism. This means that, although the writings under consideration mainly derive from the decade 1920–9, the work does not deal in a systematic manner with all the controversies appertaining to the Soviet industrialisation debate of that decade. I have impinged upon that debate only for the purpose of illustrating Bukharin's use of his theory of equilibrium. The balance of this work may therefore appear to some to be somewhat skewed, insofar as many of the actors in the dramas of the Soviet 1920s either do not appear or are only mentioned in passing. This is quite deliberate, since this book does not aspire to be a history of the Soviet industrialisation debate nor even a complete intellectual biography of Bukharin. On the contrary its focus is much more restricted in scope, since it attempts to examine in depth some of the most fundamental and enduring ideas which animated Bukharin's intellectual and political activity.

In the process I demonstrate that much of the criticism directed against Bukharin on questions of basic theory is misplaced.

Furthermore I shall demonstrate that there can be no doubt that Bukharin's contribution to Marxist theory is such that it should be required study for those who wish to understand the development of Marxism in the first third of this century.

If one examines two of Bukharin's major writings, *The Economics of the Transition Period* and the *Notes of An Economist*, written in 1920 and 1928 respectively, the first impression is of a considerable change of position. The first text is redolent with apocalyptic phrases, whilst the second is noteworthy for its cautious, one might even say pragmatic, tone. The change is certainly true as far as policy prescriptions are concerned. However, when one examines the underlying themes of these two works there emerges a certain consistency and continuity.

This underlying consistency is given its clearest expression in Bukharin's seminal work *Historical Materialism*, written in 1921. In that book Bukharin expounded his theory of equilibrium as applied to society as a whole, and to particular aspects of the social process. Using the method of historical materialism Bukharin attempted to show that, despite continual disturbances and contradictions, all social formations have a tendency towards equilibrium. When this equilibrium is disturbed it must be re-established, even though sometimes with a different fulcrum point, for the particular formation or society to survive. Should this equilibrium not be restored then it is possible for catastrophe to overtake the social formation, which will result in its destruction. This is the underlying theme which colours Bukharin's approach to social, political and economic questions.

In *The Economics of the Transition Period* Bukharin focused upon the disequilibrium of revolution, drawing upon his experiences in Russia. After 1921 he seems to have concluded that the New Economic Policy (NEP) of that year had established a new equilibrium, albeit a fragile one, which could only survive if it were subjected to changes of a slow, evolutionary nature. The *Notes of An Economist* are the end result of a continual development of the ideas of equilibrium, and its allied concept of proportionality, applied in the conditions of Soviet society in the 1920s.

Given this overall perspective we can understand, therefore, Bukharin's continual injunctions for proportional growth, of the need to maintain proportionality within the existing equilibrium between the various sectors of the Soviet economy and society. Hence the emphasis upon the 'Worker–Peasant Alliance' which runs through his pronouncements of that period.

Because of the dominance of equilibrium theory in Bukharin's intellectual equipment I have devoted considerable space to an analysis of his work *Historical Materialism* and a rebuttal of the critics of that essay. The rest of this work is a selective examination of Bukharin's application of his version of historical materialism and equilibrium theory up to the time he was effectively silenced in 1929. In this examination I have relied upon the published writings of Bukharin, but some of the texts used are new translations by Oliver Field, to whom I owe a debt of gratitude for this work. Until Soviet archives are open to inspection (and if Bukharin's papers have survived), we shall not know if Bukharin set down in writing further analyses of Soviet society in the 1930s comparable to those he made in the previous decade. However, given the weight of evidence currently available I doubt if Bukharin made any substantial revisions to his basic theory: rather, I suspect, we shall find that he elaborated upon it in the light of experience.

The method I have used, in the first chapter of this book particularly, has been that of a close, almost textual, analysis of *Historical Materialism*. This was necessary because so many of Bukharin's critics have been somewhat remiss in their use – or non-use – of actual texts. This may seem rather cumbersome to some, but it is necessary since Bukharin has for many years been badly treated by friend and foe alike. It has seemed almost open season on Bukharin for many years, in which those who had a particular thesis or prejudice to display would grab bits from here and there to sew together their own particular portrait of Bukharin, often with little relevance to the actual subject. All too often writers have pounced on short extracts, mostly a sentence here or there, to 'prove' that Bukharin stood for this, that or whatever, and this seems eminently unsatisfactory when dealing with an historical figure and a set of ideas. It is for this reason that I have combed my way through *Historical Materialism* and other texts, so that I could establish what the arguments were in Bukharin's own words before drawing conclusions. The result is that readers will have before them much of the evidence upon which to base an assessment of my own interpretations. They may or may not agree with me, but they will be able to arrive at an independent viewpoint.

I would like to say a word at this point regarding the title of this work, since it sets out to defend Bukharin's theory of equilibrium *and* at the same time rehabilitate his book *Historical Materialism*. It is impossible to defend one without at the same time defending the other, so I have chosen to place equal weight upon the two in the first part of the book. Bukharin's theory of equilibrium follows on from, and is an integral part of, the classical Marxist conception of historical materialism. This may seem to be controversial to some, but the evidence for this will become clear as the reader goes through the texts. Bukharin was not alone amongst the Bolsheviks in using the concept of equilibrium, but he was alone in actually formulating a theory of equilibrium. And he drew the inspiration for his theory directly from Marx and Engels. It would never have crossed Bukharin's mind that his theory of equilibrium was in any way inconsistent with Marxism, nor for many years after he wrote it did such a thought occur to others inside the Bolshevik Party. It was only after the victory of Stalin in 1929 that such an idea began to be hawked around until quite liberal minded people in the western academic world began to repeat this nonsense. Therefore, a defence of equilibrium theory is a defence of *Historical Materialism and* historical materialism: they are inextricably interwoven. To remove one would be to remove a pillar of support for the other. The rehabilitation of *both* aspects of Bukharin's work is an urgent necessity for the re-establishment of Marxism as a viable tool of social, political and economic analysis. Certainly, the theory of equilibrium has little comfort for those who engage in ultra-leftist phrasemongering, but then the Marxism of Marx never did provide such support. Concomitantly, those who seek a comfortable reassurance about the delights of the market or 'market socialism' will find nothing for themselves in these pages.

Essentially then, this book is a rehabilitation of Bukharin as a Marxist theorist. Having debunked the myth of Bukharin's flawed Marxism which is still prevalent, I have provided no grounds for the creation of a new one.

Three further aspects of this work should be noted, since they will, no doubt, occasion some surprise in certain circles. First, in my examination of the disputed points of theory between Bukharin and Preobrazhensky I come down on the side of Bukharin. It has long been fashionable to hold Preobrazhensky up as a model of theoretical rectitude, as opposed to Bukharin's supposed inconsistencies and backsliding; this is wrong. On the formal level of Marxist theory an examination of the actual evidence will reveal that Bukharin wins hands down in the dispute, as I demonstrate.

Secondly, the evidence now available indicates that, on many of the crucial points under dispute regarding Soviet industrialisation, Trotsky and Bukharin were in substantial agreement by the end of the 1920s and into the early 1930s. Moreover, a number of the ideas propounded by some present-day Trotskyists are directly descended from Bukharin, particularly his theory of equilibrium. Neither of these propositions is acknowledged by the majority of Trotsky's latter-day followers: all too often they prefer the myths of yesteryear.

Thirdly, there has been a tendency in certain academic circles to present Bukharin as the progenitor of 'market socialism', at least as purveyed in parts of Eastern Europe today. Bukharin would have been scandalised by these attempts to saddle him with the blame for this intellectual monstrosity. As will be seen from the present text Bukharin saw the market and socialism as being incompatible in the long run: for him socialism meant the naturalisation of economic life – not its further commoditisation. However, Bukharin *did* acknowledge the need for markets during the long period of transition between capitalism and socialism that he envisaged.

The present work, then, is not merely an exercise in historical investigation into ideas; it has direct bearing upon the modern, current world. How, and in what form should nations industrialise and modernise; who benefits from this process and at what cost to the majority? These and similar questions are still very pertinent. They were first discussed in depth in the Soviet Union during the 1920s; yet are still largely unresolved. Bukharin's theories of equilibrium and proportionality – balanced growth – are still of direct relevance to the resolution of such disputes.

Since 1945 we have witnessed two variants of growth models imposed upon developing countries. The first is the Stalinist command economy; this has run into problems of varying magnitude, and the countries enduring it have all suffered from totalitarian repression to some degree or other. The need to totally subordinate consumption to the development of heavy industry in the Stalinist model could not have any other result than an authoritarian political regime: they are but two sides of the same coin. The second variant has been the 'free enterprise' one; this too has had its share of economic and environmental disasters, coupled with brutal exploitation and repression. There is evident need for a 'third way' i.e. a socialist way to be developed; Bukharin's ideas will be found to have a significant contribution to make to such a venture, if they are seriously applied.

1
Historical Materialism and the Theory of Equilibrium

The Critics

The evolution of Bukharin's ideas in the decade 1920 to 1929, from that of being on the left of the Bolshevik Party to that of leader of its right wing, is sometimes regarded as the result of changes in his basic theoretical ideas; this is an erroneous proposition. There is sufficient evidence to show that changes in policy prescriptions by him flowed from the same basic theoretical conceptions, which were relatively constant amid these changes. I will argue that one can only understand the changes in Bukharin's views on the Soviet economy and its related political problems in the 1920s by relating them to his theory of equilibrium.

The purpose of this chapter will be to examine Bukharin's theoretical conceptions regarding social, political and economic equilibrium and relate them to some basic propositions of Marxism.

The most fully rounded-out exposition of Bukharin's theory of equilibrium is to be found in his book *Historical Materialism: A System of Sociology*[1] which was first published in the autumn of 1921. Therefore it is to that book that one must turn to understand the basic underpinnings for Bukharin's theory of equilibrium. The book itself has had a chequered career; it was written for use as a textbook in the education of members of the Communist Party of the Soviet Union and affiliates of the Communist International. It was used as such until Bukharin's fall from power in 1929, going through many editions in the Russian and in translation into other languages.[2] However, it was not without its critics even when it was first published, one of the most notable of these being Georg Lukacs.[3] The main thrust of Bukharin's critics' objections centred upon his understanding – or rather, alleged lack of it – of dialectics and his 'vulgar' materialism. Such criticisms accord with Lenin's comments on Bukharin in his political testament, when he said 'Bukharin is not only a most valuable and major theoretician of the Party, he is rightfully considered as the favourite of the whole Party: but his theoretical views can be classified as fully Marxist only with great reserve, for there is something scholastic about him (he never studied, and, I think, never fully understood dialectics).'[4]

Lenin's comments have reverberated down the years, tending to influence the views of most commentators on Bukharin's abilities as a Marxist theoretician. Even Bukharin's biographer, Stephen F. Cohen,[5] who is generally favourable towards his subject's abilities, does not wholly reject such criticism. In his discussion of *Historical Materialism* Cohen says:

> It is curious that a rigid economic determinism should have been attributed to *Historical Materialism*, because Bukharin went to great lengths to exorcise this allegation and the notion of monistic causality from Marxism. An astute non-Marxist reviewer rightly observed that Bukharin strained towards monism but approached pluralism.[6]

However, Cohen, near the end of his discussion of this topic, also says:

> In the last analysis, as reflected in his treatment of technology, he made internal equilibrium dependent on the interrelations between society and nature. The impetus of pervasive change was external to the social system. In this and other respects, his 'Marxist sociology' was frequently inconsistent and sometimes crude, though the validity of the mechanical equilibrium model continues to divide sociologists.[7]

Another commentator, Alfred G. Meyer, was even more damning:

> ... a good deal of patience is required from the reader if he wants to work his way through the initial section [of *Historical Materialism*] dealing with the philosophic basis of Marxism, as Bukharin understood (or misunderstood) it. This section is orthodox Marxism at its worst.[8]

Lukacs, who wrote his criticism before Lenin's views were widely known, sums up his critique of Bukharin as follows:

> A really thorough discussion of [his] ... theoretical aim ... would have shown how Bukharin's basic philosophy is completely in harmony with contemplative materialism; that instead of making a historical-materialist critique of the natural sciences and their methods, i.e. revealing them as products of capitalist development, he extends these methods to the study of society

without hesitation, uncritically, unhistorically and undialect-
ically.[9]

Several questions arise from this unanimous set of opinions, from
rather diverse sources, it must be said. First, is it true that Bukharin
misunderstood the philosophical basis – or component – of
Marxism, and if he did, to what extent? Secondly, does his
misunderstanding, if he indeed does misunderstand, vitiate or
invalidate his contribution to Marxism? Can his theory of
equilibrium be validated on its own terms, that is, as Bukharin
expounded it? And, fourthly, how far can his theories of
equilibrium be considered to be a part of Marxist theory in general,
and its political economy in particular?

These are the four main questions to be pursued here. I shall
proceed by a textual analysis of Bukharin's presentation and
compare it with relevant texts from other writers where
appropriate.

Methodology

In his introduction to *Historical Materialism* Bukharin advanced
certain propositions that are important for an understanding of his
viewpoint, in particular his rejection of the idea of the neutrality
of the social sciences. He said:

> Each class has its own practice, its special tasks, its interests and
> therefore its view of things. The bourgeoisie is concerned chiefly
> with safeguarding, perpetuating, solidifying, extending the rule
> of capital. The working class is concerned in the first place with
> the task of overthrowing the capitalist system and safeguarding
> the rule of the working class in order to reconstruct life. It is not
> difficult to see that bourgeois practice will demand one thing, and
> proletarian practice another ...[10]

Bukharin, therefore, argued that it is not merely that different
ends are presupposed and pursued by various classes, but that the
very problems they define as needing solution will be different.
Moreover, this will not only affect the selection of problems but
also the method of analysis of the material relating to them. This is
not to say that he was suggesting that the method of posing
problems and their analysis were directly and immediately
attributable to the class origins and viewpoint of social scientists.
The point he was making is that the *total* circumstances of a class or

group within society will influence its viewpoint and the practice flowing from them. This seemingly schematic approach is modified, clarified and amplified in later chapters, especially in the one dealing with the role of intellectuals and the question of intellectual labour. Bukharin continued: '... he who would understand social life on its present basis must also understand, at the outset, that all is changing, one form of society follows upon another.'[11] And, he argued, proletarian science – by which we take him to mean Marxism – does understand, and therefore: 'It is superior because it has a deeper and wider vision of the phenomena of social life, because it is capable of seeing further and observing facts that lie beyond the vision of bourgeois social science.'[12]

What did Bukharin mean here, when he wrote of a 'deeper and wider vision'? What did he mean by 'facts that lie beyond the vision of bourgeois social science'? Marx wrote that 'all science would be superfluous if the outward appearance and the essence of things directly coincided.'[13] Bukharin seems to be following through Marx's idea on this point, and this accords with his own view of himself as being an orthodox Marxist.

However, we need to know, or at least try to understand, what both writers meant on this point. Both writers were positing the necessity and the power of the use of abstractions when dealing with political, economic and social phenomena. But even the simplest abstraction is not an idea lacking any foundation in empirically observable phenomena. On the contrary, such abstractions are based upon and reflect a particular concatenation of historical facts.

The starting point, for Marx, when dealing with social, political and economic phenomena, appears to be abstractions. He seems to begin his analysis at the level of the abstract and move, step by step, to the level of the concrete. One could say that he attempts to discern the essence, the essential elements of a phenomenon, before examining the concrete, or particular, manifestations that reveal themselves to the casual and unreflective observer. However, the abstraction that Marx (and Bukharin) started with, or from, is not an artifice, a mere speculation, but is based upon the real historical world. Marx said:

The concrete concept is concrete because it is a synthesis of many definitions, thus representing the unity of diverse aspects. It appears therefore in reasoning as a summing up, the result, and not the starting point, although it is the real point of origin, and thus also the point of origin of perception and imagination.[14]

This synthetic conception, therefore, not only allows us to perceive the concrete, that is, interpret phenomena; it also forms the basis for our 'imagination'; and this imagination allows us to predict or forecast the possible or probable course of events upon the basis of this perception. Marx further pointed out: 'the simplest economic category, e.g., exchange-value, presupposes population, a population moreover which produces under definite conditions, as well as a distinct kind of family, or community, or state.'[15]

So, for Marx and Bukharin, real abstractions are historically determined ones, and are not universal in the sense of being supra-historical. Their method is one that attempts to get behind – without ignoring – the immediately observable facts or appearances, to discern the inner essentials of problems. In this respect the method is a rejection of positivist methodology.

Bukharin proceeded to say that there are a variety of social sciences, each with their own field of study, and 'One will study the economic life of society (science of economics) or even the special universal laws of capitalist economy (political economy).'[16] Here Bukharin attempted to distinguish between science 'in general' and particular applications of the investigative method to specific social systems. Since it is clear that when he wrote 'universal laws' he was not referring to any supra-historical laws, but to laws that are universal *within* the capitalist mode of production, no matter how they are manifested in specific historical circumstances, we may infer, then, that he was adopting an essentialist viewpoint. Moreover, Bukharin divided each branch of the social sciences into two parts, history and theory.

> And among the social sciences there are two important branches which consider not only a single field of social life, but the entire social life in all its fullness ... One of these sciences is history; the other is sociology ... History investigates and describes how the current social life flowed at a certain time and in a certain place ... Sociology takes up the answer to general questions, such as: what is society? On what does its growth or decay depend?[17]

For Bukharin then, history and sociology are the two main branches of the social sciences. Moreover, these two branches stand in a particular relationship to each other.

Since sociology explains general laws of human evolution, it serves as a *method* for history. If, for example, sociology establishes the general doctrine that forms of government depend upon the forms of economy, the historian must seek and find, in any given epoch, precisely what are the relations, and must show what is their concrete, specific expression. History furnishes the material for drawing sociological conclusions ... Sociology in its turn formulates a definite point of view, a means of investigation, or, as we now say, a method of history.[18]

On the basis of the above Bukharin then advanced the view that historical materialism was the 'proletarian sociology' of the working class, and that the whole of his book was devoted to developing this theory.[19] Thus Bukharin's definition is somewhat different to that which might be generally acceptable in academic circles – because it is wider in scope. He was aware, however, that even such a wide definition of sociology would not be unanimously acceptable amongst Marxists; Lenin in particular had a somewhat scathing attitude towards what he considered to be 'bourgeois sociology'. Bukharin put forward several possible objections to his own definition of historical materialism as a sociology; but rejected them all, because:

All such arguments are in error ... For the theory of historical materialism has a definite place, it is not political economy, nor is it history; it is a general theory of society and the laws of its evolution, i.e. sociology. In the second place, the fact that the theory of historical materialism is a method of history, by no means destroys its significance as a sociological theory. Very often a more abstract science may furnish a point of view (method) for the less abstract sciences. This is the case here also ...'[20]

This point certainly has substance, since historical materialism cannot be reduced to either being a school of political economy nor merely a method of historical enquiry. The claim advanced for historical materialism is that it is above all a comprehensive method of totalising politics, economics and history into a multi-faceted whole. And such a synthetic analysis will enable the enquirer to delve beneath the surface of social problems to reveal their essential qualities, as opposed to the outward appearance of matters.

The possible objections which Bukharin posed and then rejected were:

historical materialism should under no circumstances be considered a Marxist sociology, and that it should not be expounded systematically; they [the critics] believe that it is only a living *method* of historical knowledge, that its truths may only be applied in the case of concrete and historical events.[21]

The possible basis for such objections seems to stem from the fact that Marx did not set down, in an extended and systematic manner, his own concept of historical materialism for publication. Moreover in the one instance where he *did* attempt such an exposition he decided not to publish it. This unpublished (in his own lifetime) essay is his Introduction to *A Contribution to the Critique of Political Economy*, published in 1859. In the shorter Preface to that work he gave his reason for not publishing the Introduction as follows:

I am withholding a general introduction I had drafted, since on closer consideration it seems to me confusing to anticipate results which have still to be proved, and the reader who really wishes to follow me will have to decide to advance from the particular to the general.[22]

Let us note, however, that Marx said he was 'withholding', i.e., not repudiating, such a general introduction, and even in his Preface he did set out some short comments on his general views and method:

In the social production of their existence, men enter into definite, necessary relations, which are independent of their will, namely, relations of production corresponding to a determinate stage of development of their material forces of production. The totality of these relations of production constitutes the economic structure of society, the foundation on which there arises a legal and political superstructure and to which there corresponds definite forms of social consciousness. The mode of production of material life conditions the social, political and intellectual life-process in general. It is not the consciousness of men that determines their being, but on the contrary it is their social being that determines their consciousness.[23]

In the light of the above we can see why Marx chose not to use the Introduction, since he wanted the method he used to unfold with the reading of the *Critique*, and there was justification for his doing so at that time. The *Critique* was Marx's first substantial work where he advanced his own particular interpretation and critique of political economy.[24] Therefore he did not wish to become engaged in controversy about historical materialism, i.e., his method, as such, but rather chose to stand on the concrete results of the method. But we can see from the above extracts from the Preface that he said enough to indicate the scope and nature of his critique; and in general Bukharin's views accord with those of Marx. Bukharin seemed to be arguing – without directly referring to Marx – that what for Marx was an expository device should not be turned into a set of iron-clad rules. And, as we can see from Marx's Introduction, he was not averse to setting out the basic propositions of historical materialism for publication: for him it was only a matter of timing. (The fact that the time never did arrive for Marx is not surprising, since only a part of what he wrote was published in his lifetime. If we are to believe his biographers, Marx was never satisfied with what he wrote, and Engels had to constantly beseech him to publish.) Marx and Engels had worked out their basic materialist and dialectical method in *The German Ideology*,[25] but this was not published in either of their lifetimes, mainly because it was a highly polemical work and most of those whom Marx and Engels had argued with on these issues rapidly became marginal to their main concerns. Engels explained the matter later: 'We abandoned the manuscript to the gnawing criticism of the mice ... as we had achieved our main purpose – self-clarification'.[26]

The conclusion to be drawn from this discussion is that, in so far as historical materialism does strive to explain the general processes of society, Bukharin's description of it as a 'system of sociology' is undoubtedly correct. The reason why some of his critics shied away from this conclusion is that they feared to be tarred with any association with 'bourgeois sociology', which many saw as an attempt to provide a counter-theory to Marxism. Bukharin, on the other hand, had the intellectual toughness not to burke the issue.

Laws of Social Movement

In the first chapter of *Historical Materialism* Bukharin examined 'Cause and Purpose in the Social Sciences', and in particular causation and teleology. He pointed out: 'Everyone has observed that in nature and society there is a *definite* regularity, a *fixed* natural law. The determination of this natural law is the first task of science.'[27] Here he introduced the concept of *regularity*, and this was the first step towards his theory of equilibrium, since without regularity there can be no equilibrium, a point which will be developed later. And with regularity must be some cause:

> This causality in nature and society is objective; it exists whether men are aware of it or not. The first step of science is to reveal this causality and free it from the surrounding chaos of phenomena. Marx considered the earmark of scientific knowledge to be its character as 'a sum of many determinations and relations', as opposed to a 'chaotic conception'.[28] ... the great majority of present-day bourgeois philosophers find the function of science to be not the discovery of those causalities that exist objectively, but the invention of such causalities by the human person. But it is clear that the succession of day and night, of the seasons, the uniform sequence of natural and social phenomena, are independent of whether the mind of the learned bourgeois will have it so or not. The causality of phenomena is an objective causality.[29]

Bukharin had touched upon a fundamental question here, since he outlined what he considered to be the materialist point of view, as opposed to the idealist one. This question of the objective nature of phenomena and causality both in nature *and* society has implications for Bukharin's approach to the question of equilibrium, as we shall see later. For him this objectivity was an important factor in rejecting teleological explanations of either natural or social phenomena or events. In this matter he closely followed Marx, who wrote, in a letter to Ferdinand Lassalle in January 1861:

> Darwin's book is very important and serves me as a natural-scientific basis for the class struggle in history ... Despite all deficiencies, not only is the death-blow dealt here for the first time to 'teleology' in the natural sciences but its rational meaning is empirically explained.[30]

It is important to note here the use of the phrase 'natural-scientific' which Marx said is the rational explanation for the class struggle, since Bukharin was criticised for allegedly turning towards a version of positivist scientism. If this was indeed the case, then critics of Bukharin should also turn their attention to Marx instead of using Bukharin as a stalking horse, since there is a close affinity between

Marx and Bukharin on this issue.

However, for Bukharin the key to both causality and regularity lay in 'finding the necessary conditions from the given or accepted facts'[31]; because 'both in nature and society there exists objectively ... a law of nature that is causal in character.'[32] And 'any law of cause and effect may be expressed by the following formula: If certain phenomena are actually present, there must necessarily be also present certain other phenomena corresponding to them.'[33] Bukharin argued that the use of empirical data for ascertaining the 'necessary conditions' for causality had been given 'but little attention'[34], although both Marx and Engels used such data extensively. And, as we saw with Marx's reference to Darwin and his empirical data, this was the case indeed, since Marx was able to extend the interpretation placed upon the data, in a way probably quite unforeseen by Darwin.

In this respect Bukharin argued that:

> The whole of *Capital* is built upon it. Given: a commodities-producing society with all its elements; how explain its existence? *Answer*: it can exist only under the condition that the law of value exists; countless commodities are exchanged against each other; how may we explain this? It is possible only if we assume the existence of a money system (social necessity of money). Capital is accumulated on the basis of the laws of commodity circulation. This is possible only because the value of labour-power is lower than that of the product turned out, etc.[35]

So, capitalism, which seemingly is an abstract conception, is specifically historical, and one must build this 'abstraction' by use of historically specific data that can be empirically observed. Moreover, these facts exist independently of people's will. Only when such facts occur *regularly*, that is, not occasionally nor by chance, will they assume and identify a *causal* relationship with each other and provide the *necessary conditions* for the construction of the analytical category, capitalism. And the phenomenon so categorised has an independent concrete existence separate and apart from – and historically prior to – the category itself. But, Bukharin pointed out:

> Social determinism, i.e. the doctrine that all social phenomena are conditioned, have causes from which they necessarily flow, must not be confused with *fatalism*, which is a belief in a blind, inevitable destiny, a 'fate', weighing down upon everything, and

to which everyone is subjected. Man's will is nothing. Man is not
a quantity to be considered among causes; he is simply a passive
substance. This teaching denies the human will as a factor in
evolution, which determinism does not.[36]

Therefore, although causality incorporates cause and effect, their
relationship determines each particular whole; this does not mean
that such relationships and totalities are predestined. How then
can Marxists say that socialism is inevitable? Bukharin replied to
such a question as follows:

Socialism will come inevitably because it is inevitable that men,
definite classes of men, will stand for its realisation, and they will
do so under circumstances that will make their victory certain.
Marxism does not deny the will but explains it. When Marxists
organise the Communist Party and lead it into battle, this action is
also an expression of historical necessity, which finds its forms
precisely through the will and the actions of men.[37]

We can see, therefore, that Bukharin, far from having a mechanical
conception of movement, social change or being imbued with
fatalism, on the contrary, posited people's will as one of the
necessary conditions for change; even if that will is not sufficient a
condition on its own to radically change or transform society. There
is no rachet-like effect of a continuous advance in an upwards
direction, and this fits into Bukharin's overall conception of
equilibrium, as we shall see.

Dialectics

How then did Bukharin regard the process of change? We have
seen that there must be regularity, causality and the necessary
conditions in the expression of phenomena. By what method does
one assess the process? Bukharin gave the following answer: 'the
dialectical method of interpretation demands that all phenomena
be considered in their indissoluble relations; [and] that they be
considered in their state of motion.'[38] And, although there is
ceaseless motion this is not unilinear growth, because: 'while we
may not always observe growth, there is always motion and
alteration, though it may end in destruction or dissolution.'[39]

So the dialectical resolution of problems does not always result in
a positive solution, but on the contrary may end in the mutual
destruction of the parts of the totality in motion. Nor are all

categories – e.g. capitalism, commodity production – universal or supra-historical ones, therefore:

> we must consider and investigate each form of society in its own peculiar terms [because] each ... system has peculiar traits that require special study. By this means only can we grasp the process of change. For, since each form has its special traits, it also must have its special laws ... of motion [and] each form must be studied in its internal process of change [and] each form of society must be considered in its growth and necessary disappearance, i.e. in its relation to other forms.[40]

From this we can see that for Bukharin the process of change had *two* aspects, the internal processes of the form, and relationship of this form to other forms, i.e., external processes. But what is the relationship between the two aspects? Which is the most important and takes precedence? It is here that Bukharin introduced the concept of contradiction, since:

> The basis of all things ... the laws of change, the law of constant motion [means that] changes are produced by constant internal contradictions, internal struggle. Hegel said: 'Contradiction is the power that moves things.' There is no doubt of the correctness of this law ... For, if there is no conflict, no clash of forces, the world would be in a condition of unchanging, stable equilibrium, i.e. complete and absolute permanence, a state of rest precluding all motion. Such a state of rest would be conceivable only in a system whose component parts and forces would be so related as not to permit of the introduction of any conflicts, as to preclude all mutual interaction, all disturbances. As we already know that all things change, all things are 'in flux', it is certain that such an absolute state of rest cannot possibly exist. We must therefore reject a condition in which there is no 'contradiction between opposing and colliding forces', no disturbance of equilibrium but only an absolute immutability.[41]

Thus contradiction and its resolution lie at the heart of Bukharin's conception of equilibrium. And this contradictory equilibrium is a condition pertaining to nature and society. Moreover, he did not see contradiction and equilibrium as separate aspects of phenomena, but saw them as inseparable, that is, the one posits the other and is dependent on that other.

[For] it is clear that we are dealing with one phenomenon, that of *equilibrium*. This being the case, where do the contradictions come in? For there is no doubt that conflict is a *disturbance* of equilibrium. It must be recalled that such equilibrium as we observe in nature and in society is *not* an absolute, unchanging equilibrium, but an equilibrium *in flux*, which means that the equilibrium may be established and destroyed, may be re-established on a new basis, and again disturbed.[42]

Bukharin thus specified that equilibrium is not a static condition but a *mobile* one. For there can only be an equilibrium where there exist forces or tendencies which are opposed, in contradiction to each other, and since all of the parts are subject to change it means that equilibrium is a series of unique moments of change. Therefore we have a condition which is in motion and at rest at one and the same time. From this:

It follows that the 'conflict', the 'contradiction', i.e., the antagonism of forces acting in various directions, determines the motion of the system ... Hegel observed this characteristic of motion and expressed it in the following manner: he called the original condition of equilibrium the *thesis*, the disturbance of equilibrium the *antithesis*, the re-establishment of equilibrium on a new basis the *synthesis* (the unifying proposition reconciling the contradictions). The characteristic of motion present in all things, expressing itself in this tripartite formula (or triad) he called *dialectic*.[43]

But, how does the dialectic operate? Upon or within society?

Equilibrium: Society and Nature

Bukharin presented a series of propositions, giving what he considered to be the three main forms of equilibrium, and he clearly regarded these as an expression of dialectics at work. These are:

1. **Stable equilibrium.** This is present when the mutual action of the environment and the system results in an unaltered condition, or in a disturbance of the first condition which is again re-established in the original state ... Stable equilibrium is not always the complete absence of motion; there may be motion, but the resulting disturbance is followed by a re-establishment of

equilibrium on the former basis. The contradiction between the environment and the system is constantly being reproduced in the same *quantitative relation* ...

2. Unstable equilibrium with positive (favourable) indication (an expanding system). In actual fact, however, stable equilibrium does not exist. It constitutes merely an imaginary, sometimes termed the 'ideal', case. As a matter of fact, the relation between environment and the system is never reproduced in precisely the same proportions; the disturbance of equilibrium never actually leads to its re-establishment on exactly the same basis as before, but a new equilibrium is created on a new basis ... If we consider human society ... and assume that the relation between it and nature is altered in such a manner that society – by means of production – extracts more energy from nature than is consumed by society (either the soil becomes more fruitful, or new tools are devised, or both), this society will *grow* and not merely mark time. The new equilibrium will in each case be actually new. The contradiction between society and nature will in each case be reproduced on a new and 'higher' basis, a basis on which society will increase and develop. This is a case of unstable equilibrium with positive indication ...

3. Unstable equilibrium with negative indication (a declining system). Now let us consider the quite different case of a new equilibrium being established on a 'lower' basis ... in the case of society, let us assume that the relation between it and nature has been altered in such a manner that society is obliged to consume more and more and obtain less and less (the soil is exhausted, technical methods become poorer, etc.). New equilibrium will here be established in each case on a lowered basis, by reason of the destruction of a portion of society. We are now dealing with a declining society, a disappearing system, in other words, with motion having a negative indication.[44]

In the above Bukharin's treatment of equilibrium does not take into account disturbances arising *within* the system. However, we shall examine that aspect later. In his first two cases we can clearly see the influence of Marx's reproduction schemas from Volume II of *Capital* (Chapters XX and XXI). Bukharin's stable equilibrium can be considered to be analogous to simple reproduction and unstable equilibrium with positive indication, as being akin to expanded reproduction. The third case, unstable equilibrium with negative indication, is a new contribution of Bukharin's which he first formulated in *The Economics of the Transition Period*, written in

1920. Given the importance of the economic aspects of this third case it will be dealt with in a separate chapter, since it warrants extended treatment.

Two problems arise out of the first two cases of equilibrium and their close affinity to Marx's reproduction schemas. First, is Bukharin's use of the basic concepts correct? That is, do the premises and purposes of the schemas warrant an extension to the wider application in the manner that Bukharin suggests? Second, was Bukharin in fact postulating that disequilibrium arises only from external causes?

Let us examine the second question first, since it will condition our understanding of the first question. Bukharin certainly did not ignore internal contradictions, because he proceeded to say:

> Thus far we have spoken only of the contradictions between the environment and the system, i.e. the *external* contradictions. But there are also internal contradictions, those that are within the system. Each system consists of its component parts (elements), united with each other ... Between them there are a number of contradictions, differences, imperfect adaptions ... In other words, here also there is no absolute equilibrium ... This may be seen best by the example of the most complicated system ... human society. Here we encounter an endless number of contradictions; we find the struggle between classes, which is the sharpest expression of 'social contradictions', and we know that 'the struggle between classes is the motive force of history' ... But these contradictions do not of themselves destroy society.[45]

Accordingly we have a combination of internal and external contradictions which are a part of, and help to determine, the overall totality. Then the question is posed – which are the determining contradictions, those between the elements of a system or those between the system and its environment? Here we arrive at a vital distinction, one that has led a number of Bukharin's critics to place him firmly in the camp of mechanical materialism. But what did Bukharin actually say on this point?

> Let us consider the question in the following form: we have seen ... that the character of the equilibrium between society and nature determines the fundamental course of the motion of society. Under these circumstances, could the internal structure continue for long to develop in the opposite direction? Of course not. In the case of a growing society, it would not be possible for

the internal structure of society to continue *constantly* to grow worse. If, *in a condition of growth*, the structure of society should become poorer, i.e., its internal disorders grow worse, this would be equivalent to the appearance of a new contradiction ... between the external and the internal equilibrium, which would require the society, if it is to continue growing, to undertake a reconstruction, i.e., its internal structure must adapt itself to the character of the external equilibrium. *Consequently, the internal (structural) equilibrium is a quantity which depends on the external equilibrium (is a 'function' of this external equilibrium).*[46]

The above passage, taken out of its context, could lead the unwary to conclude that Bukharin was positing that the evolution of society is wholly and immediately dependent upon its relationship with nature, and that various modes of production are the result of this dependency. Such a conclusion would be unwarranted, even though Bukharin did lay stress upon the primacy of nature in the society/nature relationship. How did he accord this primacy? By recognising humanity as being a part of nature, i.e., by adopting a materialist conception of the part of humanity in nature and interaction with it. In so far as humanity is one of the animal species (albeit a unique one) it is, in the final instance, subject to natural law. Any other concept leads one to an idealist viewpoint of evolution, being and history. As Bukharin said:

A consideration of society as a system involves the recognition of 'external nature' as its environment, i.e., chiefly the terrestial globe with all its natural properties. Human society is unthinkable without its environment. Nature is the source of foodstuffs for human society, thus determining [its] living conditions. But nothing could be more incorrect than to regard nature from the teleological point of view: man, the lord of creation, with nature created for his use, and all things adapted to human needs. As a matter of fact, nature often falls upon the 'lord of creation' in such a savage manner that he is obliged to admit her superiority. It has taken man centuries of bitter struggle to place his iron bit in nature's mouth.[47]

This passage, then, puts the primacy of nature, in the equilibrium between nature and society, in its proper *historical* setting. Bukharin was advancing a known, and continually attested fact – that human society cannot ignore its relationship to given – at any one time – climatic, geographical and ecological conditions; or it ignores them at its peril. For example, the law of gravity is 'given' and no one person unaided could overcome it and escape the gravitational field of the earth to enter outer space. However, as we all know, within the last two decades or so people have been able to leave earth and reach the moon. But this was not done in contradiction to any natural laws – on the contrary, it was only by an extension of knowledge of natural 'laws' that a means was found to counter the force of gravity by the use of a countervailing force. Moreover we are also aware that nature often does still deal savage blows to the 'lord of creation', as Bukharin put it, through such events as hurricanes, floods or snowstorms that can bring the most advanced metropolis to a grinding halt for days on end, indicating the precariousness of social 'control' of nature. Bukharin's ideas, in this respect, are very close to those of Marx, when Marx wrote:

> Physically man lives on those products of nature, whether they appear in the form of food, heating, clothes, a dwelling, etc. The universality of man appears in practice precisely in the universality which makes all nature his *inorganic* body – both in as much as nature is (1) his direct means of life, and (2) the material, the object, and the instrument of his life activity ... Man lives on nature – means that nature is his *body*, with which he must remain in continuous interchange if he is not to die.[48]

Since the above was taken from the *The Economic and Philosophic Manuscripts* of 1844 it could be argued that this is the opinion of the young, immature Marx. But there are definite threads of continuity in his work that are consistent and abiding – witness:

> Labour is, in the first place, a process in which both men and Nature participate, and in which man of his own accord starts, regulates, and controls the material reactions between himself and Nature. He opposes himself to Nature as one of her own forces, setting in motion arms and legs, head and hands, the natural forces of his body, in order to appropriate Nature's productions in the form adapted to his own wants. By thus acting on the external world and changing it, he at the same time changes his own nature ... The soil ... in the virgin state in which it supplies man with necessaries or means of subsistence ready to hand, exists independently of him, and is the universal subject of human labour.[49]

Since the second extract is taken from the first volume of *Capital* it could hardly be said that it does not represent the viewpoint of the mature Marx. Nor is Marx introduced here as an authority, since he is only expressing an opinion, and at the same time using good sense. The extracts from Marx do show, however, that Bukharin was firmly in the Marxist tradition when he posited that the internal equilibrium of society is a function of the equilibrium of society and nature; and that in the last instance it is nature that must be accorded primacy. This does not preclude us from averring that in this exchange (equilibrium) between society and nature it is society which is the most active, indeed conscious, and therefore the most potent factor – within certain constraints – of this exchange. As Marx said, people change nature and in the process change themselves. Bukharin developed this aspect, by saying:

> Human society works in nature and on nature, as the subject of its labour. But the elements existing as such in nature are here more or less constant and therefore *cannot explain changes*. It is the social technology which changes, which adapts itself to that which exists in nature ... Technology is a varying quantity, and precisely its variations produce the changes in the relations between society and nature; technology therefore must constitute a point of departure in an analysis of social changes.[50]

For many Marxists this is the most controversial premise of Bukharin's approach to the development of society. The precise role of technology in change is still a matter for debate, not, one supposes, that there will be anyone who would deny *any* role to technology in change. However, just as Lenin's remarks about Bukharin in his testament have echoed down the years, so too has Lukacs' criticism of him. The criticism by Lukacs was contained in a review of *Historical Materialism*, in which he argued that:

> The discussion of the role of technique in social development highlights ... false 'objectivity'. Bukharin attributes to technology a far too determinant position, which completely misses the *spirit* of dialectical materialism ... It is obvious that this final identification of technique with the forces of production is neither valid nor Marxist. Technique is a *part*, a moment, naturally of great importance, of the social productive forces, but it is neither simply identical with them, nor ... the final or absolute moment of the changes in these forces.[51]

This is a powerful indictment of Bukharin, from a Marxist

perspective, since – as Lukacs argues – it is not technology *per se* that historically determines a mode of production or the changes in modes of production, but the mode of production which, in the final analysis, determines the technology used. But there can be no doubt that these two aspects have a powerful reciprocal effect upon each other. However, despite Lukacs' assertion, Bukharin did in fact locate technology in its social setting, and in three specific ways. First, in the sense that machinery (specific *forms* of technology) can only be considered as machines when they are used in their particular environment. Secondly, the distribution of labour and its specific functions will be determined by the state of technology. And, third, the uses to which technology is put is determined by the class structure of society. On the first aspect, Bukharin said:

Any specific machine will at once lose its significance as a machine outside of human society; it becomes merely a portion of external nature, a combination of pieces of steel, wood etc. When a great liner sinks to the bottom, this living monster with its powerful engines...loses its *social* significance ... the steamer ceases to be a steamer; having lost its *social* existence, it is excluded from society, has ceased to be a portion of society, to perform its social service, and is now merely an object...which does not come into direct contact with human society.[52]

So he posited technology, and its products, as having been both created by society and only having an existence within it. Moreover, tools are only significant when they are distributed and stand in relation to each other in a particular manner and are used by human beings. This would seem to accord with Lukacs so far. Bukharin continued:

In speaking of the social technology, we of course meant not a certain tool, or the aggregate of different tools, but the whole *system* of these tools in society ... In other words, we may consider the special technology as a whole, in which each of the parts at a given moment is socially necessary.[53]

And, to emphasise the point:

The social technology, we reiterate, is not therefore a mere aggregate of the various instruments of labour, but is their connecting system. On any individual part of the system depends all the rest of the system. At any given moment, also, the various parts of this technology are related in a certain proportion, a certain quantitative relation.[54]

Here we do not have technology *per se* but *social* technology and the concept of proportionality within the system. This latter point was to have particular significance for Bukharin's attitude in 1928–9, when the First Five Year Plan was being implemented. In the present text Bukharin made the elementary, but none the less important, point that it is useless to have ten times more people and machinery producing ten times more coal than can be used with a given state of development of industry. And, conversely, factories will stand idle and workers will be unemployed if insufficient coal or power is produced.

> This being the case, it is also clear that each given system of social technology also determines the system of labour relations between persons ... Technical devices naturally also determine the *type of worker*, the degree of his skill, and also working relations, the productive conditions.[55]

It is quite clear that Bukharin was at that point still writing about the *technical* conditions of the labour process, which at any *given* time will determine both the number of workers and the degree or type of skill required. He pointed out that even a simple enumeration of the types of jobs and skills will elicit an indication of the degree of complexity of the technology at any given time. Moreover, such types of skills are an indication of the division of labour.

This point needs to be understood in the way that Bukharin was using the concept 'division of labour'. He was not suggesting that technology determines the division of labour as such, only that it will determine the *particular* divisions, and these will change as technology changes. It is at this point that we come to one of Lukacs' criticisms of Bukharin. Bukharin wrote: 'Under a different system of technology, slave labour would have been impossible [in the ancient world]: the slaves spoil delicate machinery, and slave labour does not pay.'[56]

If we take this sentence in isolation then it would seem that Bukharin was adopting the theoretical stance that Lukacs imputes to him. But Bukharin immediately followed on from the above to say: 'Thus, even such a phenomenon as the labour of imported slaves can be explained, *under the given historical conditions*, by the tools with which social labour works.' [emphasis added][57]

My reading of this is quite different to that of Lukacs. What Bukharin was saying was that in those circumstances where slave labour was the dominant mode of production, the parameters of social technology were severely circumscribed. Consequently, the tools with which slaves worked made it necessary to import slaves to enable production to continue because of the existing social technology. That is to say, in a society based upon slave labour, certain technologies could not be introduced or there was no incentive for their development. Far from Bukharin suggesting that it was the tools (technology) which determined the import of slaves, he was saying that the use of such labour would restrict the types of tools and techniques that could be used. And *consequently* – because of the low reproduction rate of slaves in antiquity – slave labour would have to be imported. In other words he was suggesting a reciprocal relationship between the mode of production and the technology it produces and uses.

Bukharin emphasised the historical nature of the technological division of labour and said: 'The division of labour constitutes one of the fundamental conditions of production. The modern division of labour is determined by the ... character, description, and combination of machines and tools, that is, by the technical apparatus of capitalist society.'[58] It is not particularly difficult to draw the conclusion from this that, far from technology being an independent factor, its development and application are often the result of class forces operating within society. Since for Marx (and Bukharin) the process of production and reproduction was also one of the reproduction of class relations, technology would usually reinforce this process.

Thus what Bukharin was saying was that with a given state of technology, which implied a given set of tools, the *particular* divisions of labour would be determined. And with this the need for a particular type of labour force is also determined. A modern example of this would be the introduction of microcomputers into schools to cater for the demand arising from the use, on an expanding scale, of microchip technology in industry and commerce. Bukharin concluded that:

A constantly progressing realignment of classes may totally change the form of society. This will particularly be the case if the class at the bottom comes out on top, a process which is to be described in the following chapters. For the present we shall merely state that class relations also – the most important part of production relations – change with the changes in the productive forces.[59]

It should be noted that Bukharin said that class relations are the 'most important part of production relations'. In this respect it would seem that Lukacs' criticism of Bukharin – as an orthodox Marxist – cannot be sustained. Bukharin remained firmly in the camp of historical materialism by ascribing the primacy of class relations to the changes in the forces of production. Bukharin was also wholly correct to ascribe the primacy to nature (i.e. the external) in the relationship between society and its environment. The problem with most of Bukharin's critics on this matter, and in particular Lukacs, is that they fail to take a comprehensive look at what he said, and rather concentrate upon short extracts or even sentences which are taken out of the overall context of Bukharin's work.[60]

Equilibrium and Social Classes

So far we have dealt with questions relating to equilibrium between systems, that is, between nature and society. Let us now turn to the question of *internal* equilibrium. Given the manner in which Bukharin expressed his ideas up to this point, it will come as no surprise that he first of all examined conditions of equilibrium before embarking upon an examination of social dis-equilibrium. There is no doubt that this method of enquiry is correct, since only by understanding what is significant for equilibrium can we also understand what is significant for dis-equilibrium.

We have seen how Bukharin used the concept of social technology as one of the basic elements in his approach to social equilibrium. He introduced the idea of the division of labour and gave numerous examples of this and its relationship to social technology. He then proceeded to say:

All the persons enumerated participate in one way or another in the labour process and therefore have certain definite relations to each other. In classifying them, we may divide them according to their trades and callings; but we may also divide them according to their *classes*.[61]...

It is obvious that locksmiths, lathe-workers, machine workers, stevedores, are in one class, while the engineer, the specialist, etc., are in another class; the capitalist, who has control of all, is in another class ... The greatest difference here is the productive function, in the productive significance, in the character of the relations between men; the capitalist in his factory distributes and arranges his workers as he might things or tools; but the workers do not 'distribute' the capitalists ... they 'are distributed' by these capitalists. This is a relation of 'master' and 'servant', as Marx says, with 'capital in command'. It is their different function in the production process that constitutes the basis of the division of men into different social classes.[62]

Moreover, Bukharin said, the distribution of the material products of society will also be determined by the mode of production. And in a society where use-values are overwhelmingly produced as commodities this distribution will be based upon exchange via the market, that is, through the medium of money. And 'this distribution may not be considered as independent of production. On the contrary, it is determined *by* production and, together with it, constitutes a section of *material social reproduction*.'[63]

We should note, however, that here Bukharin was using the term 'distribution' in a particular manner, one that includes what would usually be considered to be distribution but also other features which are not normally considered as coming within the purview of that term. As we have seen he also wrote about the distribution of people in the production process, and earlier he wrote about the distribution of machines and instruments in the pattern of social technology and its equilibrium.

He proceeded to further widen this definition of distribution by saying:

But this varying 'distribution of persons', depending on their varying assignments in production is also connected with a distribution of the means of labour: the capitalist, the owner ... controls these means of labour (factory and machinery) ... while the worker has no instruments of production aside from his own labour power ... It is therefore obvious that the varying function of classes in production is based upon the distribution of instruments of production among them ... The current class relations in capitalist society, namely, the relations between capitalists and workers, are bound up with a *thing*: the instruments of production in the hands of the capitalists, controlled by the latter, not owned by the workers. These instruments of production serve the capitalists as tools for the obtaining of profits, as a means of exploiting the working class. They are not mere things, they are things in a special social significance, in that they here serve not only as means of production, but also as a means of exploiting wage labourers. In other words, this *thing* expresses the relations between classes...In the last analysis, this *thing,* in our example, is capital.[64]

Bukharin indicated that these special relationships are 'particularly important in society. It is they which determine in the first place the outline of society, its system or, in the words of Marx, its economic structure.'[65]

However, the particular structure or system of society is not immediately reducible to these economic relations; there are numerous other factors, 'psychical relations, "mental" relations; society produces not only material objects: it also produces ... "cultural values": art, science ... it produces ideas in addition to things. These ideas, once they have been produced, may be developed into large *systems of ideas.*'[66] And these systems of ideas are embodied in certain elements and social structures, i.e. what is normally considered to be the 'superstructure' of society. And Bukharin cast a wide net in this respect, including within it the state, political parties, trade unions, manners, customs, morals, sciences, philosophy, religion, art, and language.[67] All these expressions, Bukharin said, are determined by the base of society, for 'it is on the basis of the economic conditions that law, customs and morals are evolved in any society; they change and disappear with the economic system.'[68]

Although there are many different interests and conflicts between classes and groups within classes, these are regulated mainly by law, that is, by the state. This is of course the standard Marxist approach. However, Bukharin continued beyond that point, because although 'contradictions are here found at every step ... yet society and certain groups within it continue their relatively permanent existence.'[69] This is because there are 'supplementary norms [which] impress themselves on the minds of men, apparently from some inner source, and appear sacred to them, being voluntarily adhered to. Of such nature, for example, are the rules of morality ... binding upon all decent people.'[70] Bukharin was here writing about customs and culture which form an 'invisible sea' in which every member of society 'swims' from birth to the grave, often being unaware that many habits, manners, customs, even turns of speech, are not natural or innate, but are the product of specific social conditions. The ordinary 'common' life and 'common sense' are products of social conditioning which are particular to a mode of production *and* the national-historical-geographical particularities within that mode. This implies that Bukharin's vision is able to understand and explain quite diverse forms within a given mode of production. He correctly rejected the idea that such phenomena are in any way supernaturally inspired, arguing that:

> A close observation forces us to recognise two fundamental conditions: first, that these laws are subject to change; second, that they are connected with class, group, occupation, etc. It is also obvious that 'in the last analysis' they are likewise conditioned by the level attained by the productive forces.[71]

And here we arrive at a key element in Bukharin's theory of equilibrium, since he said:

> In general, these rules indicate the line of conduct conducive to a preservation of the society, class, or group in question, and requiring a subordination of the individual to the interests of the group. These norms are therefore *conditions of equilibrium* for holding together the internal contradictions of human social systems, whence it results that they must more or less coincide with the economic structure of society. It is impossible, for instance, in any society, for the system of its *dominant* manners and customs to be in permanent contradiction with its fundamental economic structure. Such an opposition would mean the complete absence of the fundamental condition for social equilibrium.[72]

It is in this passage that we can see the intricate mechanism that Bukharin conceived as social equilibrium. This is not a rigid or mechanical application of economic determinism, but the expression of the subtlety of the nuances of the relationship between economic structures and their forms, between these forms and the ruling ideology – and here ideology is not only the formal or legal system of ideas, but also – and perhaps more important – what is usually called 'common sense'. Rather than posing 'base' and 'superstructure' as two different parts of the social whole, it is clear that Bukharin integrated them into a cohesive totality, each acting upon, and being acted upon, by the many diverse elements of the whole. Moreover, Bukharin's approach enables one to locate the state proper in the wider framework of ideology, morals, customs, etc., rather than to exclusively concentrate upon the state as being reducible only to 'armed bodies of men'. Hence Bukharin's salutary conception of aggregates plays an important part, since it emphasises that it is 'the existence of a special *relationship* [which] turns a simple aggregate into a real one.'[73] He is thereby contrasting statistical aggregates, 'a sum of crabs in a basket is not a real unity',[74] with a real social totality, since these exist as true aggregates composed of people who form a *system* of mutually interacting elements; and 'this sort of aggregate excludes the concept of an arithmetical sum, because it is much greater and more complex than that sum.'[75]

Bukharin summed up his approach to internal equilibrium as follows:

> We have examined ... the phenomena of social equilibrium; but we must not lose sight of the fact that we are dealing with a mobile equilibrium ... We are dealing...with a process of contradictions, not of rest: we are not discussing a condition of absolute adjustment, but a struggle between opposites, a dialectical process of motion.[76] ...
>
> Again we emphasise that the law of social equilibrium is a law of mobile equilibrium, that includes antagonisms, contradictions, incompatibilities, conflicts, struggles, and – this is particularly important – that it cannot dispense, under certain circumstances, with catastrophes and revolutions, which are absolutely inevitable.[77]

This is the process, the dialectical process, of contradictory motion which produces social change, so that we can see that each situation of equilibrium is the result of change and the basis for change at one and the same time. Therefore:

> The process of social change is closely connected with changes in the condition of the productive forces. This movement of the productive forces, and the movement and regrouping of all social elements involved in it, is nothing more or less than a process of constant disturbance of social equilibrium, followed by re-establishments of equilibrium. Indeed, a progressive movement of the productive forces implies above all that a contradiction has arisen between the social technique and the social economy: the system loses its equilibrium.[78]...
>
> We may conceive of the restoration of social equilibrium in either of two ways: that of a gradual adaption of the various

elements in the social whole (evolution), and that of violent upheaval (revolution). We have seen from history that revolutions do sometimes occur; they are historical facts. It will be interesting to learn under what circumstances the adaption of the various elements of society proceeds by evolution, and under what circumstances by revolution.[79]

The interesting point in the above is that Bukharin posed the possibility of gradual evolutionary change within society, and did not see revolution as being the sole method of change. Which alternative is possible or likely can only be determined by an examination of a whole series of factors. And because 'not every conflict between the productive forces and the production relations results in revolution ... our task therefore will be to differentiate between the various aspects of these relations, and to determine what is the species of production relations in which a conflict would lead to revolution.'[80]

Bukharin laid down as a set of general propositions that:

Revolution ... occurs when there is outright conflict between the increased productive forces, which can no longer be housed within the envelope of the production relations ... i.e. property relations, ownership in the instruments of production. This envelope is then burst asunder. [Therefore] the cause of revolution is the conflict between the productive forces and the productive relations, as solidified in the political organisation of the ruling class. These production relations are so emphatic a brake on the evolution of the productive forces that they simply must be broken up if society is to continue to develop. If they cannot be burst asunder, they will prevent and stifle the unfolding of the productive forces, and the entire society will become stagnant or retrogressive, i.e. it will enter a period of decay.[81]

In so far as he considered capitalism, Bukharin thought that the growth of the productive forces was fettered by the emphatic brake of capitalist property relations, and thus the only possibility for the future progressive development was by means of a revolutionary overthrow of these relations. But to be truly progressive such a revolution must not only overthrow these capitalist property relations; there must also be instituted new, socialist, property relations.

It is here that Bukharin's particular conception of equilibrium comes to the fore, since – as he indicated – should there not be a revolution there is the possibility of stagnation and decay. Equally important is the possibility that a revolution might fail: this brings with it an unstable equilibrium with negative indications, since no society can pass through the traumas of failed revolution without paying some grievous penalties. But it is also possible that stagnation leading to decay might trigger off a crisis of inner collapse. This means that there is no guarantee that the resolution of social contradictions will always be at the point wished for by the major protagonists. This becomes a key idea when examining the development of the Soviet Union after 1917.

2

The Legend and Reality: Bukharin's Critics

Having explored Bukharin's exposition of historical materialism and his theory of equilibrium, let us pass on to examine some of the criticisms levelled against him in a little more detail.

The Methodology of the Critics

I pointed out in the previous chapter that the majority of Bukharin's critics did not attempt to verify their statements about Bukharin's ideas; instead they tended to make unsubstantiated assertions. This is indicative of the generally low level of scholarly concern on the part of Bukharin's critics, most of whom seem to have had an axe to grind. For instance, it is noteworthy that Lukacs, in his review of *Historical Materialism*, only quotes one complete sentence from the book and for the rest is content with odd phrases. The bulk of the article is taken up with Lukacs' own views as to what he thought Bukharin had meant, not what Bukharin actually said.

Gramsci, in his *Prison Notebooks*, does not once quote directly from Bukharin in 53 pages. In so far as he was writing in prison it is almost certain that Gramsci did not have access to a copy of Bukharin's book. The result is that Gramsci made some crass, blunders by apparently relying upon memory – memory going back several years moreover, seeing that he was arrested and imprisoned in 1927 and wrote his notes on Bukharin in the 1930s. Most of what Gramsci said about the book is what he thought should have been in it, rather than what *was* in it. It was as though Gramsci was more concerned to put his own thoughts on paper rather than considering the substance of his subject's ideas. At one point Gramsci asserted something directly contrary to the facts, that is, 'The Manual [*Historical Materialism*] contains no treatment of any kind of the dialectic' (p. 434). Yet, as we have seen, Bukharin dealt at length with this topic, and devoted a whole chapter to it. At another point Gramsci engages in a rather convoluted discussion of 'aggregates', presumably intending this to be a criticism of Bukharin, yet what he says has little relationship to what Bukharin actually wrote. It must be said that Gramsci's notes bear heavy traces of his long imprisonment and poor health. At times Gramsci resorts to abuse rather than argument: the whole section on Bukharin is woolly, and elliptical, with long asides on other writers. These notes comprise a travesty of what Bukharin actually said.

Thus, contrary to what a recent writer said,[1] Gramsci does not provide a 'substantial critique' of Bukharin – rather an incoherent set of notes that would best have been left to gather dust. Indeed, Gramsci in his more lucid moments appears to have been aware of some of the problems brought on by the ill-health besetting him, and wrote in one of his prison notebooks:

> Like those in the other books, the notes in this one have been written straight down without revision and are intended as memoranda. They all need to be revised and checked minutely, as they contain imprecise statements, false comparisons, and anachronisms. Since they were written in the absence of the works referred to, it is possible that after such a check they may have to be radically altered, and the very opposite of what is asserted here may well turn out to the case.[2]

So we may take it that Gramsci's criticisms of Bukharin would have been subject to considerable revision and in some cases dropped if he had lived to revise them in the light of a rereading of the actual text. It is a a great pity that Gramsci's comments should have been given such wide currency without his own caveat being constantly put before the reader.

In like vein Karl Korsch also criticised Bukharin in his *Marxism and Philosophy*, never attempting to come to grips with the substance of Bukharin's ideas. Marcel Liebman in 'Bukharin, Revolution and Social Development' in the *Socialist Register 1975*, whilst purporting to criticise Bukharin, uses the article's three and a half pages to discuss *Lenin's* conception of dialectics, without quoting Bukharin once nor directly counterposing Lenin and Bukharin. Raya Dunayevskaya, in his two books, *Marxism and Freedom* and *Philosophy and Revolution*, launches many attacks upon Bukharin, but again on the basis of odd phrases, with never one full sentence quoted.

Even Stephen Cohen, Bukharin's biographer, is occasionally cavalier in his treatment of Bukharin's ideas and texts. On page 117 of Cohen's book there are four lines supposedly 'quoted' from *Historical Materialism* that put a different interpretation upon some of Bukharin's ideas than those that I advance. When the reference for this 'quotation' is examined, however, we find 'Chapters V–VI; Ataka p. 119'. In other words, what purports to be a coherent statement by Bukharin is actually some phrases taken from two chapters of one book, spread out over 39 pages – some taken from one page in a separate collection of articles.

This brief look at the methods of Bukharin's critics indicates a need for caution on the part of readers towards any statement purporting to give Bukharin's opinions. It is for this reason that I have concentrated upon only two of Bukharin's critics in the rest of this chapter: Gustav Wetter and Georg Lukacs. Only these two writers have actually attempted to come to grips with the substance of Bukharin's ideas. Lukacs' criticisms have had a wide currency on account of his own international reputation, and thus, despite the deficiencies in his text, it is necessary to deal with him. Gustav Wetter, on the other hand, is little known, yet does attempt to deal with Bukharin in a coherent manner.

Wetter and Bukharin's 'Mechanism'

Wetter, in his book *Dialectical Materialism*,[3] expounds his views on the Soviet philosophical debate of the 1920s between the dialectical materialists and the so-called mechanists. Wetter placed Bukharin in the so-called mechanist school. It should be noted, however, that there is no direct evidence that Bukharin intervened in those philosophical debates. Wetter's categorisation of Bukharin, therefore, rested upon inferences drawn from Bukharin's writings upon other topics, in particular *Historical Materialism*.

Wetter characterised the mechanist school in the following terms:

The primary characteristic of the mechanist school is its fundamentally hostile attitude towards philosophy ... Hence the mechanists stand accused, in contemporary dialectical materialism, of a certain 'positivism', in as much as they deny the right to existence of any special discipline of philosophy...[4]

A further difference between dialectical materialism and mechanism lies in the mechanists' conception of the dialectic. They attribute all motion to impulses arriving from without, and thereby abandon that attribute of matter which dialectical materialists regard as most essential, namely its inner liveliness, that spontaneity which they describe ... as the self movement of matter.[5]

In his critique of Bukharin, Wetter argued that Bukharin retained a residue of Bogdanov's influence, as follows:

> ... his kinship with empirio-criticism shows itself in this, that he appears to derive the whole process of knowledge from the combination of sensations, and assumes that it is man himself who constructs his world from the chaotic mass of sensory elements. Science, according to this view, is concerned not with discovering general laws from among isolated facts, but with merely systematizing the products of knowledge.[6]

This was an odd claim to make about Bukharin, since the whole of *Historical Materialism* was precisely directed towards establishing such general laws of knowledge, and laws of development. The evidence that Wetter presented to substantiate this claim is the following extract from Bukharin's book: 'Science classifies, arranges, clarifies, eliminates the contradictions in, the thoughts of men: it constructs a complete raiment of scientific ideas and theories out of fragmentary knowledge.'[7]

It is difficult to understand how Wetter thought he could sustain his argument with this quotation, since Bukharin specifically mentioned 'theories' which within the context of his main point, can be said to correspond to Wetter's 'general laws'. It would seem somewhat ridiculous to suggest that Bukharin's theoretical position was that there were *no* general laws.

Moreover, when we examine the context from which Wetter extracted his quotation from Bukharin, his assertion becomes even more puzzling. The chapter in question is 'Equilibrium Between Social Elements', and the source of the quote is where Bukharin deals with the question of *art* and social life where he says: 'We shall now take up another order of social phenomena – art. Art is as much a product of the social life as is science or any other outgrowth of material production.'[8]

The quotation that Wetter gave is immediately followed by:

> But social man not only thinks, he also feels; he suffers, enjoys, regrets, rejoices, mourns, despairs, etc.; his thoughts may be of infinite complexity and delicacy; his psychic experiences may be tuned according to this note or that. Art systematizes these feelings.[9]

This is followed by a lengthy discussion of art. His reference to science was merely inserted to contrast it with art; it was a preliminary – almost throwaway – aside to indicate that science and art cannot be collapsed into each other, but that each must be studied separately as a specific field of enquiry. Bukharin was not purporting to establish a particular definition of science at that point in his discourse. Moreover, had Wetter so wanted, he could have found Bukharin adopting the exact opposite stance to that which was attributed to him, to wit:

> Everyone has observed that in nature and society there is a *definite* regularity, a *fixed* natural law. The determination of this natural law is the first task of science. This causality in nature and society is objective; it exists whether men are aware of it or not. The first step of science is to reveal this causality and free it from the surrounding chaos of phenomena. Marx considered the earmark of scientific knowledge to be its character as 'a sum of many determinations and relations', as opposed to a 'chaotic conception' ...[10]
>
> What constitutes such a law of cause and effect? Such a law is a necessary, inevitable, invariable and universal relation between phenomena.[11]

It was entirely tendentious, therefore, for Wetter to have asserted that Bukharin was not concerned to assimilate knowledge in a manner which establishes 'general laws'.

However, Wetter continued by saying: 'Much more important than this epistemological standpoint is Bukharin's celebrated "equilibrium theory", which was so violently attacked by the Russian dialectical materialists. It derives from the mechanistic view that Bukharin takes of the dialectic.'[12] So we arrive – once more – at equilibrium theory and its alleged inconsistency with dialectics. Wetter asserted that, despite Bukharin's proclaiming himself as a dialectical materialist, and despite the fact 'the term "internal contradiction" is repeatedly employed by him'[13] there is such a difference between Lenin and Bukharin as to throw doubt upon the latter's credentials as a dialectical materialist. Wetter argued that:

> Lenin sees the heart of the dialectic in the unity of opposites, and these dialectical opposites lie, moreover, in the inner nature of all things and phenomena as such: 'Dialectic in the proper sense is the study of contradiction in the nature of things as such.' Hence it follows that things in dialectical opposition do not merely negate and exclude one another, but also presuppose and

confirm one another; the bourgeoisie not only negates the proletariat but presupposes it; for without the proletariat there can be no question of the bourgeoisie either.[14]

Now it is true that Bukharin does not use exactly the same phrases as Lenin, or Wetter, and it might be possible to convict him on the principle of 'the dog that did not bark' being significant. If one reads Bukharin looking for set phrases then one may indeed be disappointed. But any serious reading of *Historical Materialism* will soon convince one that Bukharin did have an adequate grasp of unity in contradiction. Even where he seems at his most 'mechanistic' he is in fact applying the dialectic. For instance, in discussing Hegel, he said: 'It is quite possible to transcribe the "mystical" (as Marx put it) language of the Hegelian dialectics into the language of modern mechanics.'

A critic looking for 'mechanism' could seize upon this with relish; but they would be unwise to do so, since Bukharin immediately followed this with:

Not long ago, almost all Marxians objected to the mechanical terminology, owing to the persistence of the ancient conception of the atom as a detached isolated particle. But now that we have the Electron Theory, which represents atoms as complete solar systems, we have no reason to shun this mechanical terminology.[15]

So when Bukharin wrote about mechanics, it was to the then modern theories of physics that he was referring, and as such incorporated the elements which Wetter said were missing. As we shall see, Bukharin's reference to electron theory was relevant to later passages.

The point that Wetter was pursuing here is that:

Whereas for Lenin the internal unity of opposites gives rise to self-movement, a genuine movement *ab intra*; motion, for Bukharin, is the product of antagonisms between opposing forces. The origin of motion lies outside things, motion is conceived of mechanically as local motion, occasioned by an impulse supervening from without.[16]

Wetter was confusing the issue here by posing some opposition between on the one hand internal contradictions and movement, and on the other movement in time and space. Nowhere in the writings of Bukharin (or Lenin) can be found anything to suggest, let alone substantiate, the idea that there could be matter *without* motion, or motion without matter. In other words this was such a fundamental idea that it was almost taken for granted. None the less, Bukharin did spell out, quite clearly, his view on the question:

> there is nothing immutable and rigid in the universe. We are not dealing with rigid things, but with a process. The table at which I am writing at this moment cannot be considered an immutable thing: it is changing from second to second. To be sure, these changes may be imperceptible to the human eye or ear. But the table, if it should continue to stand for many years would rot away and be transformed into dust.[17]

Bukharin saw everything in motion, but according to Wetter, Lenin would have Bukharin's table decay because of 'inner contradictions', whilst apparently Bukharin would see decay caused by some external forces. Wetter in fact posed a false dichotomy here. The table cannot be extracted from its environment; the wood it was made from was only able to grow by a combination of internal and external 'motion', such as rain, sunshine, soil, chemicals and capillary action. Similarly, the process of decay would be a combination of action and re-action of the wood to its environment.

Lenin's study of contradiction in the nature of things 'as such', does not thereby exclude this 'things' environment, since it is *inconceivable* without it. All motion and rest is relative, not absolute.

Wetter proceeded to examine Bukharin's theory of equilibrium and the necessary conditions for change therein, and ended with the following quotation from Bukharin:

> It is quite clear that the internal structure of the system (its internal equilibrium) must change together with the relations existing between the system and its environment. The latter relation is the decisive factor; for the entire situation of the system, the fundamental forms of its motion (decline, prosperity, or stagnation) are determined by this relation only. Consequently, the internal (structural) equilibrium is a quantity which depends on the external equilibrium (is a 'function' of this external equilibrium).[18]

Wetter's comment on this was:

The dialectical materialists very properly object to this explanation that makes it impossible to continue to speak of 'internal contradictions' as it does of the origin of motion, since the former is in fact derived from the relation of the system to its environment. Moreover, this solution offers no answer to the question as to the actual origin of motion: for if this motion be ascribed to the disturbance of equilibrium between 'system' and 'environment', the question still arises, as to how this disturbance comes about. Mitin is correct when he observed that, if Bukharin is to remain consistent, he has no alternative but to assume some sort of supernatural power, which has ordinarily been described as the 'First Mover', or simply as God the creator.[19]

In that passage Wetter had quite clearly presented the central issue. But in so doing he revealed his own misunderstanding. We have seen that Bukharin held the view that everything is in motion and hence in contradiction both internally and externally, that is, in relation to its environment. Therefore he saw the question, quite correctly, not as being how to explain motion, but rather how to explain non-motion, how to explain rest (equilibrium). Since matter and motion are inseparable, a condition of rest can only be a relative one, not absolute. It is Wetter who sought to discover the origin of motion, and who was seeking the 'First Mover'. When he posed the question as an either/or, or internal versus external origin, he was posing the problem in terms of a motionless system in motionless environment; and then he asked 'how will motion start?'. If such a system could exist, could be achieved, then the question of internal or external mechanical origin of motion would become irrelevant. The question would then become *who* was the first mover, i.e. was it God?

Looking at the passage that Wetter quoted from Bukharin on this question, it is true that Bukharin posed the conditions as being that internal equilibrium is a fundamental function of the external equilibrium; but Wetter's interpretation implied a unilinear, one way, relationship, and drew the conclusion, by implication, that the internal equilibrium is a *passive* factor in the relationship. But there is nothing in what Bukharin actually wrote to sustain such a view. His whole argument was based upon a *reciprocal* relationship in which the environment plays a decisive role. But this decisive role, final determination, is itself only conditional, having no *absolute* meaning.

Let us take a simple and contemporary example: the problem of oil supplies. Oil is a part of the environment – part of the natural resources available to society. Though it has not always been present, but it can be counted as a 'given' in the nature/society relationship. The enormous increase in the consumption of oil over the last few decades is the result of changes in the internal equilibrium of industrial society. This has reacted upon the environment: once assumed to be a limitless resource, oil is now seen as finite. In other words the system is conditioned by its relationship with the environment and, as we know, there is now some urgency in finding new sources of energy. This in turn will, no doubt, have repercussions upon the environment and perhaps there will emerge a new equilibrium between it and the system (society). But each new development will affect both the system and the environment. The germane point here is: do we count oil solely as an external factor in relation to society or is it an internal one? And the answer is that it is both.

If there emerge new sources of energy because oil supplies run out, will the changes (movement) in society be due to external factors – no more oil – or to internal factors, the system itself having used up all the oil? To pose the question in this manner is really meaningless, since we are dealing with a reciprocal relationship.

As we have seen, Bukharin specifically rejected the possibility of a stable equilibrium. And since he posited that all equilibria – in society – have either a positive or negative indication, the idea of motion *and* equilibrium are inseparably embedded in his theory.

In this respect Bukharin closely followed Engels, who also said:

> *Motion and equilibrium.* Equilibrium is inseparable from motion. In the motion of the heavenly bodies there is *motion in equilibrium* and *equilibrium in motion* (relative). But all specifically relative motion, i.e., here all separate motion of individual bodies on one of the heavenly bodies in motion, is an effort to establish relative rest, equilibrium. The possibility of bodies being at relative rest, the possibility of temporary states of equilibrium, is the essential condition for the differentiation of matter and hence of life.[20]

Wetter's attempt to place Bukharin in the mechanist camp and in opposition to 'orthodox' Marxism is therefore spurious; even if that 'orthodoxy' appears in the form of Lenin's notes.

Lukacs, Technology and Society

Turning to Lukacs and his criticism of Bukharin, we find – unfortunately – arguments of the same order and substance. Lukacs maintained that:

> Bukharin sets out a precise parallel between the hierarchy of power in the structure of economic production on the one hand and that of the State on the other. He closes with the remark: 'Thus we see here that the structure of the state apparatus reflects that of the economy – i.e. *the same classes* occupy the same positions in both.' This is undoubtedly correct as a developmental tendency. It is also true that a long-run, major contradiction between the two hierarchies usually leads to a revolutionary upheaval. But concrete history will not fit into Bukharin's over-schematic, simplified formula. For it is perfectly possible that a balance of economic power between two classes in competition may produce a state apparatus not really controlled by either ... so that the economic structure is by no means simply reflected in the state.[21]

It should be noted that the section of *Historical Materialism* to which Lukacs was referring is entitled 'The Outline of the Superstructure'; therefore, precisely because it is an outline, it cannot be considered as anything more than a preliminary statement. This being the case it should surprise no one that Bukharin's statements appear to be somewhat categorical, without the qualifications and nuances that an extended treatment would entail. Moreover, Lukacs' suggestion of a state not wholly controlled by a particular class does not in itself contradict Bukharin's proposition – it merely elaborates it. This elaboration would be one suggesting the a-typical, whilst Bukharin outlined the typical.

Lukacs moved on to say:

> But we must not confine ourselves to details. More important than such oversights, Bukharin deviates from the true tradition of historical materialism in several not inessential points ... This remark applies particularly to the introductory philosophical chapter, where Bukharin is suspiciously close to what Marx aptly called bourgeois materialism. Bukharin apparently does not know of the critique of this theory by Mehring and Plekhanov ... which sharply restricts its validity for an understanding of the historical process because of the particular place of history in historical, dialectical materialism.[22]

The first thing to note about the above is that Lukacs rather gave the game away by admitting that his previous thrusts at Bukharin were aimed at 'oversights'. Now, either he was criticising Bukharin for 'oversights', in which case he acknowledged that Bukharin was aware of the substance or he was insinuating that Bukharin was ignorant.

Secondly, we have the dubious manner of argument: first, that he said Bukharin 'is suspiciously close', not *is* a bourgeois materialist. None the less, this remark has the effect of painting Bukharin in that hue; second, he had recourse to authority: Marx says ... and therefore Bukharin must be wrong. However, it is not clear what precisely Bukharin was 'guilty' of. Finally, we have the debating ploy of 'of course Bukharin has not read', which was rather cheap and, in the case of Bukharin, very unwise since both of the writers mentioned by Lukacs were quoted by Bukharin! Of all the Bolshevik leaders, Bukharin was universally recognised by serious writers to have been the most widely read and erudite, not only in Marxist literature but of all material relating to the topics he dealt with.

Having set the scene, Lukacs moved on to make what can only be described as an astounding claim, viz: 'Of course, Hegel is mentioned from time to time, but the essential comparison of his and Marx's dialectic is absent.'[23] Yet, in *Historical Materialism* we find:

Since Hegel, being an idealist, regards everything as a self-evolution of the spirit, he of course did not have any disturbances of equilibrium in mind, and the properties of thought as a spiritual and original thing was therefore, in his mind, properties also of being. Marx wrote in this connection: 'My dialectic method is not only different from the Hegelian, but is its direct opposite. To Hegel, the life-process of the human brain, i.e. the process of thinking, which, under the name of "the idea", he even transforms into an independent subject, is the demiurgos of the real world, and the real world is only the external, phenomenal form of the "idea". With me, on the contrary, the ideal is nothing else than the material world reflected by the human mind and translated into forms of thought ... With him (Hegel) it (dialectics) is standing on its head. It must be turned right side up again, if you would discover the rational kernel within the mystical shell.'[24] For Marx, dialectics means evolution by means of contradictions, particularly, a law of 'being', a law of movement, a law of motion in nature and society.[25]

Thus we can see that Lukacs could only make that particular charge against Bukharin by what would seem to be an almost wilful disregard of the evidence. Could it be perhaps that Lukacs acknowledged that Bukharin did use the above passage from Marx, but thought he did not understand it? If he did, he did not say so. Or was it that Lukacs was not as familiar with the contents of Bukharin's work as he perhaps imagined he was? We can only speculate upon such points. Whatever the case, it is patently obvious that Bukharin *did* in fact make the key distinction between Hegel's use of the dialectic and Marx's, i.e. he emphasised Marx's *materialist* dialectic. This would seem to have been Lukacs' real concern, but he could not bring himself directly to challenge Marx, therefore he closed his eyes to the evidence and asserted that 'Bukharin rejects all the elements in Marxist method which derive from classical German philosophy.'[26] The reason why Lukacs put this forward becomes clear when we examine the following:

> The closeness of Bukharin's theory to bourgeois, natural-scientific materialism derives from his use of 'science' (in the French sense) as a model. In its concrete application to society and history it therefore frequently obscures the specific feature of Marxism: that all *economic or 'sociological' phenomena derive from the social relations of men to one another*. Emphasis on a false 'objectivity' in theory leads to fetishism.[27]

The key idea here seems to be that which Lukacs himself emphasised, yet it is incomplete, since it posits economic and social relations as though hanging in mid-air, without any material basis. The emphasis that Lukacs used led *him* to distort Marx's historical materialism. Marx expressed the matter as follows:

> In the process of production, human beings work not only upon nature, but also upon one another. They produce only by working together in a specified manner and reciprocally exchanging their activities. In order to produce, they enter into definite connection and relations to one another, and only within these social connections and relations does their influence upon nature operate, i.e., does production take place.[28]

It can be seen that Marx did not only consider 'social relations of men to one another' but also placed them in the context of their 'relations with nature'. Bukharin also put social relations within the same frame of reference, and in this sense was more in keeping with Marx than was Lukacs. Therefore when Lukacs criticised Bukharin in this manner he was implicitly criticising Marx also. That is, of course, not something to be condemned in itself; Marx cannot be placed in a category which places him beyond criticism. But the attempt to counterpose Marx to Bukharin in this way only introduced confusion and side-stepped the central issues.

The precise issue upon which Lukacs was focusing becomes evident from the following:

> Bukharin attributes to technology a far too determinant position, which completely misses the *spirit* of dialectical materialism. (It is undeniable that quotations from Marx and Engels can be found which *it is possible* to interpret in this way.) Bukharin remarks: 'Every given system of social technique *determines* human work relations as well.'[29]

It will be seen that Bukharin was first charged with a nebulous 'offence', that is, missing the 'spirit' of dialectical materialism. This is a catch-all accusation; rather like the charge of 'dumb insolence' that could be brought in the armed forces, the 'crime' is wholly in the eyes of the beholder but does not exist as a verifiable *act*. And, Lukacs admitted, Marx and Engels could be summoned as witnesses for the defence: but even *their* statements were suspect. Perhaps this meant that Lukacs felt competent to divine the 'real spirit' of any such statements as opposed to the actual words used? However, we lesser mortals can only rely upon the words we have before us...

All this, of course, lays the ground for the specific charge of allowing technology the determining role, and this is supported by one sentence, which can be shown to have been taken out of context. The section of Bukharin's work which the particular sentence is taken from is entitled 'Social Technology and Economic Structure of Society'. Bukharin pointed out that: 'In speaking of the social technology, we of course meant not a certain tool, or the aggregate of different tools, but the whole *system* of these tools in society.'[30]

He then proceeded, at length, to discuss how certain tools can operate or be operated within the context of this social technology. To cite one example, he pointed out that to have a textile *industry* presupposes mining, iron making, machine making, etc., and all of these will require specific types of labour and skills. What Bukharin was therefore concentrating upon, at that point in his text, was the necessary proportionality of specific, concrete use-values and labour, as opposed to value and abstract labour characteristic of commodity production of the capitalist type.

After this exposition Bukharin said: 'Thus, as there is a definite relation and a definite proportion between the various branches of production; there is also in social technology a certain definite relation between its parts as well as a definite prevailing proportion.'[31]

It was only *after* this that he said: 'This being the case, it is also clear that each given system of social technology also determines the system of labour relations between persons.'[32]

Note that he said 'relations between persons' not relations between classes. He was saying that with a given system of social technology there are required specific, concrete types of labour, which determine the work relationships between people. But if the system changes these relationships also change. In fact what he was writing about at that point was the changes in labour markets which technical change induces, that is, the creation of new skills and the de-skilling of other workers. This recurrent phenomenon has meant that various strata of the workforce have become defunct, whilst new ones appear, or that certain strata have become relatively smaller or of less economic importance. A quite recent example of this process at work has been the reduction in the number of dockworkers as a result of containerisation. Another example might be the dramatic changes – de-skilling – in the Swiss watch industry with the introduction of microchip technology into chronometers and watches.

Lukacs attempted to show, with one isolated sentence, that Bukharin had put forward the idea that *class* relations are determined by social technology. However, it is clear from any serious examination of what Bukharin actually wrote that he was suggesting something quite different, namely that a given technology determines the given *technical* division of labour.

None the less, Lukacs continued:

He [Bukharin] insists: 'If technique changes, the division of labour in society also changes.' He asserts that 'in the last analysis' society is dependent upon the development of technique, which is seen as the 'basic determinancy' of the 'productive forces of society', etc. It is obvious that this final identification of technique with the forces of production is neither valid nor Marxist.[33]

But it is not at all clear why Lukacs objected to the idea that if techniques change, then so will the division of labour. One can only point to the empirically observable fact that this is the case, verifiable practically any day of the week. Since Lukacs claimed to be a more 'orthodox' Marxist than Bukharin it would seem appropriate to enquire as to what Marx said on this topic. In *Capital* we find:

> Modern industry never looks upon or treats the existing form of a process as final. The technical basis of that industry is therefore revolutionary, while all earlier modes of production were essentially conservative. By means of machinery, chemical processes and other methods, it is continually causing changes not only in the technical basis of production, but also in the functions of the labourer, and in the social combination of the labour-process. At the same time, it thereby also revolutionizes the division of labour within the society.[34]

But the main aim of Lukacs was to couple this question with his second objection, i.e. that technique is the final determination of the productive forces of society. However, there is no logical reason why the two aspects should be linked in this way – they are separate issues.

With the first aspect out of the way, we can now turn to the second. It is significant that Lukacs did not quote directly more than the occasional phrase from Bukharin on this point, because in reality the textual evidence points in the opposite direction to that suggested by Lukacs.

For instance, Bukharin wrote:

> we have seen from the example of the two different societies chosen (the ancient and the modern) that *the combinations of the instruments of labour* (social technology) are the deciding factor in the combinations and relations of men, i.e., in social economy. But there is another phase of the production relations, namely, the question of the *social classes*, which is to be discussed later in detail.[35]

What Bukharin was referring to here was the division of labour and the necessary proportionality of the distribution of labour with a given technology. Obviously, the question of social class does impinge upon such a distribution, but for the purposes of analytical exposition the two aspects can be separated. Moreover, Bukharin's remarks were set in the context of an examination of the *differences* engendered by the type of social system under scrutiny.

Regardless of this, Lukacs plunged on, saying:

> Technique is a *part*, a moment, naturally of great importance, of the social productive forces, but it is neither simply identical with them, nor (as some of Bukharin's earlier points would seem to imply) the final or absolute moment of the changes in these forces. This attempt to find the underlying determinants of society and its development in a principle other than that of social relations between men in the process of production ... that is in the economic structure of society correctly conceived – leads to fetishism, as Bukharin himself elsewhere admits.[36]

It can be seen that Lukacs himself made a similar error to that which he imputed to Bukharin. Lukacs said that technique is a part, a moment, in the formation of the social productive forces, but also that it is social relations which are decisive. In so far as he ascribed primacy to social relations he severed the link between social conditions and the material basis for them. It is historically well attested that a number of technological innovations were present in some societies but were not used because the social conditions for their application were lacking. For example, printing and gunpowder were available in ancient China, but were not widely used. On the other hand such new techniques were taken to Western Europe and extensively applied.

From this it might be inferred that Lukacs was correct in assuming that technology is only a 'moment' in social change. But he failed to understand the crucial importance of the necessary *union* of new techniques and the appropriate social conditions which develop the forces of production, the combination of which provides the engine of social change. What was lacking, again, in Lukacs' account was the reciprocal of technique and social conditions upon economic development. Moreover, Lukacs failed to confront the problem of a lack of technology and its effects upon development. The social conditions for change may be present, but unless the necessary techniques are, or become, available, the initial impulses will be dissipated. Thus there is a voluntarist element in Lukacs, which is absent in Bukharin.

Bukharin was able to understand, also, that the introduction of new technology, or the products of it, could lead to far reaching social change. This is particularly so when this new technology is introduced into a particular society from outside. In this respect Bukharin's theory specifically allows for the reciprocal effects of technology and social conditions, and thus does not rely upon monocausal explanations.

The Theory of Equilibrium

It is now possible to return to the questions posed at the start of Chapter 1, and also provide a summary of Bukharin's theory of equilibrium.

The first question posed was, did Bukharin misunderstand dialectics and/or the philosophical component of Marxism? The answer to this must be a qualified *no*. As I have demonstrated, Bukharin proceeded on the basis of historical abstractions, and in this respect his method was in the tradition of Marx and Engels. He saw historical materialism as a *general* method of investigation, and – again – there was nothing in this view that directly contradicted Marx and Engels. However, the qualification that should be added is that Bukharin rather heavily relied upon illustrations which tended towards the mechanistic, and his exposition has in some instances provided ammunition for his critics. There is also, in certain passages, a tendency to reduce the social to the natural. However Bukharin did not make such a fundamental mistake – it was rather that he sometimes oversimplified his text, having in view his readers, i.e. ordinary party members. That is not to say that society is not a part of nature, but that it is a special part of it, with the ability to change the relationship in a conscious and predetermined manner. Bukharin in no way denied this, and the allegation that he accorded primacy to the external (i.e. nature) in the determination of internal social equilibrium can only be upheld by a tendentious use, or misuse, of quotations taken out of context. Lenin's remarks notwithstanding, Bukharin cannot be held to have either misunderstood or misused the dialectical method. That is not to say that his particular presentation, or use of the method, is one that would accord with the use to which his critics put it; but to expect this is to assume that Bukharin saw problems in *exactly* the same light as they did. Moreover, one should not approach Bukharin with preconceived judgements. Most of his critics do this and rarely, if ever, is Bukharin mentioned without the somewhat ritualistic reference to Lenin's testament. In terms of the actual writings of Marx and Engels, Bukharin's use of historical materialism cannot be faulted in any major respect.

The second question posed was related to the first, since it asked:

does Bukharin's understanding or misunderstanding of dialectics vitiate his contribution to the development of Marxist theory? The answer to this question must be an unqualified no. He made numerous contributions which were original and trail-blazing, for example, on imperialism, the theory of the imperialist state, the economics of the transition period, and his critique of marginalist economics.

This does not imply an uncritical attitude towards Bukharin. Sometimes his mistakes were of historical importance. However, if one wants to understand both his mistakes and his positive contributions, it is first of all necessary to understand his writings and his ideas. He must be judged on his own terms, his own merits and de-merits; and by placing him in the period in which he lived.

This brings us to the theory of equilibrium. What are the essential elements of this theory? First, there is the concept of regularity both in nature and society, and this regularity of phenomena is necessary for any generalisation to be made, since one cannot generalise from the accidental. Coupled with this is the acknowledgement of the objective nature of the material world, i.e. a materialist viewpoint. And, as a complement to these two aspects, there is causality. That is, every cause must result in some effect and every effect is related to some cause; thus there is an interconnection between events in the material world. Secondly, Bukharin incorporated the dialectical notions of continual movement and change, with the Hegelian concepts of thesis, antithesis and synthesis, that is, a change from quantity to quality at some point. This brings to the fore the question of necessary conditions, since if we have cause and effect, movement and change, we must know under what conditions such movements will take place. However, what may be necessary presuppositions for change may not in themselves be sufficient for change to take place. This means that only when necessary conditions reach a critical point will they become sufficient for change to occur.

Thirdly, there is the relationship between the internal system and the environment, but these are not rigid or predetermined entities, i.e., what can at one time be considered 'internal' is also 'external' when looked at from a different perspective. Bukharin pointed out that for the individual, society is the immediate environment, yet society itself is set in the natural environment, and so on.

Fourthly, we have a *formal* definition of equilibrium, taken from Van Halban, which says:

The precise conception of equilibrium is about as follows: 'We say of a system that it is in a state of equilibrium when the system cannot of itself, i.e., without supplying energy to it from without, emerge from this state.' If – let us say – forces are at work on a body, neutralizing each other, that body is in a state of equilibrium; an increase or decrease in one of these forces will disturb the equilibrium.[37]

However, since Bukharin viewed the question of equilibrium from a dialectical point of view, i.e. constant motion, his view was that equilibrium is always an *unstable* state, never at rest: either there is motion forwards or backwards. This view of equilibrium, as being inherently unstable, is not precisely the same as a theory of dynamic equilibrium, since it does not necessarily suppose progression, only the possibility of it.

The fifth point, therefore, is that for Bukharin, contradiction is at the heart of equilibrium. And it follows that equilibrium is a *mobile* state. This must not be taken to mean, however, that such motion is of the order which will *necessarily* guarantee a qualitative change in the terms of the equilibrium. Whilst for some it may appear strange that a revolutionary such as Bukharin should develop a theory of equilibrium, such a view is itself odd since it starts from the premise that a stable equilibrium is the only form of equilibrium, and by implication that internal forces are inert. Bukharin's conception of equilibrium starts from the premise of opposed or contradictory forces which are united, which are not inert but are in motion as a part of the same totality.

This led Bukharin to consider that for most of the time society was in a state of unstable equilibrium with positive indications, and that *historically* the breakdown of that situation was not frequent. It is this aspect perhaps more than any other which distinguished Bukharin both from the vulgar evolutionists and vulgar voluntarists.

There is no justification for the view that Bukharin believed that the final and determinate cause of disequilibrium within society was located externally. Only by a misunderstanding of the various stages of his exposition is such a view tenable. The merit of his theory of equilibrium is that it attempts to synthesise the natural, social, economic and ideological factors into an account of the stability and instability of society at given stages of historical development.

Coming to our final question, was Bukharin's use of the underlying conception of Marx's schemas of reproduction valid? Again the answer is yes, and I shall deal more fully with this point in the next chapters. Here I will say the following: Marx's model as expressed in the schemas is essentially an equilibrium one, and there is an affinity between it and Van Halban's equilibrium theorem. The affinity is superficial, however and the real substantive affinity is between Bukharin's unstable equilibrium and Marx's schemas. The schemas of Marx are built upon the premise of Say's Law of Markets, i.e. of general equilibrium between supply and demand, but this is done precisely to show that crisis could occur even if such equilibrium did obtain.[38] In this respect Marx's schemas seek to demonstrate the necessary conditions for equilibrium for total social capital and total social production. But they do not establish both necessary *and* sufficient conditions for such equilibrium. Bukharin's use of the model is well articulated in his analysis of the necessary conditions for proportionality and balanced growth within an economy. When we come to examine his attitude towards Soviet economic development we shall be able to locate his equilibrium model in the context of the debate of the 1920s.

3

Equilibrium and Economic Growth

Reproduction in the Economy is a Process of Equilibrium

As we have seen, equilibrium was central to Bukharin's approach relating to social, political and economic problems. With reference to the economy he said: 'To find the law of this equilibrium is the basic problem of theoretical economics and theoretical economics as a scientific system is the result of an examination of the entire capitalist system in its state of equilibrium.'[1]

It is here, therefore, that we shall examine Bukharin's use of the concepts of simple and expanded reproduction (which Marx used in volumes I and II of *Capital*) in the exchanges between society and nature. Bukharin first posed this exchange as follows: 'Considered as a whole, we find that the process of reproduction is a process of constant disturbance and re-establishment of equilibrium between society and nature. Marx distinguishes between simple reproduction and reproduction *on an extending scale*.'[2]

In the case of simple reproduction there is no growth, either of means of production or of the total social product. Marx was of course examining reproduction in its particular *capitalist* form, and hence tended to emphasise this aspect. Bukharin, on the other hand, was initially posing the problem in a more general manner. Yet there is sufficient relationship between the two to consider the similarities.

Marx made the point that: 'Production in general is an abstraction, but a sensible abstraction insofar as it actually emphasises and defines the common aspects and thus avoids repetition.'[3]

And in the specific case of capitalist production, and simple reproduction in particular, he said:

If we study the annual function of social capital – hence of the total capital of which the individual capital forms only fractional parts, whose movement is their individual movement and simultaneously integrating link in the movement of the total capital – and its results, i.e., if we study the commodity-product furnished by society during the year, then it must become apparent how the process of reproduction of the social capital takes place, what characteristics distinguish this process of reproduction from the process of reproduction of an individual capital, and what characteristics are common to both. The annual product includes those portions of the social product which replace capital, namely social reproduction, as well as those which go to the consumption fund, those which are consumed by labourers and capitalists, hence both productive and individual consumption. It comprises also the reproduction (i.e. maintenance) of the capitalist class and the working class, and thus the reproduction of the capitalist character of the entire process of production.[4]

From the above passage we can see that an examination of the production, circulation and consumption of the total social product presents different problems from those posed by the movement of a single capital. For the individual capital the external relations are given in a narrow manner, that is, its main problem is seen as that of the transformation of its commodity-value-product into the money-form of value. It is assumed that it will find on the market, readily available, the correct quantity and quality of means of production and labour-power necessary for it to restart its production cycle. In other words, the assumption is that the transformation from money-capital to commodity-capital and back to money-capital again will find no external barriers, other than the market.

When we examine the reproduction of the total social product, however, other problems emerge. What was previously assumed to be given for a single capital now needs to be explained. The renewal of one production cycle now depends upon the results of the previous one, i.e., to start this production cycle there must be produced means of production of the correct quantity and quality with which to repeat the process. Marx posed the question as follows:

How is the *capital* consumed in production replaced in value out of the annual product and how does the movement of this replacement intertwine with the consumption of ... the capitalists and ... the labourers? ... So long as we looked upon the production of value and the value of the product of capital individually, the bodily form of the commodities produced was wholly immaterial for the analysis, whether it was machines, for instance, corn, or looking glasses. It was always but a matter of illustration, and any branch of production could have served that purpose equally well ... This merely formal manner of presentation is no longer adequate in the study of the total social capital and of the value of its products. The reconversion of one portion of the value of the product into capital and the passing of another portion into the individual consumption of the capitalist as well as the working class form a movement within the value of the product itself in which the result of the aggregate capital finds expression; and this movement is not only a replacement of value, *but also a replacement in material and is therefore as much bound up with the relative proportions of the value-components of the total social product as with their use-value, their material shape.*[5] [emphasis added]

Marx resolved this question by positing that the total social productive capital and the total social product is divided into two major departments of production.[6]

Department I produces all means of production and Department II produces all means of consumption. In his schemata of reproduction Marx suggested that if equilibrium is to subsist for total social production, then there must exist definite proportions between the two departments *and* proportionality in the exchanges between the two departments.

Although Marx highlighted the necessity of the proportionality between use-values in such exchanges in the passage just quoted from, in his own analysis he still concentrated upon the creation of value and surplus-value in his examination of the capitalist production process. This concentration, upon the value aspects, can be misleading, and in fact has led to a certain neglect by many Marxists of the material, use-value, aspects of reproduction and the centrality of this use-value in the reproduction schema.[7]

Bukharin was not one of those who neglected the material aspects of the reproduction schemata. On the contrary, he began by examining the material aspect of production in general, and the exchange aspects of this material production, saying:

We have seen that in the process of production, the means of production are used up (the raw material is worked over, various auxiliary substances are required ... machines themselves, and the buildings in which the work is done, as well as all kinds of instruments ... wear out); on the other hand, labour-power is also exhausted (when people work, they also deteriorate, their labour-power is used up, and a certain expenditure must be incurred in order to re-establish this labour-power). In order that the process of production may continue, it is necessary to reproduce in it and by means of it the substances that it consumes.[8]

He then proceeded to elaborate what he meant by this consumption, for example, that cotton is turned into fabric, so new cotton must be grown; fabric is worn out, so that new fabric must be woven, etc. And the same applies to all material aspects of production. Therefore: 'If this replacement proceeds smoothly and at the same rate as the disappearance, we have a case of simple reproduction, which corresponds to a situation in which the productive social labour remains uniform, with the productive forces unchanging.'[9]

And, Bukharin concluded:

It is clear that this is a case of stable equilibrium between society and nature. It involves constant disturbances of equilibrium (disappearance of products in consumption and deterioration) and a constant re-establishment of equilibrium (the products reappear); but this re-establishment is always on the old basis.[10]

Looking at extended reproduction, he said:

But where the productive forces are increasing, the case is different. Here ... a portion of the social labour is liberated and devoted to an extension of social production (new production branches; extension of old branches). This involves not only a replacement of the formerly existing elements of production, but also the insertion of new elements into the new cycle of production. Production here does not continue on the same path, moving in the same cycles all the time, but increases in scope. This is *production on an extending scale*, in which case equilibrium is always established on a new basis; simultaneously with a certain consumption proceeds a larger production; consumption consequently also increases, while production increases still further. Equilibrium results in each case on a wider basis; we are now dealing with *unstable equilibrium with positive indication*.[11]

In so far as Bukharin was discussing the relationship between society and nature he focused his attention almost wholly upon the material aspects of the exchanges. Yet it is clear that his approach was overwhelmingly based upon Marx's reproduction schemata, and it would seem to be an entirely legitimate use of the concepts embodied in Marx's work. The schemata of Marx concentrate upon equilibrium *between* the elements of social production and *assume* that the equilibrium between social production and nature is pre-established.

Bukharin, since he was writing for a somewhat different purpose – at that point in his exposition – did not assume or leave implicit the equilibrium between society and nature, but instead desired to show that it is a necessary basis, precondition, for the situation that Marx dealt with. In this respect there is a difference of emphasis between the two writers, but at the same time there is a fundamental unity of purpose and method between them. I would suggest that it is probable that Marx, as a materialist, would not have disagreed with Bukharin's exposition of the case, since Marx's own illustrations of simple and extended reproduction were implicitly based upon the same assumptions. Indeed, the only correct way to read Marx's reproduction schemas is to firmly grasp the interconnection between the value and use-value aspect of the model and the relationships they seek to demonstrate.

In one respect Bukharin's presentation of the reproduction process is superior to Marx's since he also included the necessity for a proportional distribution of labour within it. This is not to say that Marx was unaware of the need for such a proportional distribution of labour, but this was not directly discussed in his own exposition of the schemas of reproduction.

Marx's Reproduction Schemas

Marx formalised his ideas about simple and extended reproduction in Vol. II of *Capital* (Chapters XX and XXI), but did not live to put this part of his work in order for publication, so it was left to Engels to prepare the various drafts for the printer. An examination of Volume II will quickly reveal the unfinished nature of parts of the material, but there is sufficient there to enable the reader to arrive at an understanding of Marx's ideas.

It is the unfinished nature of those parts dealing with the schemas of reproduction that has given rise to a number of controversies regarding the interpretation of them. Possibly the most famous controversy was initiated by Rosa Luxemburg in 1913 with the publication of her book *The Accumulation of Capital*.[12] Luxemburg was vigorously criticised by a number of leading Marxists at that time, such as Otto Bauer and Karl Kautsky, and while she was in prison during the First World War she wrote a reply to her critics. This *Anti-Critique* was only published after her death,[13] and Bukharin joined the debate only in 1924 with his own book, *Imperialism and the Accumulation of Capital*.[14]

Let is look briefly at Marx's presentation of his schemas before examining Bukharin's ideas.

Marx built a model of simple reproduction upon the following assumptions:

- Only two departments of production; Dept. I produces all means of production and Dept. II produces all means of consumption.
- There are only two classes considered who play a direct economic role: workers and capitalists. All revenue passes through the hands of these two classes in its first movement. The fact that some of this revenue passes through other hands, particularly after the first movement, is ignored. Thus the division of surplus-value into industrial profit, commercial profit, interest, rent, etc., is ignored. Also those classes or groups that provide services in exchange for revenue are similarly ignored.
- All production is carried out upon a capitalist basis; exchanges with non-capitalist economic forms are excluded.
- Foreign trade is excluded from consideration, since it is assumed that such trade will not affect the value of production, but merely affect its material form.
- There is the same organic composition of capital in both departments of production. Therefore we are dealing solely with an exchange-value schema, not a prices of production one.
- There are no changes in technology or productivity of labour, hence no change in the organic composition of capital.
- All capital, constant and variable, has one turnover once per production period.
- The rate of surplus-value, s/v, is assumed to be 100 per cent, or 1, in both departments.
- All commodities are sold, or realised, at their exchange-value.
- The only relation between the two departments of production is that of exchange, i.e. there is no movement of capital from one department to the other.
- Under simple reproduction all surplus-value is consumed unproductively by the capitalists.

These are a set of highly restrictive constraints, and Marx set out his schema for simple reproduction as follows:

Dept. I   4000c + 1000v + 1000s = 6000   means of production
Dept. II 2000c + 500v   + 500s   = 3000   means of consumption

---

6000C + 1500V + 1500S = 9000 value of total social product

It can readily be seen that the sum of constant capital (C) used up in the two departments is equal to the sum of means of production produced in Dept. I; and the sum of capitalist consumption (S) plus workers' consumption (V) is equal to total means of consumption produced by Dept. II. But since Iv + Is exists in the form of means of production (constant capital), whilst IIc exists in the form of means of consumption, for production to continue these two quantities must be exchanged. This is because the capitalists and workers of Dept. I cannot consume the products of that department in their natural form, whilst the products of Dept. II cannot be used as means of production in their natural material form.

Therefore the condition of equilibrium between the two departments is that an exchange should take place, and that IIc = Iv + Is.

Moving on to extended reproduction, all previous assumptions hold except that now a portion of the surplus-value will be accumulated in the form of constant and variable capital, that is, as c or v. For purposes of exposition we shall assume that the surplus-value is divided equally between accumulation and unproductive consumption. A numerical model will take the following form:

Dept. I   4000c   + 1000v   + 1000s   = 6000   means of production
Dept. II 1454.5c + 363.5v   + 363.5s = 2181.5 means of consumption

---

5454.5C + 1363.5V + 1365.5S = 8181.5   total exchange-value

It can now be seen that the sum of constant capital used up in the two departments during the production cycle is less than the total means of production produced by Dept. I. Moreover, the sum of v + s is greater than the product of Dept. II. It follows that with extended reproduction a part of the surplus-value is embodied in the physical form of means of production. Therefore, for equilibrium to subsist a part of the surplus-value must be accumulated as constant capital, and only a further portion may be accumulated as variable capital. On the assumption that 50 per cent of the surplus-value is accumulated, we would have:

Dept. I   400c   + 100v   + 500uc
Dept. II 145.5c + 36.5c + 181.5uc

545.5c + 136.5v + 681.5uc = 1363.5 total s.v

A quick calculation will show that the sum of constant capital used up in the production cycle – 5454.5 – plus the constant capital accumulated from surplus-value is equal to the product of Dept. I, i.e., 6000. Similarly, we now find that the sum of variable capital advanced in production plus the variable capital accumulated from surplus-value added to the sum of unproductive consumption (uc) is equal to the product of Dept. II, i.e., 2181.5.

Further, if we designate the surplus-value accumulated as variable capital as Δv, and that accumulated as constant capital Δc, we find: $Iv + I\Delta v + Iuc = 1600 = IIc + II\Delta c$.

And this is the basic condition for equilibrium assuming extended reproduction.

Bukharin's Algebra of Reproduction

Rosa Luxemburg, in her discussion of Marx's reproduction schemata brought forward a number of criticisms of them. These criticisms were basically of two kinds: the first was that there would not be sufficient demand within the system for accumulation to take place; the second is that if the organic composition of capital rises then again there will be insufficient demand for all the surplus-value to be realised and hence accumulation will be choked off. The essence of Luxemburg's critique is that for accumulation to proceed there must be a *third* market, that is, petty commodity production, feudal economy, etc., for the whole of the surplus-value to be realised. And it was this need for a 'third market' that Luxemburg regarded as the driving force behind imperialism.[15] Interesting as Luxemburg's ideas are, they need not detain us here seeing that what I am concerned with is Bukharin's response to them and the results of that response.[16]

Bukharin was the most sophisticated of Luxemburg's critics, and in the process of writing his critique of her work he developed a more refined version of Marxist accumulation theory than had obtained hitherto. And it is this aspect that I wish to deal with, rather than the controversy surrounding Luxemburg. Bukharin gave us the first fully algebraic exposition of accumulation in the Marxist tradition; and as such his contribution marked a turning point in discussions of the reproduction schemas, since he was able to formulate general conditions of capitalist development.

Let us, therefore, examine what he said:

> As is well known, Marx outlined in general terms the course of the total social reproduction, proceeding from a whole series of premises to simplifying the situation ... How is a mobile equilibrium possible in the growing capitalist system? – this is how Marx formulated his question. By and large, the *most abstract* (supremely theoretical) solution is as follows.[17]

And here we may summarise Bukharin as follows:

For simple reproduction:

$$C + V + S \quad = W = \text{value of total social production} \quad (1)$$
$$c_1 + v_1 + s_1 = w_1 = \text{value of means of production} \quad (2)$$
$$c_2 + v_2 + s_2 = w_2 = \text{value of means of consumption} \quad (3)$$

Subscripts refer to Marx's departments of production, therefore

$$w_1 + w_2 \quad = W \quad (4)$$
$$c_1 + v_1 + s_1 = c_1 + c_2 \quad (5)$$
$$c_2 + v_2 + s_2 = v_1 + v_2 + s_1 + s_2 \quad (6)$$

By elimination equations (5) and (6) may be reduced to:

$$c_2 = v_1 + s_1 \quad (7)$$

Equation (7) is the fundamental one for simple reproduction. Turning to extended reproduction, Bukharin said:

> If we let α_1 indicate that part of the surplus-value which serves for the personal consumption of the capitalists, and β_1 that which is turned into capital, thus, if we make $s_1 = \alpha_1 + \beta_1$ and correspondingly $s_2 = \alpha_2 + \beta_2$, if we further let β_{c1} indicate that part of the surplus-value which is accumulated as a part of the constant capital, and β_{v1} that part of the surplus-value which is to be accumulated as a part of the variable capital, and thus posit β_1

$= \beta_{c1} + \beta_{v1}$ and correspondingly $\beta_2 = \beta_{c2} + \beta_{v2}$ thus the general formula for the product of both departments takes on the following form:[18]

$$
\begin{array}{c}
\overbrace{\phantom{c_1 + v_1 + \alpha_1 + \beta_{c1} + \beta_{v1}}}^{\beta_1} \\[-4pt]
\text{I} \quad c_1 + v_1 + \alpha_1 + \beta_{c1} + \beta_{v1} \\
\hline
\text{II} \quad c_2 + v_2 + \alpha_2 + \beta_{c2} + \beta_{v2} \\[-4pt]
\underbrace{\phantom{\beta_{c2} + \beta_{v2}}}_{\beta_2}
\end{array}
$$

From the above the following equations may be derived:

$$c_1 + v_1 + \beta_{c1} + \beta_{v1} + \alpha_1 = c_1 + \beta_{c1} + c_2 + \beta_{c2} \tag{8}$$
$$c_2 + v_2 + \beta_{c2} + \beta_{v2} + \alpha_2 = v_1 + \beta_{v1} + \alpha_1 + v_2 + \beta_{v2} + \alpha_2 \tag{9}$$

By elimination (8) and (9) may be reduced to:

$$v_1 + \beta_{v1} + \alpha_1 = c_2 + \beta_{c2} \tag{10}$$

And equation (10) is the fundamental one for expanded reproduction. Thus, for the first time, Bukharin formulated a set of simple, yet sophisticated, equations for illustrating the reproduction of capital in the algebraic manner. The simplicity is self-evident; the sophistication lies in the possibility of considerable elaboration in discussions of growth theory.

These equations were a major advance, since they generalised Marx's formulation, and incorporated both equilibrium and proportionality. Since he first published his equations there has been a considerable literature developed which is devoted to expanding and refining this algebraic approach, but it was Bukharin who helped lay the foundation for this later work.[19] It should be said, of course, that in the 1920s Bukharin was working in a particularly rich culture for this type of intellectual endeavour. It was a period of intense debate, not only amongst politicians but also between many outstanding economists working within the Marxist tradition.

What was implicit in Bukharin's work can now be stated explicitly. Starting with Dept. I, and using the following equations, we find:

$$s_1/(c_1+v_1) \qquad\qquad = p_m = \text{the rate of profit margin} \qquad (11)$$
$$\alpha_1/s_1 \qquad\qquad\qquad = \underline{b} = \text{the rate of unproductively}$$
$$\text{consumed surplus-value} \qquad (12)$$
$$\text{Therefore } (1- \underline{b}).p_m = g' = \text{the rate of accumulation} \qquad (13)$$

This means that with a given rate of profit margin and a given rate of unproductive consumption of surplus-value, there is determined the rate of accumulation in Dept. I; and with a given production function the rate of growth in that department is also determined. Therefore, given p_m and g', it is also possible to determine the proportions for Dept. II which will lead to equilibrium.

$$\text{Let } (c_1/w_1).(1+g') = \underline{x} \qquad\qquad (14)$$
$$\text{Then } \underline{x}/(1- \underline{x}) = n = \text{proportionality coefficient} \qquad (15)$$
From this we may derive $w_1/n = w_2$
And, it follows, that $c_1/n = c_2$, $v_1/n = v_2$, $s_1/n = s_2$.
All of the above assumes that there is an equal organic composition of capital in both departments.

Let us look at a numerical example, giving Dept. I a numerical value of:

$$6000c_1 + 1200v_1 + 1800s_1 = 9000 = w_1$$

Therefore $s_1/(c_1+v_1) = p_m = 0.25$, assuming that $\alpha_1/s_1 = \underline{b} = 0.4$; then:
$$(1- \underline{b}).p_m = g' = 0.15.$$

Given these constraints, we find that $n = 3.2875112$. And, allowing for rounding, this gives us for the two departments;

$$\text{I} \qquad 6000c + 1200v + 1800s = 9000 \ = w_1$$
$$\text{II} \qquad 1826c + 365v \ + 548s \ = 2739 \ = w_2$$

With g' given for both departments, we find that:

$c_1.g' = \beta_{c1} = 900$, $v_1.g' = \beta_{v1} = 180$ and $\alpha_1 = 720$, $c_2.g' = \beta_{c2} = 274$, $v_2.g' = \beta_{v2} = 55$, $\alpha_2 = 219$.
And: $c_1 + \beta_{c1} + c_2 + \beta_{c2} = 9000 = w_1$
$$v_1 + \beta_{v1} + \alpha_1 + v_2 + \beta_{v2} + \alpha_2 = 2739 = w_2$$
Therefore $v_1 + \beta_{v1} + \alpha_1 = 2100 = c_2 + \beta_{c2}$
Thus proportionality and equilibrium may be maintained.[20]

Sweezy's and Rosdolsky's Critique of Bukharin

Paul Sweezy, in his book *The Theory of Capitalist Development*, criticised Bukharin's equations as follows: 'Bukharin in his formal presentation of the expanded reproduction scheme, makes the error of assuming that capitalist consumption always remains the same ... he seems incapable of imagining an increase in capitalist consumption.'[21] Roman Rosdolsky, in his work *The Making of Marx's 'Capital'*, picked up and elaborated Sweezy's critical remarks, spelling out the details of Bukharin's supposed error, to wit:

> ... it was Bukharin who first formulated the general relation of equilibrium for extended reproduction $cII + \beta cII = vI + \alpha I + \beta vI$. However, he derived two other, totally incorrect formulae from this one, namely: $cII = vI + \alpha I$ and $\beta vI = \beta cII$. It is in fact correct that in the *initial year* of Marx's first scheme $cII = vI + \alpha I$ and also $\beta vI = \beta cII$.
>
> However, this is only the case because Marx was not able to ascertain the correct proportions between cI and cII. In the succeeding years of the first scheme, and in all the years of the second, cII is necessarily smaller than $vI + \alpha I$, and βcII greater than βvI. In other words, Bukharin completely forgot that the extended reproduction ... must not only lead to growth of c and v but also to that of α, i.e. to the growth of the individual consumption of the capitalists. Nevertheless, this elementary mistake remained unobserved for almost two decades.[22]

However, both Sweezy and Rosdolsky failed to notice a clear statement to the contrary of what they asserted, made by Bukharin himself. Bukharin, in formulating his equations for extended reproduction, assumed that the 'economy' under consideration was moving from a state of simple reproduction to one of extended reproduction. Therefore it is logical that, at that point, there would be no growth of α. That Bukharin was capable of 'imagining' that capitalist consumption would grow, along with c and v, is stated explicitly two pages later (in the English text) than the reference cited by his critics:

> In the following cycle the capital of the starting stage is reproduced again, the unproductively consumed part of the

surplus-value grows – *for the first time* – the part of the latter which is to be accumulated even more and so on.[23]

So it is clear that Bukharin did not make the elementary mistake that Rosdolsky attributed to him. However, this does not dispose of the problem presented by the secondary equations that Rosdolsky brought forward. Could it be that Sweezy and Rosdolsky were correct? The answer must be yes.[24] The problem arises because of the undifferentiated nature of α. As far as the constant and variable capital is concerned the values which are *replaced* – $c + v$ – are clearly distinguished from the increments β_c and β_v, and these latter represent *additional* values and use-values.

Sweezy resolved this problem by the introduction of further algebraic notations which distinguished between unproductive consumption of the level pertaining to the *previous* production period and that which is additional, new, unproductive consumption. Let us call these two quantities a and a' respectively, then $a + a' = \alpha$.

We may now amend Bukharin's secondary equations in line with the above to read: $c_2 = v_1 + \underline{a}$ and $\beta_{c2} = \beta_{v2} + \underline{a'}$.

It is obvious from Bukharin's written statement that he was considering a transition from simple to extended reproduction, and he visualised a' = 0. Thus Sweezy's and Rosdolsky's criticism on the main point – does or does not unproductive consumption increase through time – can definitely be rejected. The criticism of Bukharin's secondary equations is sustained because he failed to distinguish between a and a', but in the context of his assumptions this was not strictly necessary. The fact that Bukharin's secondary equations gave rise to these criticisms indicates that he should have spelled out his intentions much more clearly.

There is one aspect of Bukharin's treatment of the assumed change from simple to extended reproduction that both Sweezy and Rosdolsky failed to notice or comment upon. The aspect in question relates to the problem of where the extra means of production for accumulation would come from.

Given that the original model is assumed to be both closed and in equilibrium, there is no surplus constant capital to draw upon. This being the case, if the production of constant capital is to increase – an absolute necessity for accumulation to occur – then this can only be done by a transfer to Dept. I of part of the constant capital normally allocated to Dept. II. This would lead to a *decrease*, in the initial stages, of the production of the means of consumption. That is, of course, unless one assumes a big leap in productivity in Dept.

II sufficient to compensate for the loss of the constant capital transferred to Dept. I.

It follows that – unless the capitalist class were prepared to be altruistic and reduce its own unproductive consumption – there would be a decline in real wages for the productive workers. But to pursue this point further at this stage would take us beyond our immediate concerns, since it impinges upon questions related to money, prices, rates of realised surplus-value, and to the problem of crises. All I will say here is that Bukharin was far too sanguine in his treatment of such a transition, even allowing for the fact that it was being treated at a purely abstract level.

Equilibrium and Effective Demand

The problem raised by Rosa Luxemburg regarding an unrealisable surplus arising in Dept. II, stemming from an increase in the organic composition of capital, needs to be touched upon here. She argued that Marx's schema of reproduction became unbalanced if one assumed such an increase in the organic composition of capital.[25] This particular answer was arrived at by taking a schema that was built as an equilibrium model and then changing one of the terms: naturally it produced dis-equilibrium.

Marx, in his schemas, assumed an organic composition of capital of 4c : 1v or 5c : 1v, and also that Dept. I always accumulated 50 per cent of its surplus-value, whilst Dept. II adjusted its unproductive consumption and accumulation of surplus-value to accommodate to this pattern. In the schema with a different organic composition of capital in the two departments, in Marx's illustration both departments still accumulated capital at the same rate, even though their rate of unproductive consumption was different.

Luxemburg suggested that, whilst leaving only one half of the surplus-value to be consumed unproductively, the other half should be accumulated at an increasing rate of organic composition of capital; that it should rise progressively from 5 : 1 to 6 : 1 to 7 : 1, etc. Now, leaving aside the case where there were different organic compositions of capital, we can see what happens.

To remind ourselves, the basic equation for extended reproduction is: $v_1 + \beta_{v1} + \alpha_1 = c_2 + \beta_{c2}$. With a given rate of profit margin, p_m, and a given rate of unproductive consumption of surplus-value, $\underline{b}$, there is obtained a specific g', i.e. rate of accumulation. Moreover, with an unchanged organic composition of capital we find: $\beta_c/c = \beta_v/v = \underline{a}'/\underline{a}$. And, if we say that G = the rate of growth of the total social product W, then on the assumption of an unchanged organic composition of capital we find that: $\beta_c/c = \beta_v = \underline{a}'/\underline{a} = g' = G$.

It now becomes clear that if, as Luxemburg suggested, the rate of increase in unproductive consumption remains constant, but the rate of increase in productive workers' consumption declines, whilst G remains constant, then there will emerge the surplus of unsold consumption goods that she postulated. However, if we drop the highly restrictive assumptions of Luxemburg, equilibrium is possible. If instead of a constant rate of unproductive consumption of surplus-value we now assume $\underline{a}'/\underline{a} > \beta_c/c > \beta_v/v$ and that $\underline{a}'/\underline{a} > G$ then, if $\Sigma\alpha + \beta s + \beta v/ S = 1$, the basic equation for extended reproduction can hold.[26]

This is not to dismiss the problems of realisation and effective demand that Luxemburg pointed to, rather I merely point out that equilibrium growth is *possible* even with a rising organic composition of capital.

Growth Theories Compared

The reason I touched upon the problem of realisation and the related questions of a rising organic composition of capital is that they relate to both growth and crisis theory. Here we shall deal only with growth theory and shall tackle crisis separately, even though they are intimately connected. In this section I want to compare a Marxian approach to growth – based upon Bukharin's equations – with that of Harrod. To enable us to do this I shall introduce some new notations and categories. Up to now we have ignored the specific role of fixed capital; this we shall now rectify.

Let F = fixed capital and cc = circulating capital, then we have:

$$F_1 + cc_1 + v_1 + s_1 = h_1$$
$$F_2 + cc_2 + v_2 + s_2 = h_2$$
$$h_1 + h_2 = H$$

Let T = time, i.e. the projected life span of fixed capital then: $F/T = d$ = depreciation
$H - (\Sigma F - \Sigma d) = W$ = total social product.

With any given value of w_1 there will be a maximum amount of constant capital (fixed and circulating) which is available for accumulation, and this is determined by:

$$\frac{w_1 - \Sigma(d+cc)}{\Sigma(F+cc)} = g = \text{maximum rate of accumulation of constant capital}$$

The actual rate of accumulation will, therefore, be determined by:

$$\frac{S}{\Sigma(F+cc+v)} = p' \text{ and } \Sigma\alpha/S = \underline{b} \therefore (1-\underline{b}).p' = g'$$

It may be that g' = g, but this is not necessarily the case. But from the above we can say:

$$\Sigma(d + \beta_F + cc + \beta_{cc}) = w_1$$
$$\Sigma(v + \beta_v + \alpha) = w_2$$

And for equilibrium: $v_1 + \beta_{v1} + \alpha_1 = d_2 + cc_2 + \beta_{F2} + \beta_{cc2}$.

It will be seen that g' is dependent upon two variables, the rate of profit (i.e., the social rate of profit p') and the proportion of surplus-value consumed unproductively. If we assume, as in more orthodox models, that savings equals investment – and that investment and accumulation are analogous – then we can see that savings are a *result* and not a precondition. That is to say that savings are a function of the rate of profit and unproductive consumption.

In more orthodox economics we find that Y = national income, which in our model is equivalent to v + s, and this is what we designate net national income.

In Harrod's model of growth we find that $G_{a'}$ = the rate of actual growth, $G_{w'}$ = warranted rate of growth and $G_{n'}$ the rate of growth dependent upon the growth in population. $G_{a'}$ is an ex-post definition, whilst $G_{w'}$ is ex-ante.

$G_{a'}$ = s'/v', where s' = the average and marginal propensity to save and v' = the capital-output ratio.

$G_{w'}$ = s'/v'$_r$ where r expresses capitalist requirements for additions to capital stock.

$G_{n'}$ = 1 + t + (1xt), 1 = rate of population increase and t = the rate of productivity increase.

In trying to compare the two models we find that there are problems arising from differences in nomenclature and these hide quite different approaches. For instance, if S' = aggregate savings and s' is as defined above, then S' = s'w'W' + s'pP where W' and P are wages and profits respectively, but in our Marxian model s'w'W' = 0.

This is a valid assumption when using a purely exchange-value model, but may present problems when dealing with a model that uses current monetary units of account. The next problem is that of the capital-output ratio, since output is measured as Y in the Harrod model and not W. And the same problems arise when determining the aggregate production function. These differences arise from orthodox economics treating its subject matter as being a purely technical problem, whilst the Marxian approach is one that is based upon an analysis of class relationships.

My term $\underline{b}$ can be seen as being analogous to the propensity to unproductive consumption, but this is *not* the same as the Keynesian propensity to consume.

The nearest approximation that we can find between our g' and Gw' is:

$$F + cc + v = K, \quad v + s = Y, \quad \therefore \quad K/Y = v'_r$$
$$\beta/Y = s' \quad \therefore \quad s'/v'_r = g'$$

However, it will be noted that the above depends upon the propensity to save and not the propensity to unproductive consumption. The difference is critical, since total productive consumption has a relationship to unproductive consumption, whilst the Harrod equation is indiscriminate as to the nature of consumption; nor does it take into account the rate of profit.

In our equation if the rate of profit declines and all other factors remain constant, then the rate of accumulation will also decline. Similarly, if the rate of unproductive consumption declines, then – *cet. par.* – accumulation increases. The significant difference is that our interpretation of the capital-output ratio includes variable capital, not merely fixed capital stock. Since our v is advanced to purchase labour-power, *then the rate of exploitation will have a determining role in the outcome for output.*

I must stress that the equation $(1 - \underline{b}).p' = g'$ is *not* one that Bukharin himself put forward, but has been derived by myself from his set of simple equations for equilibrium conditions. What I have been concerned about in this short section has been to compare some simple forms of growth equations deriving from quite different traditions. It can be seen that in terms of the formal equations it is possible to make some juncture, but in so doing it is also possible to lose sight of the quite different perspectives from which they derive.

There are two aspects of contradiction combined in the equations derived from Bukharin which are not present in the Harrod formulation. It is obvious that the aggregate demand for consumption goods must grow at the same rate as the production of such commodities if equilibrium is to be maintained; but there is an inherent drive within the capitalist system to reduce the amount of variable capital advanced or employed for the purchase of labour-power as a proportion of the total capital advanced. In other words there is a contradiction between the need to expand markets and the need to reduce costs, which implies a conflict between the micro and the macro needs within the system.

The second aspect of contradiction within Bukharin's equations is that between accumulation and unproductive consumption. At first sight this appears as a simple conflict of competing demands upon a given quantity of surplus-value. However, on closer inspection, the problem becomes more complex. The fundamental equation for extended reproduction is, as we know: $c_2 + \beta_{c2} = v_1 + \beta_{v1} + a + a'$.

The c's of Dept. II are necessary productive consumption of constant capital, whilst only v and β_v of Dept. I are necessary productive consumption, the α part of the equation (i.e. $a + a'$) are unproductive consumption. This suggests, *given the assumptions of the model*, that the unproductive component is a necessary one for expanded reproduction. Therefore the simple conflict between accumulation and unproductive consumption which appears at the micro level may be transformed into its opposite at the macro level. Thus this contradiction is an essential element in Bukharin's equilibrium growth model.

The tradition of which Bukharin was a part, and helped to develop, was the forerunner of much post-1945 growth theory in the capitalist world, if often unackowledged. The Soviet debate of the 1920s was the first in history to face the problems of growth in a conscious manner, and they were not merely theoretical discussions since the results could have had a profound effect upon the actual outcome of events. However, what actually happened was something quite different to that visualised by nearly all the participants. Bukharin's contribution to analysing growth theory has, by and large, remained underplayed in the existing literature. Whilst a number of writers have commented upon his contributions to debates upon current policy problems, little has been said about the theoretical basis of these contributions.

That Bukharin argued for balanced and proportional growth can be seen to arise from his earlier work on equilibrium theory and in his formulating an algebraic approach to the problems of analysis posed by Marx's reproduction schemas. These points will be amplified as we proceed.

4
Equilibrium and Crisis Theory

Theories of Crisis

Since Marx did not live to articulate a comprehensive theory of capitalist economic crisis, after his death there developed a number of theories of crisis which drew upon various aspects of his writings. These various theories may be defined in a number of ways. The greatest division among them is:

a) crises as seen to be leading to the collapse of the capitalist system. This is usually referred to as the catastrophic version; and today this has few, if any, adherents; and

b) cyclical crises, which *may* provide the conditions for a revolutionary overthrow of capitalism, but are not sufficient in themselves to bring about its automatic collapse.

However, there are still to be found undertones of catastrophism in many Marxist writings, even though the authors would reject any explicit adherence to such ideas.

The second variant is the one that has produced the greatest number of specific theories of cyclical crisis. And these maybe categorised as:

1. Excess commodity theory (underconsumption)
2. Excess capital theory
3. Disproportionality
4. Crises arising from the decline of the rate of profit.

Of course, all the theories propounded incorporate all of the above elements, but each gives pre-eminence to one particular factor.

Bukharin's own theory of capitalist crisis can be said to be one of disproportionality. And, indeed, his theory is firmly rooted in his conception of equilibrium. The loss of equilibrium is seen as being both a root cause of the crisis when it occurs and its manifestation. There does, however, appear to be some confusion among various commentators as to Bukharin's basic position: some, such as Itoh, place him in the underconsumptionist school, while others place him – correctly – in the disproportionality school; but the latter, e.g. Sweezy, Mandel, Day, do not always attribute the same meaning to this.[1]

Bukharin's Contribution

We shall therefore examine what Bukharin said, and then appraise its coherence. Let us start with the following:

> In his theoretical grasp of the capitalist system of relations of production, Marx proceeds *from the fact of its existence*. Since this system exists, it means that – whether well or badly – social needs are satisfied ... [therefore] there must be a definite *equilibrium* of the whole system ... There may well be all sorts of deviations and fluctuations here; the whole system expands and becomes complicated, develops and is continuously in motion and oscillating but, taken as a whole, it is in a state of equilibrium.
>
> To find the law of this equilibrium is the basic problem of theoretical economics and theoretical economics as a scientific system is the result of an examination of the entire capitalist system *in its state of equilibrium*.[2]

The important point to note here is that for Bukharin this state of equilibrium contained deviations and fluctuations, thus what he was postulating is not a static equilibrium nor even a dynamic one – dynamic in the sense of an orderly balanced growth. On the contrary, as we noted earlier, his equilibrium model is a mobile one. He said:

> Gradually, complicating factors are introduced, the system starts to oscillate, and becomes mobile. These oscillations, however, still conform to laws and, despite the most severe violations of the equilibrium (crises), the system as a whole remains... a crisis does not overstep the limits of the oscillation of the system... through all the movements and oscillations, the equilibrium is restored time and again.[3]

Even though it was suggested that such crises *may* at some point lead to a collapse of the system, this is not inevitable nor even highly probable. In capitalist society:

> The development of the productive forces is by no means a

smoothly rising curve. On the contrary, it must be clear, a *priori* that in an antagonistic society, a society based on productive and social anarchy, there cannot be an uninterrupted development of the forces, for in such a society the laws of equilibrium are and can only be realized by means of continual or recurrent disruptions of the equilibrium. Consequently, the starting point for the restoration of the equilibrium must be its disruption, the function of which in the present case is to restore the balance, but at the same time on an even more deeply contradictory basis. And since every violation of the equilibrium is inevitably bound up with a decline in the productive forces, it goes without saying, that in an antagonistic society, the development of the productive forces is made possible *only by means of their periodic destruction.*[4]

Now this does not merely pose the cyclical nature of development under capitalism, although of course this is implied, but rather it suggests that even in those periods of upturn or growth there will be oscillations and deviations, so that the cycle itself is contradictory. This is the difference between seeing growth as depicted by a statistical average on an ascending curve, or as a trend line indicating upwards motion and growth but which includes decline and ascent combined. It is this conception of uneven and combined development, in which the whole may be growing at some point in time, but within that overall growth there will be sectors in decline.

So capitalism develops in this combined and uneven manner, and crises are not merely periods of 'no growth'; on the contrary:

Capitalist society ... can maintain a relative equilibrium only at the price of painful crises; the adaptation of the various parts of the social organism to each other and to the whole can be achieved only with a colossal waste of energy.[5]
[This is why] ... the examination of the social and, moreover, irrational and blind system from the viewpoint of its equilibrium, has nothing in common ... with *harmonia praestabilitata*.[6]

Given these suppositions, Bukharin maintained that 'the law of crises is the law of the inevitable periodic disturbance of equilibrium of the system and its restoration.'[7] And '... as is well known, the crises we are talking about here are *crises of overproduction.*'[8]

The question remains as to the cause and the manifestation of these crises, since merely to assert that crises are the result of the disturbances of equilibrium does not in itself locate the precise nature of the process – it merely poses it. Bukharin arrived at the following conclusion:

Marx, as you know, gave us a theory of *capitalist crises.* These crises he showed to be caused by a general lack of planning ('anarchy') of the capitalist methods of production, by the impossibility of attaining correct *proportions* between the various elements of the process of reproduction under capitalism, especially between production and consumption. In other words he showed the cause to be the *incapability of capitalism to maintain an equilibrium among the various elements of production. This does not, of course, mean that Marx avoided the problems of class and the class struggle.* Mass consumption, its level, the value of labour-power itself – according to Marx the factor of the struggle is inherent in all these. The whole mechanism of contradictions developing between production and consumption, between the growth of production and the relations of distribution, *contains in itself,* the class struggle, taking the form of economic categories.[9]

Therefore, basing himself on Marx, Bukharin rejected the idea that there can be no general overproduction; instead he argued that there is a causal relationship between the various branches of production which offer each other markets for their respective goods. He thus posited a chain of relations:

This chain, however, *ends* with the production of means of consumption which no longer enter in material form, i.e. as use-values, directly into any process of production but into the process of personal consumption ... As a result, one can indeed envisage a situation in which we have before us an over production in all links of the chain which expresses itself in an over-production of means of consumption, i.e. in an over-production in relation to the *consumer market,* which is precisely the expression of a *general over-production.*[10]

Such over-production is only a relative one, that is, relative to effective demand, effective monetary demand being the only form of demand that the capitalist market recognises. Having disposed of these points, Bukharin then moved on the question of whether such a general over-production is one of the over-production of capital (excess capital) or the over-production of commodities (excess commodities). His answer was:

> It is ... obvious that there can be no over-production of capital if there can be no over-production of *commodities*. For what does the production of capital mean? The process of the production of capital is clearly nothing other than the process of capitalist production; in other words, of the production of commodities under conditions of *capitalist* production, not under conditions of simple commodity production. The production of capital is, therefore, a production of *capitalistically* produced commodities. Hence, an over-production of capital is also an over-production of commodities.[11]

Nor can there be permanent over-production; this over-production is relative and cyclical. Moreover, over-production is not the cause of such crises, 'rather it is the expression of crises.'[12] Therefore, the basic and fundamental cause of crises for Bukharin was the 'disproportion of social production. The factor of consumption, however, forms a component part of this disproportionality.'[13] Thus disproportionality was seen as being of a different order to that of merely being a disproportionality between individual branches of industry (as, for instance, Hilferding suggested[14]). Disproportionality between the branches of production was therefore seen as a result of the basic disproportion, i.e. that between production and consumption. This was not an 'under-consumptionist' position, however, since Bukharin located this underconsumption in the over-production of *capital*. On this point he said:

> capitalism is continually promoting the tendency to develop production quickly on the one hand ... and to depress the wage on the other (pressure of the reserve army [of the unemployed]). In other words: it is the tendency of capitalism *to push production beyond the limits of consumption*. For this kind of disproportionality only appears if an over-production of means of production has taken place and *manifests itself* externally as an over-production of means of consumption.[15]

And since this over-production of capital arises from the anarchy of capitalist production, Bukharin asked:

> where is the planlessness of the economy, its anarchy expressed?

In the fact that there is no proportionality between the individual *branches* of production and the scale of *personal* consumption. This is precisely why Marx speaks about the proportional application of capital (1) 'in the various spheres of production' and (2) 'according to its [society's] needs'. *Both* factors belong to the concept of the proportionality of social production. Or to express it in more popular terms: let us assume that we had a complete proportionality in every branch of production, in the sense of their unilateral connection in one direction: from means of production to means of consumption ... Would we then have a guarantee against the occurrence of a crisis? No. For it can happen that more cloth is produced than is used, and, as a result, also more machines, iron and coal than is necessary. In other words: the disproportionality of the entire social production consists, not only in the disproportionality between the branches of production, but also in the disproportionality between production and consumption.[16]

How does such disproportionality come about according to Bukharin? He related his answer to the production of labour-power as a commodity. Posing the problem in terms of the equilibrium equation for extended reproduction – $v_1 + \beta_{v1} + \alpha_1 = c_2 + \beta_{c2}$ – he asked what would happen if the value $c_2 + \beta_{c2} - \alpha_1 > v_1 + \beta_{v1}$. The answer Bukharin gave was that there would be over-production of consumption goods, because there would be 'a disproportion between production and consumption. It is obvious that, in the production of means of production ... the level of the wage is not determined by a calculation of the values which will be produced in the production of the means of consumption.[17]

Having come very close to the heart of the matter, Bukharin then slid off into a discussion of the role of workers' consumption in the circulation of capital; all of which is correct, but he failed to explicate the mechanism by which such a disproportionality comes about. Then, whilst resolutely throwing underconsumption out of the window he allows it to creep in through the back door again with his discursive discussion of the role of labour-power as a commodity and its place in the circulation process. Although he maintained that crisis is the result of the over-production of capital the actual mechanism, he suggested, is located in the circulation process. In fact Bukharin came very close to Rosa Luxemburg's proposition regarding a surplus of consumption goods arising from an increase in the organic composition of capital.

We have already seen that at the *formal level* Luxemburg's thesis of the need for a 'third market' to realise the value of these consumption goods is not necessary. It was pointed out that *if* unproductive consumption is increased equilibrium may be maintained. Bukharin's reference to the level of wages paid in Dept. I indicated a possible line of enquiry that would have been much more fruitful had he pursued it more vigorously *and* had begun to examine the role of *fixed* capital in the cyclical process.

Many of the elements of a rounded theory of capitalist economic crisis were present in Bukharin's writings, but overall they remained too disconnected to rise to the level of a coherent theory. Therefore it remains for us to sketch out a more articulated theory based upon Bukharin's ideas of disproportionality and dis-equilibrium.

Bukharin's Presentation: A Reformulation and Critique

As a preliminary statement we can say that the equation: $v_1 + \beta_{v1} + \alpha_1 = c_2 + \beta_{c2}$ is at best only ever achieved as a momentary or fleeting condition. Such an equation is basically made up of two parts: viz $v_1 + \beta_{v1} + \alpha_1 > c_2 + \beta_{c2}$ which indicates that business conditions are good, and $v_1 + \beta_{v1} + \alpha_1 < c_2 + \beta_{c2}$ which indicates business conditions are poor. The equation for equilibrium conditions is, in reality, a combination of these two dis-equilibrium conditions. Or, put another way, the equilibrium equation represents an average of a graph of fluctuations.

The critical question is, what forces are at work that will push the economy away from this average, either in an upward or downward direction? In so far as we deal with cyclical fluctuations here, they will be those which were characteristic of an unregulated capitalist economy typical of the nineteenth century. That is to say we shall not attempt to consider changes induced by monopolisation or state intervention on the scale we have witnessed since, say, 1945. To try to encompass these modifications would be beyond the scope of our present remit.

Let us accept Bukharin's proposition that the final cause of capitalist economic crisis is the fundamental contradiction between the social character of production and the private appropriation of wealth. This means that the capitalist system is the cause of the crises encountered, and therefore such crises must be ascribed to endogenous factors. Such crises do not have an accidental character, they are a part of the very process of capitalist production and reproduction.

I shall also argue that crises have a *material* basis, which relates to the periodic replacement and expansion of *fixed* capital. However, there is no intention of dealing with the question of long-waves. Linked with this periodic replacement and expansion of fixed capital will be the proposition that the direct cause of the outbreak of crises is that the sale of means of consumption falls relative to the volume of their production.

The last statement may seem to imply that a variant of the underconsumptionist thesis is being adopted, but as Marx pointed out, consumption by workers almost invariably reaches a high point immediately before a crisis breaks out.

Crises of the 'classical' type which we are going to consider usually involve a sudden and sharp deterioration of business conditions – not a gentle decline. Therefore it is not a feature of such crises that they were immediately preceded by a lack of effective demand on the market for consumer goods. (However, credit had normally been greatly extended.) Moreover, at the beginning of such crises the *production* of consumer goods either remained at a high level or actually continued to increase. Concomitantly the production of raw materials normally continued to be maintained or increased. The point being emphasised here is that it is only possible to understand the suddenness of the onset of the downward spiral by keeping in view the *production* of fixed capital. And in particular the role played by this element in such cycles.

Rather than attempt to start our exposition of the cycle from the point of crisis, we shall be able to understand the role of fixed capital if we begin at the point of depression. It is characteristic of fixed capital that it has an assumed lifespan – without taking into account the problem of technological obsolescence – and therefore its replacement may be said to be time-proportional. This time-proportionality determines the value of depreciation in the value of commodities produced with the aid of such fixed capital, that is to say, it is an element of the total value of the commodities.

Now, if the depression has been preceded by a particularly deep-going crisis, equilibrium may be established at such a low level of activity that the volume of fixed capital currently being produced may well be considerably smaller than that which would allow for the time-proportional replacement of fixed capital at the *previous* average rate. That is to say, in the depths of a depression there may well be a negative reproduction of fixed capital if the wear and tear is greater than its replacement. (This may in turn lead to a build-up of idle money-capital arising from unused depreciation funds.)

In the classical trade cycle, which is agreed to have been

normally of between nine and twelve years, the time proportional factor was of the same order. Whilst it is true that, in the main, the replacement of fixed capital is usually accompanied by an increased production capacity because of advances in technology, we do not have to take this into account when dealing with the basic theory of the cycle. The reason for this is that the renewal of fixed capital is normally to maintain existing production levels. The fact that such increased production capacity is the result of replacement is of no immediate consequence, since that capacity may not be used fully in the initial production period.

The mere replacement of productive capacity means in reality, however, that during a depression there will be an increase in the demand for consumer goods. Why this occurs is as follows: if Dept. I, particularly those sections producing fixed capital, starts increasing production to meet *replacement* demand, then more wages are paid out in that department. Then, with a given volume of consumption goods being produced and a relatively stable demand by capitalists for consumer goods, the increased demand in the form of extra wages being paid in Dept I, will tend to push up the price of these consumer goods, produced by Dept. II. At the same time, since there is an increase in the production of fixed assets, which by definition can only be a part of surplus-value, this means that the volume of surplus-value and its rate begins to increase.

The increase in the price of consumer goods is thus accompanied by a faster rate of growth in Dept. I than in Dept. II. However – and here we come to the point that Bukharin was attempting to make – a growth in production by Dept. I does not necessarily lead to an increase in the price of consumer goods. The growth in the sum of $c_1 + v_1 + s_1$ will only lead to an increase in the price of consumer goods if the sum of $v_1 + \beta_{v1} + \alpha_1$ grows too. The possibility of this latter sum of value lagging behind the growth of the volume of production in Dept. I occurs if there is an increase in the organic composition of capital at a rate which is faster than the rate of growth of the volume of production.

However, if the crisis has been particularly sharp and the depression of sufficient duration then it is more likely that the total of $v_1 + \beta_{v1} + \alpha_1$ will increase sufficiently to push up the price of consumer goods. If the impulse from Dept. I is sufficiently strong then there will develop a period of prosperity. In such a period the sum of *money* wages will increase and so will the demand for labour-power. This will provide a better climate for the workers to push for higher *wage* rates. None the less, the decisive reason for the increase in the price of consumer goods is the rapid growth in the production of fixed capital goods. Thus the mere replacement of fixed capital can lead to an increase in the overall level of economic activity. And it follows from this that an acceleration of this replacement will have the same effect as if there had been an increase in fixed capital.

We now have an outline of the reasons for an upswing in economic activity and for an increase in the rate of surplus-value. But the faster the upswing, the more bunched replacements will be and the sooner a new crisis will loom on the horizon. It is clear that the bunched replacement of fixed capital requires a considerable growth in the rate of the production of fixed assets, but after a few years the need for such *replacement* will decline rapidly. This means that for the boom to continue it would be necessary to undertake *capacity increasing* investment, that is, increase the stock of fixed capital.

It is at this point that the system is heading for a new crisis.

The first possibility is that such an increase in productive capacity is not undertaken. Perhaps the capitalists in Dept. II are satisfied with the level of profits they are currently obtaining and do not therefore increase production. Obviously, because of the previous excessive growth in the sectors of Dept. I producing fixed capital, there would be a precipitate decline in those sectors. Such a decline would lead to a decline in total money wages being paid out and hence a decline in the demand for consumption goods. Inevitably there would follow a contraction of activity in Dept. II, thus leading to a further reduction in total money wages being paid etc.

The second possibility is certainly more 'cheerful'. Let us assume that as a result of the increased prices obtained for consumer goods, there is induced an increase in capacity in Dept. II. Contrary to expectations this growth in the production of consumer goods merely postpones and then magnifies the problem.

The nub of the problem resides in the fact that an increase of consumer goods as a share of the total social product decreases the share of surplus-value in the net national income. Moreover, it will lead to a decline in the ratio of surplus-value to the capital that is advanced. Why is this so? The reason falls into two parts: the first relates to savings and the second is to do with the nature of β_v. Consumer goods occupy a much more contradictory place in the circulation and realisation of capital than do fixed assets. Out of the total value and volume of consumer goods only α and β_v have the character of being surplus-value, since the sum of Dept. II's production is by definition $v + \beta_v + \alpha$. It follows, therefore, that out of this sum only $\beta_v + \alpha$ have the character of being realised surplus-value. If we recognise that capitalist consumption – α – is a limited quantity which is *relatively* inelastic, β_v represents that part of surplus-value embodied in consumption goods which is 'saved'. This saving does not have the character of savings 'in general', that of being saved for future consumption, but is saved by *capitalists*. Such saving is specifically used to increase productive *capital* and future *profits*. So long as βv does increase and the organic composition of capital is not increasing rapidly, it will represent future consumption by productive workers, but will still be considered as a part of the surplus-value. However, if this β_v is invested in labour-power producing consumption goods, then this will lead to an increased volume of consumer goods. And in the following production period the maintenance of an increased volume of consumer goods will require the maintenance of an adequate level of v_2: but v is *not* surplus-value. So what is invested as surplus-value in one production period is not seen as surplus-value in the following production period, but rather as a cost.

From the above we can see that so long as investment goods, particularly fixed assets, are being produced on an increased scale the effect on business conditions is favourable. But as soon as they are used to expand the production of consumer goods they will actually cause business conditions to deteriorate.

The reason for this is that as soon as the opportunities for investing in fixed capital begins to diminish – mainly because the capacity for producing consumer goods has been substantially expanded – any further growth in the production of consumer goods would reduce their price, and – *cet. par.* – the profits of the capitalists producing them would also decline.

The net result is that the slowdown in the production of fixed capital will also cause a reduction in the rate of growth of β_{v1}, or even its reduction to zero. At the same time, because of the expansion of capacity in Dept. II, stocks of consumer goods may be growing or their prices no longer rising – or no longer rising as rapidly as before – and the new productive capacities are possibly just going to enter the production stream. All these signals would be sufficient to slow down the expansion of Dept. II. If that happens at the peak of the boom it would be sufficient to precipitate a sudden and spectacular crisis.

The conditions would then be created for a rapid decline in the rate of surplus-value on capital advanced, the growth of unsold stocks of consumer goods, which would lead to a cessation of the expansion of fixed capital in Dept. II, and a further dramatic plunge in the production of fixed capital in Dept. I. Thus there begins a downward spiral into depression.

This, then, is an approximate sketch of Bukharin's theory of disproportionality crisis. It contains all the elements that have normally been placed at the centre of crisis theory in the Marxist tradition, i.e. the falling rate of profit, excess capital, excess commodities. But instead of attempting to place any one of them in opposition to the others as the key feature, it integrates them all as being the expressions of the basic contradiction of capitalism, that is, the striving continually to expand production, and in particular the production of surplus-value, as opposed to the relatively restricted consuming power of the population. As I have indicated, the material basis for this contradiction resides in the role of fixed capital in the classical cyclical movement of the capitalist economy.

In so far as we consider Bukharin's theory of equilibrium in relation to his ideas on the theory of capitalist economic crisis we can see that contradiction is a key element in explaining it. Perhaps we can say that capitalist equilibrium is made up of a series of moments of dis-equilibria. This being the case, a crisis of capitalist economy is not a crisis of society in terms of the catastrophic visions of some of the early Marxists, but, on the contrary, crisis is a *normal* condition of its longer term equilibrium. How long is that longer term is still a matter for debate.

The major weakness in Bukharin's presentation of crisis theory lies in his lack of appreciation of the role of fixed capital in the cyclical process. This lack of appreciation was to have an adverse effect upon his stance in some of the debates in the 1920s; something he came to realise and rectify later on. However, given his equilibrium theory, Bukharin was able to escape the monocausal trap that beset a number of other Marxist theorists on the question of crisis theory.

5
War Communism and the New Economic Policy

Bukharin's work *The Economics of the Transition Period*[1] has a special place in his writings and in relation to the period in which it was written. Any study of the man and the period must locate and take into account this book. The work itself has maintained an almost subterranean existence in footnotes and references in many other works, yet it was not until comparatively recently that it became accessible to the non-specialist reader. It has only ever had one edition in the Russian – in 1920 – and one German translation in 1922. The English translation had to wait until the 1970s. Because of this the title of the work was well known but its content very much less so.

The book was a pioneering effort and has all the faults, as well as the merits, of such an enterprise. Before the Russian revolution of October (November) 1917, very few Marxists were prepared to talk or write, in any other than the most general terms, on what the outline of a future socialist society would be like, or discuss the nature of the transition period to such a society.[2] Bukharin wrote his book on the basis of his own lived experiences within the revolution then in progress. If he dared to predict, it was on the basis of the evidence around him. That he should have been proved wrong on a number of points should occasion no surprise. It is indeed rare for the participants in such epoch-making events to have a complete understanding of them and their consequences. We should, however, acknowledge Bukharin's intellectual audacity in his attempt.

Alfred Rosmer gave an amusing but enlightening insight into Bukharin's character and role in 1920, and let it be recalled that he was only 32 years old in that year. When Rosmer attended the second congress of the Third International he spoke to Trotsky about Bukharin, and reported the following:

Trotsky [said] 'Bukharin is always in front, but he's always looking over his shoulder to make sure Lenin isn't far behind.' When I got to know the two men well I got a visual image of these judgements – Lenin, solid and stocky, advancing at an even pace, and the slight figure of Bukharin galloping off in front, but always needing to feel Lenin's presence.[3]

Rosmer's anecdote gives us the measure of the role that Bukharin played, not only in relation to Lenin, but also to the whole Bolshevik Party. He acted as the intellectual cavalry, seeking out new fields, harrying the enemy with his pen and probing unknown territory.

The Economics represented a landmark, indeed a turning point, in Bukharin's own career. Up to and including 1920 he had been consistently on the left of the Bolshevik Party, and this particular book was his last major offering from that stance before his subsequent evolution to the 'right' of the party. Yet any study of the book and Bukharin's subsequent writings indicate more continuity than is usually allowed for by those commentators who have only a cursory knowledge of his works. And, let it be noted, if 1920 marked the high tide of Bukharin's leftism, then it can be said to be equally true of the Bolsheviks as a whole, Lenin included. The rigours of the winter 1920–1 and the Kronstadt rebellion stripped away the exuberance and illusions about 'war communism' for all but a tiny minority within the Bolshevik Party.

The Background

What then was the period in which *The Economics* was written? It was one of revolution and civil war, following on from Russia's collapse during the First World War.

The war that had begun in August 1914 had thrown an intolerable burden upon the industry of the Russian Empire. Agriculture and the transport system were likewise soon staggering under the strains imposed by war. Although there had been considerable growth in Russian manufacturing industry between 1880 and 1914, by any criteria it was still quite inadequate to cope with the strains imposed on it by modern industrialised warfare. In terms of production and transport facilities the Russian Empire was far behind any of the other major participants in that war.

Although much of the industrial production was carried out in large modern units, these were still comparatively small islands in an ocean of small-scale production and a very backward agriculture.[4] In this respect it could be said that there was considerable unevenness within the economy as a whole. In the first stages of the war production rose, but as the war dragged on it declined rapidly. Food and raw material shortages reached famine proportions in the cities by the winter of 1916–17. The revolution of February 1917 further aggravated this situation and brought about disruption of industry. Therefore by the time of the October revolution, when the Bolsheviks assumed power, the whole economy was in a state of chaos.

Large areas of Western Russia were under German occupation until the collapse, in turn, of the Central Powers in November 1918. Since the areas under occupation contained rich grain lands as well as the industrialised sectors of Russian Poland as it was then, the food shortages in the towns and the goods famine in the countryside were further exacerbated.

It was in this situation that the Bolsheviks assumed power. Until the start of the civil war, in the summer of 1918, there was a relative lull in the social conflicts during which the Bolsheviks shared power with the Left Social-Revolutionaries and at the same time attempted to obtain the collaboration of some sections of the bourgeoisie and industrial managers in their efforts to revive industry. There was no immediate move to take into state ownership the major manufacturing industries, although there was a vigorous campaign to extend what was called workers' control, i.e. the supervision of owners and managers by rank-and-file committees. The Bolsheviks, on the insistent urging of Lenin, moved with caution in relation to nationalisation during this period. It is true that certain measures of nationalisation had been undertaken in the first months of Soviet government – for example, the Merchant Marine had been taken over in January 1918 and the sugar industry nationalised in May of that year – but the main efforts had been directed towards a stabilisation and regularisation of the tottering economy on the existing basis of ownership.

Lenin's theme in this early period was the need to install an efficient system of accounting and control, and to bring all factories and mines back to full production as soon as possible, even if this meant employing former owners and managers at high salaries. The most radical measures had been initiated from below, the workers seizing factories and, above all, the peasants dispossessing the landlords and sharing out the land among themselves. The latter move was endorsed by the Soviet government, but it was an acknowledgement of an accomplished fact over which it had little or no control.

The reason for the caution on the part of the Bolsheviks can be found in their expectation of an early revolution in Germany and in other countries of Europe. They reasoned that if such events occurred, particularly in Germany, the problems regarding supplies of industrial and processed goods would be solved, if not immediately, then at least fairly quickly.[5] This policy was not without its critics within the Bolshevik Party, and the Left Communists – among whom was Bukharin – pressed for more and far-reaching measures to be taken against capitalist property. Such were the tolerant conditions still prevailing that the Left Communists were able to publish their own journal – *Kommunist* – and Lenin had to argue policy questions with them publicly; just as had been the case over the Brest Litovsk peace treaty.[6]

The situation changed radically in the summer of 1918. First, civil war began in earnest, fuelled by Western intervention, and second, there was a fear of further German intervention. These threats came on top of sabotage and flight by the owners of industry, and these factors themselves led to further complications. There was a wave of factory seizures by workers' committees, very often on a local and fragmentary basis. These were followed by a Soviet Government decree on 28 June 1918 which nationalised all branches of industry.[7] Later, in November 1918, all internal and foreign trade was nationalised, the latter having little practical significance at that time, since foreign trade had by then all but ceased in those parts of the country in the control of the Soviets. However, the state monopoly of foreign trade was to become of critical importance later on.

Thus the civil war was powerfully to reinforce the centrifugal tendencies at work within the economy, and as Carr noted:

> the machinery of exchange and distribution established by recent decrees was quickly pushed aside; and for some time the most effective instruments in extracting grain from the peasant were the 'iron detachments' of workers from towns and factories reinforced by the local committees of poor peasants.[8]

Another source, and consequence, of the economic chaos was inflation: like all the belligerents in the war, a part of the Russian expenditure upon arms and munitions had been met by an increase in the note issue of the central bank or treasury. There had been a budget deficit ever since 1914, rising in the case of Russia to 81 per cent in 1917. The budget for the first half of 1918 had been estimated at 17.6 milliard roubles expenditure, but revenue at only 2.8 milliard.[9] So, although the Bolsheviks did not start the inflationary process, they were unable to stop it either, despite their wish to do so in the first few months of Soviet rule.

Given this chaotic situation, the Bolsheviks, when faced with the necessity to fight a civil war as well as combat foreign intervention, had to take urgent and drastic measures to supply the towns with food and the fledgling Red Army with weapons and munitions. There was evolved – it would be wrong to say planned – a system for the production of war materials, and the provisioning of the towns which subordinated all else to survival. Victor Serge succinctly summarised the system of 'war communism' that emerged as follows:

> War communism could be defined as follows: firstly, requisitioning in the countryside; secondly, strict rationing for the town population, who were classified into categories; thirdly, complete 'socialisation' of production and labour; fourthly, an extremely complicated and chit-ridden system of distribution for the remaining stocks of manufactured goods; fifthly, a monopoly of power tending towards the single Party and the suppression of all dissent; sixthly, a state of siege and the Cheka.[10]

The first official steps on the road to 'war communism' came in May 1918 with the decree which conferred upon the Commissariat of Supply extraordinary powers for the collection of grain. This was to be the legal basis for the armed detachments of workers who were supposed to confiscate surplus grain and the hoards of speculators. This was later changed to requisitioning fixed amounts of grain, which often went beyond taking surpluses. Thus began the process which eventually led to the peasants ceasing to sow grain and ultimately to the New Economic Policy.

In the towns money soon ceased to circulate in a meaningful manner; workers were given rations; all state services were provided free; school meals were given free to the children, even theatre tickets were distributed among factory workers free. Many Bolsheviks saw in all this the realisation of their aims as communists, but the reality was far from what the founding fathers of Marxian socialism had envisaged as being communism or socialism.

It was in this feverish atmosphere of gunsmoke and (if one was lucky) subsistence rations that Bukharin tried to peer ahead and formulate some theoretical propositions regarding the transition to socialism. Much of what he wrote was, essentially, a defence and even a celebration of 'war communism'. However, Bukharin's ideas were not formed solely by what was currently happening in Soviet

Russia; rather he viewed what was happening there as a part of a much larger upheaval on a world scale.

Imperialism: Apogee and Collapse

To understand Bukharin's particular views on the transition period to socialism it is necessary to understand how he viewed the then current stage of capitalist development.

In 1915 he had written his book *Imperialism and World Economy*, and the first few chapters of *The Economics* is taken up with a summary restatement of that work, particularly in the light of German experience during the 1914–18 war. He took as his starting point the capitalist world economy:

> Contemporary capitalism is world capitalism. This means that the capitalist relations of production dominate the entire world and connect all parts of our planet with a firm economic bond. Nowadays the concrete manifestation of the social economy is a world economy. The world economy is a *real* living unity.[11]

As we have seen previously, Bukharin distinguished between arithmetical sums and what he called 'real aggregates', or perhaps what we might call totalities. He argued against those who saw the world economy as being merely a summation of national economies, and instead he posited that the world economy is a *system* with its own particular equilibrium. However:

> The question now arises: just what are the consciously functioning parts of the world capitalist economy? In theory one can conceive of world capitalism as a system of individual, private enterprises, but the structure of modern capitalism is such that the economic subjects are the collective capitalist organisations – 'the state capitalist trusts'.[12]

What then was qualitatively different about the imperialist epoch, as compared to the previous era of capitalist development? Among the crucial features was the fact that:

> *Finance capital* did away with the anarchy in production within the major capitalist countries. Monopolistic employers' associations, combined enterprises, and the penetration of banking capital into industry created a new model of production relations, which transformed the unorganised commodity

capitalist system into a finance capitalist *organisation*. The unorganised relationship of one enterprise with another, through buying and selling, has to a considerable extent been replaced by an organised relationship through the 'controlled holding' of shares, 'participation' and 'financing', which find personal expression in the 'Dirigenten' of the banks, industry, the enterprises and trusts. By the same token, the exchange relation expressing the social division of labour and the separation of the socio-production organisation into independent capitalist enterprises is replaced by a *technical* division of labour within an organised 'national economy'.[13]

Here we see how Bukharin viewed the changes wrought by finance capital in the national capitalist economies. It is not merely that 'state capitalist trusts' compete on the world market, but that their creation has brought about a new and different model of production relations. Commodity circulation has been replaced by the circulation of products within the national economy, in much the same manner as products circulate within an oligopoly or conglomerate firm. In this respect his view of the division of labour is quite important:

> one should not confuse ... *two* things: the fragmentation of social labour, which *arises from* the fact of the social division of labour on the one hand, and the fragmentation of social labour, which negates this very division of labour on the other hand... 'enterprises' ... stand in various relationships to each other: either they are bound to each *other* by buying and selling (heterogeneous enterprises), or they are in competition with each other (homogeneous enterprises).[14]

These two types of social division of labour represent very different relationships: the heterogeneous enterprises form a complementary division of labour, whilst the homogeneous ones are antagonistic. And since capitalist commodity production is spontaneous – that is, unplanned social production, they are anarchic. But Bukharin pointed out:

> Usually, the anarchy of capitalist production is seen in the light of market competition and of that alone. Now, we can see that market competition expresses only *one* part, only one model of the 'life' of separate commodity producers, i.e., that model of relations which is not connected with the division of social labour.[15]

Here Bukharin was pointing out that even enterprises which are not directly in competition on the market, are in reality in competition with each other for the division of surplus-value in the form of profits. He therefore suggested three forms of competition:

1. Horizontal competition between homogeneous enterprises.
2. Vertical competition, the struggle between heterogeneous enterprises.
3. Finally, by combined (complex) competition we mean the struggle that is waged by combined enterprises, i.e., capitalist units which amalgamate various branches of production, i.e., which transform the social division of labour into a technical division.[16]

Therefore, in Bukharin's view:

the units which make up the system of the modern world economy are not individual enterprises, but ... complexes, state capitalist trusts ... The capitalist 'national economy' has changed from an *irrational* system into a *rational* organisation ... This transformation has been made possible by the growth of finance capitalism and the cohesion between the economic and political organisations of the bourgeoisie. At the same time, neither the anarchy of capitalist production in general, nor the competition of capitalist commodity producers, have been ...destroyed. Not only do these phenomena still exist, they have been intensified by being reproduced within the framework of a *world* economy. The world economic system is as blind, irrational and without subject as was the former system of national economy.[17]

Without doubt Bukharin was correct in the above, in so far as there was and is such a *tendency* at work within capitalism. However, he mistook certain war-time conditions in the main belligerent states as being irreversible changes. In this he was mistaken, since state control over industry was considerably reduced once the war was over, even if it did not wholly return to pre-war conditions. Moreover, even today allowing for the enormous growth in monopoly, or oligopoly, in the advanced capitalist countries, the national economies have not yet reached that condition of 'rationality' or planning in production that Bukharin assumed had been already achieved.

Given the actual conditions prevailing in 1920 Bukharin went on to say:

The 1914–18 war raised the question of state power point blank ... from the moment the imperialist state threw tens of millions of people onto the stage of history and instantly revealed its colossal significance as an *economic* factor, the analysis of state power became a matter for theoretical and practical discussion.[18]

But not only did the war raise the question of state power and economics; for Bukharin and the Bolsheviks it signalled the beginning of the end of imperialist capitalism, the first act in the collapse of the system as a whole, a collapse that had been hotly debated in the pre-war Marxist movement in Europe. Bukharin asserted that:

The actual economic situation in Europe in 1918–20 clearly shows that this period of collapse has set in and that the *old* system of relations of production shows no signs of revival. Quite the reverse, the concrete facts all indicate that the elements of decomposition and the revolutionary severance of relations are progressing with every month that passes.[19]

The apocalyptic vision of Bukharin and the Bolsheviks was clearly stated when he wrote:

The object of this work is to demolish common, vulgar and quasi-Marxist ideas about the nature of the Zusammenbruch (collapse) of capitalism predicted by the great authors of scientific communism and the nature of the process of transforming a capitalist society into a communist one. He who imagines the revolution of the proletariat to be a peaceful transition of power from one set of hands to another, and the revolution in the relations of production to be a change in the leadership of the organisational apparatus, he, who pictures the classic model of a proletarian revolution *in this way*, will recoil in horror from the tragedy mankind endures throughout the world. Amidst the smoking, charred ruins and the roar of civil war, he will be unable to discern the grand and stately outlines of the future society.[20]

But what is the process of collapse? What is the mechanism that brings capitalism crashing down? Obviously, war is seen as an engine of destruction, not merely in the physical sense, but also in the sense of the destruction of all those social bonds that constitute the equilibrium of capitalism as a social entity.

In his discussion Bukharin introduced a quite new and novel

concept when he examined the effects of war production upon the economy and society. He pointed out the *illusory* nature of much of the growth in the gross national product to which war economy gave rise, and to the fact that it *masked a decline in real wealth*. Although it will be easily grasped that war destroys large amounts of material means of production and means of consumption, he went further and analysed its effects upon the forces of production and the accumulation of capital. He introduced a concept that he termed 'expanded negative reproduction'.

Starting from the assumption that capitalist equilibrium is a *mobile* one, it is possible to precipitate dis-equilibrium not only in an upward direction, but also in a downward direction:

> the position of the development of the productive forces is closely related to that of reproduction: the growth of the forces of production corresponds with expanded reproduction, when static they correspond with simple reproduction and their decline is expressed in the fact that an ever diminishing share of the periodically consumed products is replaced. In the last instance we have social regression.[21]

With this view Bukharin was challenging the 'truly monstrous theoretical construction that drew the conclusion about the beneficial(!) influence of war on "national economic" life.'[22]

Also, by implication, Bukharin was challenging the views of Rosa Luxemburg, and all who since followed her in this matter, in her assumption that arms production is a field for the creation of surplus-value. Bukharin argued that armaments production 'has an altogether different significance: a gun is not transformed into an element of a new production cycle: gunpowder shot into the air does not appear in a different guise in the next cycle at all. Quite the reverse. The economic effects of these elements *in actu* has a purely negative value.'[23] He pointed out that when armaments production and war reaches a certain point, when larger and larger quantities of material goods *and* labour-power are sucked into this process, it will begin to destroy the very basis of production itself. Thus 'what we have ... is not expanded reproduction, but an ever-increasing u*nder-production*. This process may be called *expanded negative reproduction*. This is what war is from an economic point of view.'[24] What Bukharin was doing was to describe the actual situation in Soviet Russia during the period of 'war communism' and civil war. The gigantic military effort was sucking out of the economy, not only surplus products, but the very means of replacing means of production and means of consumption.

In 1920 the Red Army consumed one quarter of all available wheat in Soviet held territories.[25] Moreover, it was also draining the working class: in 1917 there had been three million workers employed in Russian industry, by the winter of 1920–1 the number had declined to 1,480,000.[26] And by 1921 the population of Moscow had declined by one half and that of Petrograd by two-thirds.[27] Because of the flooding of mines in the Donets valley the supply of fuel to industry was reduced to a trickle, as Deutscher noted:

> Deprived of fuel and raw materials, the industrial centres ... were paralysed. Even towards the end of 1920, the coal-mines produced less than one-tenth and the iron-and-steel works less than one twentieth of their pre-war output. The production of consumer goods was about one-quarter of normal. The disaster was made worse by the destruction of transport.[28]

This was a situation which could only last a short time before complete economic and social collapse ensued. It seemed as though Bukharin's expanded negative reproduction was going into free-fall.

Bukharin envisaged negative reproduction taking place even before such a catastrophic situation was reached, however, and he applied this concept to the capitalist countries. One of the forms of regression was inflation:

> The huge quantity of accumulated paper values are tokens, the realisation of which lies wholly in the future and depends, on the one hand, on the conditions of capitalist reproduction and, on the the other hand, on the very existence of the capitalist system. Clearly, the huge flood of bits of paper in various forms may become totally incommensurate with the real labour process, and in conditions of a *capitalist* structure, this will be one of the indications of its collapse. Thus, negative expanded reproduction runs parallel to the accumulation of paper values.[29]

He suggested that such a situation was inherently dangerous for the capitalist system, because 'the process of reproduction is not only a process of reproducing the material elements of production', but also a process of the reproduction of the very relations of production.[30] Given the regression of reproduction then, there would be a lessening, an atrophy of these *relations*, not merely of material reproduction but of all class relations. Thus expanded negative reproduction carries with it the seeds of revolution.

The process of expanded negative reproduction, then, reacts upon the political and social equilibrium; and should it be pushed too far, this in turn will react upon the productive forces, giving a further twist in the downward spiral. Bukharin argued that just as there is a period of political disintegration, so too will there be a period of technical and productive collapse. He argued, moreover, that this was historically inevitable. This meant that there would be an *inevitable* reduction of the productive forces and 'in this way the process of expanded negative reproduction is greatly speeded up.'[31] What was posited was a series of reciprocal acts which reinforce each other, and so create a multiplier effect in a downward direction.

Here then was Bukharin's view of the world he attempted to theorise about and in which to locate the transition period to socialism. Capitalism had been transformed into a world economy composed of competing state capitalist trusts, with rational, planned organisation internally, but still anarchic as a world system. And by 1920 this system was allegedly in the process of disintegration and revolutionary collapse. This posed the question: if capitalist equilibrium had been disrupted beyond recall and expanded negative reproduction had been set in motion, how was a new socialist equilibrium to be brought into being?

There were three main aspects to Bukharin's ideas on the transition period leading to a new socialist equilibrium:

1. The relationship between town and country;
2. The naturalisation of economic relations, i.e. the destruction of commodity circulation and the substitution of product circulation.
3. The use of coercion in the transition period.

I shall deal with these items in the above order.

Dis-equilibrium: Town and Country

In the first instance Bukharin noted that the process of expanded negative reproduction was at work in agriculture just as in industry, but its material effects were mitigated by the very primitiveness of agriculture as compared to industry. But: 'the collapse of the state-capitalist system ... also entails the collapse of this system in respect of agriculture.'[32] The decay of the system was manifested by speculative trading in agricultural produce, as against the orderly methods of the state-capitalist trusts. Within the revolutionary upheaval envisaged, relations between town and countryside are disrupted. This takes three forms: (1) the rupture of credit relations, (2) the breakdown of national and local government; and (3) the breakdown of the exchange of material use-values between town and countryside.

> With the collapse of the capitalist production apparatus, the process of production almost comes to a standstill; people live on old stocks which have survived the war and have been inherited by the proletariat. Money, which in 'normal times' represented a value in itself, finally reveals itself as an intermediary symbol, without any independent value. Consequently, for people in command of large quantities of agricultural produce, almost every incentive to deliver it to the town disappears. The social economy disintegrates into two autonomous spheres: the famine-stricken town, and the country, which despite the partial destruction of the productive forces, has a fairly considerable quantity of unmarketable 'surplus' produce.[33]

Alongside this process, and as a part of it, was the revolution in the countryside, with the dispossession of the landlords, 'and the less highly developed capitalist relations are, the greater its significance.'[34]

Therefore 'the struggle can be, and usually is, accompanied by a tremendous waste of resources and the breaking-up of the physical production base (partially by dividing up large estates, implements, livestock, etc.), by a *further* reduction in the productive forces.'[35] Bukharin then asked 'how is a new equilibrium possible, an equilibrium *within* agriculture itself, and also one *between* town and country'?[36] And then, with considerable foresight, he added: 'It is a decisive question for the fate of mankind, for it is a most important and highly complicated one.'[37] This was to be a problem which plagued the Soviet government throughout the 1920s and even today remains a problem of the first magnitude. (On an international scale one could also say that the so-called North–South division is a form of this problem.)

Given that the land had been distributed to the peasants, Bukharin suggested that without the intervention of the state, that is, the *proletarian* state, the scene would be set for a 'new American-style cycle', by which he meant the development of capitalist commodity production in agriculture with a process of centralisation taking place and the development of agri-factories. However, he immediately rejected such a possibility because:

> with the abolition of a commodity economy in the town and with the socialist organisation in industry ... the dictatorship of the proletariat is inevitably accomplished either by a hidden, or more or less open, struggle between the proletariat's tendency towards organisation and the tendency of the peasantry towards commodity anarchy.[38]

And, on the assumption of the superiority of socialist organisation, the victory would go to the proletariat.

How then would the new equilibrium be achieved? Bukharin replied: 'It is obvious that only the real process of "exchanges of substances" between town and country can serve as a firm and stable basis for the influence of the town to be decisive.'[39]

It is clear that what Bukharin had in mind here was that the 'town' must provide consumer goods and means of production to agriculture on such a scale as to make it worthwhile for the peasants to produce more than for their own immediate needs. For this real exchange to take place it was necessary, of course, that industrial production should be revived. And given the conditions obtaining this posed an almost insuperable problem, since 'the rebirth of industry is itself dependent on the flow of vital resources into towns, the absolute necessity for this influx at any price.'[40]

It was this 'any price' which indicated the unequal relationship between town and countryside. Bukharin argued:

> This minimal 'equilibrium' can be achieved only (1) at the expense of the resources left in the towns, and (2) by use of force on the part of the proletarian state. This state coercion (the removal of grain surpluses, tax in kind, or some other form) is economically funded: in the first place, directly, since the peasantry itself has an interest in the growth of industry, which supplies it with agricultural machines, implements, artificial fertilisers and electric power, etc.; in the second place, indirectly, since the state power of the proletariat is the best means of protection against the restoration of the economic pressure of the large-scale landowner, banker...[41]

Now, in the conditions of 1920 in Soviet Russia, to write about all those things that industry could supply to agriculture was the 'music of the future' and the reality was that coercion was the main means

of provisioning the towns. Nevertheless, Bukharin was attempting
to look beyond 'war communism' to a situation where a genuine
exchange could be achieved. In this respect it is very important to
understand just what he meant by exchange. Bukharin envisaged a
situation where large-scale agricultural production would be
organised by the state and therefore the state 'would directly
organize the *production* process'. But for the small producers:

> their involvement in the organisational apparatus is primarily
> made possible through the *sphere of circulation*. Hence,
> nominally in the same way as under the system of state
> capitalism. The ... government organs of distribution and state
> procurement are the chief apparatus of the new system of
> equilibrium.[42]

It is important to recall that Bukharin had already argued that
under the system of state capitalism *commodity* production had
been abolished in the internal relations of such states. Therefore
when he refers to the sphere of circulation here he does not have
in mind *market* relations, but rather a system of planned
production and exchange, which may or may not have included
some form of monetary accounting. (To suggest otherwise is to
imply that Bukharin was suggesting that a proletarian state would
regress back beyond state capitalism.)

However, Bukharin did acknowledge that there would be a long
period when petty commodity production would spontaneously
arise, and that the struggle between state organised agricultural
production and petty commodity production would – as he saw it –
be a struggle between socialist and capitalist tendencies in the
economic arena.

> In the towns, the main struggle for the economic model comes to
> an end with the victory of the proletariat; in the country ... it is
> resurrected in other forms as a struggle between the state
> planning of a proletariat which embodies socialised labour and
> the commodity anarchy, the speculative licence of a peasantry
> which embodies scattered property and the anarchic element of
> the market ... a simple commodity economy is merely the embryo
> of a capitalist economy...[43]

Clearly, then, Bukharin did not adhere to any idea of 'market
socialism', since he directly counterposed plan and market.

However, he then proceeded to say: 'there resides two "souls" within the bosom of the peasant himself and the poorer he is, the greater will be the significance of the proletarian tendency.'[44]

Here Bukharin raised one of the questions that would be consistently debated throughout the 1920s. The idea of the two 'souls' of the peasant would become one of the hallmarks of his attitude in the decade of the 1920s. Thus, despite the fact that he had dealt with the relationship of town and countryside at a very abstract level Bukharin did try to grapple with some of the fundamental, enduring and *concrete* problems arising from the revolutionary transformation of the economy. He pointed to the necessity of a *reciprocal* relationship, one that had ultimately to be beneficial to all participants, and not merely based upon value money exchanges but one that entailed an exchange of real use-values. He argued against *market* exchanges, and instead pointed to the need for *planned* production and exchange. Lastly, he pointed to the danger of the spontaneous revitalisation of petty commodity production if the peasants were not drawn into the planned economy via the process of exchange. And, concomitantly, the possibility of a class struggle between workers and peasants was pointed to in deciding which model or relations would prevail.

Naturalisation of Economic Relations

As we have already seen, Bukharin argued that with the domination of state capitalist trusts in the period leading to the collapse of capitalism, commodity production had been replaced internally by the rational organisation of production. Therefore the process of the naturalisation of economic relationships had already begun *before* the transition period was embarked upon. And, in the determination of a new equilibrium between town and country this displacement of commodity production and circulation by the production of use-values and the circulation of products was further extended.

The question arises, why was this process of naturalisation considered necessary? Bukharin had already indicated a part of his reasoning when he proposed that political economy as a subject of study would disappear under socialism, because:

Theoretical political economy is the study of a social economy based upon the production of *commodities*, i.e. the study of an *unorganised* social economy... as soon as we take an organised social economy, all the basic 'problems' of politcal economy disappear: problems of value, price, profit and so on. Here 'relations between people' are not expressed as 'relations between things', and the social economy is regulated not by the blind forces of the market and competition, but by a consciously followed plan ... the end of a capitalist commodity society will also see the end of political economy.[45]

Therefore, according to Bukharin, commodities as an economic category exist because of the *social* division of labour and the anarchic manner of production and distribution. The abolition of commodity production therefore presupposes the development of a system which retains the *technical* division of labour combined with *associated social labour*.

In an analysis of the economics of the transition period, one must not only deal with 'pure' forms and categories. This analysis is therefore difficult, because there are no stable quantities here. If knowledge in its present state is generally concerned with fluid 'processes' and not with fixed metaphysical 'essences', it is in the transition period ... that the categories of being are replaced by categories of 'becoming'.[46]

In this situation the categories of political economy no longer suffice for analytical purposes:

The old categories of political economy continue to take the form of practical *generalisations* about a *continuously changing*, living, economic reality. At the same time, these categories do not enable one to penetrate the 'surface of phenomena' ... to understand the process and development of *economic life as a whole* ... By their very nature these elementary relations, which in ideological terms are represented by the categories of commodity, price, wages, profit, etc., simultaneously exist and do not exist. It is as if they are non-existent. They drag out a strange kind of illusory real, and really illusory existence ... Therefore, the old, tested tools of Marxist thought, coined by Marx on the basis of the very real existence of the appropriate relations of production, begin to misfire. But in everyday practical life, they continue to be uncritically regarded as a means for a true understanding of the phenomena of economic life.[47]

Why do these 'tested tools' no longer correspond to everyday life? Bukharin answered:

The law of value is *the law of equilibrium in a simple commodity system of production*. The law of the costs of production [plus the average rate of profit] is the law of equilibrium in a transformed commodity system, i.e., the capitalist system. The law of market price is the law of oscillation in this system. The law of competition is the law of the continual restoration of the upset equilibrium. The law of crises is the law of the inevitable periodic disturbance of the equilibrium of the system and its restoration.[48]

But if the market is no longer operative in large parts of the economy, and therefore is no longer anarchic; if costs plus average rate of profit do not determine production and investment, all of the above falls to the ground. This is despite the fact that economic calculations are still carried out in 'prices'. As Bukharin pointed out: 'The limits to the applicability of these categories will become instantly clear if we define the basic conditions of existence for the real relationships which correspond to them (i.e., to these categories).'[49]

He argued that once *conscious* control of production is established at the macro level, the result of this production loses its commodity characteristic. And:

Value emerges when we have true commodity production. Here, a constant and not a chance model of anarchic relations via exchange is obligatory ... the law of value is merely the law of equilibrium of an anarchic commodity system ... Consequently, value as a category ... is least useful of all during the transition period, where commodity production to a considerable extent disappears and there is no equilibrium.[50]

Since value is no longer a viable category in the transition period, this in turn will react upon money and prices:

One must distinguish from the cases of the *imaginary* form where price *does not rest* on a value correlation. Here price is absolutely divorced from value. Consequently, in the transition epoch, the case of the imaginary form inevitably comes close to the typical case.[51]

From the above Bukharin deduced that the monetary system would collapse, money would be devalued and 'the distribution of paper money is divorced from the distribution of products.'[52] From this it follows that wages 'become an imaginary value without content'. Therefore 'under the dictatorship of the proletariat the "workers" receive a *socio-labour ration* and not wages.'[53]

It was by developing such a line of reasoning that Bukharin reached the conclusion that it was necessary to conceptualise the naturalisation of economic relations. This naturalisation consists in the fact of planned production and distribution in the economy by means of material quantities and not by prices plus market exchanges. Prices in such circumstances become an administrative convenience or merely irrelevant. Here as in a number of places in his text, Bukharin appeared to be confusing different conditions, for example, money becomes valueless with the introduction of planning under conditions of material abundance. The disappearance of money and market relations under socialism should arise because of the lack of any compulsion to labour, brought about by a huge increase in productivity coupled with the transformation of labour into a free spontaneous activity. Such *ideal* conditions contrast sharply with the actual experiences of 'war communism': money became valueless because of the disappearance of goods, wages were replaced by rations – the rations of abject poverty not abundance – prices became imaginary because money no longer had any value, and paper money was issued by keeping the printing presses working day and night, amounting to hyper-inflation!

As a result of this confusion Bukharin was led into a contradictory position on the question of coercion.

Coercion During the Transition Period

It is in the chapter headed 'Non-Economic Coercion in the Transition Period' that we can see the confusion engendered by the foregoing circumstances being translated into a hymn of praise for violence. Bukharin started out correctly by noting the use of force in historical change, and its use in the class struggle. He rejected the idea that there can be any revolutionary change in society without force, even if that force is merely latent or potential:

In the transition epoch, when one production structure is giving way to another, the midwife is revolutionary violence. This revolutionary violence must destroy the fetters on the development of society, i.e. the old forms 'of concentrated violence' which have become counter-revolutionary ... the old state and the old model of relations of production ... Revolutionary violence must actively assist in the formation of new relations of production, after it has created a new form of 'concentrated violence', the state of the new class ... Hence, on the one hand, violence plays a destructive role and on the other, it is a force for cohesion, organisation and construction.[54]

So far there is little here that would run counter to what would be considered orthodox Marxist views. Bukharin went on, however, to make a leap that did not necessarily follow from his previous line of thought. He said:

The greater the magnitude of this 'non-economic' force which in fact *is* an 'oekonomische Potenz', the smaller the 'costs' of the transition period will be (other things being equal, of course), the shorter this transition period will be, the more quickly social equilibrium will be established on a new basis and the more rapidly the curve of the productive forces will begin to rise.[55]

What he missed here was any consideration of the degree of resistance by the dispossessed classes and those sections of the population which follows them; this surely is the determinant of the level and degree of violence necessary to reorganise social and economic life. Moreover, there seems to be an element of moral righteousness in Bukharin's attitude, in so far as he sought to clothe what could be considered necessary violence with an aura of positive good, thereby turning necessity into a virtue. And having sanctified violence as a positive good, Bukharin then proceeded to argue for coercion to be applied to the working class also:

In so far as this political power, as 'concentrated violence' against the bourgeoisie, is itself an economic force, it is the force which severs the capitalist relations of production, by putting the proletariat in charge of the material and physical framework of production ... on the other hand, this same 'concentrated violence' is partly turned inward, where it is a factor in the *self-organisation* and compulsory *self-discipline* of the workers.[56]

Bukharin argued that this self-organisation and compulsory self-discipline was a part of the process of transforming a 'class in itself' into a 'class for itself'. However, he did not seem to comprehend the possibility that *self* organisation and *compulsion* are mutually exclusive. He attributed the actual cohesive organising role to the vanguard of the working class (read Communist Party) which led the various strata of that class with their differing levels of consciousness. Therefore: 'compulsory discipline is absolutely inevitable, and the less voluntary internal discipline is, i.e., the less revolutionised a given section or group of the proletariat is, the more strongly its compulsory nature will be felt.'[57]

And what would the concrete form of this compulsion take?

One of the main forms of compulsion of the new model, operating within the working class itself, is the abolition of the so-called 'freedom of labour'. 'Freedom of labour' in capitalist society was one of the many myths of that society, since in reality the monopolisation of the means of production by the capitalists *forced* the workers to sell their labour-power. This is what that 'freedom' amounted to: in the first place, to the relative possibility of *choosing* your own master (moving from one factory to another), the possibility of being 'fired' and getting 'the sack'; in the second place, this 'freedom' implied *competition between workers themselves*. In this latter meaning, 'the freedom of labour' was already partially overcome by the *workers' organisations* in the capitalist period, when the trade unions partly abolished competition between workers by uniting them and making them stronger in their struggle against the capitalist class ... Under the proletarian dictatorship, the question of an 'owner' no longer arises, since the 'exploiters have been expropriated'. On the other hand, the remaining disorganisation, lack of solidarity, individualism, parochial narrow-mindedness and the defects of capitalist society are apparent in the form of the failure to understand general proletarian tasks, which are expressed most forcibly in the tasks and demands of the Soviet dictatorship, the workers' state. Since these tasks must be accomplished ... from the proletariat's point of view, the abolition of the so-called 'freedom to labour' is essentially *in the name* of the real and not mythical freedom of the working class ... Hence, a regime of compulsory labour service and state distribution of workers ... already shows a comparatively high degree of organisation throughout the entire apparatus...[58]

What we have here is a process of logical reductionism. The abstraction 'working class' is opposed to 'backward' sections of the real class and the needs of this abstraction are to be imposed upon reality. Thus the new reality is that a small group of people substitute themselves for the class as a whole and decide what is best for all. This is, of course, in a situation where there is a 'dictatorship of the proletariat', where the proletariat itself is only a small minority of the whole population. Thus we have a recipe for the dictatorship of the leadership of the ruling party, since they are presumed to know what the historical tasks of the proletariat are. This particular passage is Bukharin at his sophistical worst, since he rails against the 'freedom to labour' in a manner that dodges the real freedom that workers can obtain by forming trade unions; this was not a negation of the 'freedom to labour', but rather a redefinition of that freedom in a positive manner.

Moreover, Bukharin greatly underrates the real freedom involved in the freedom to 'choose one's own master', since it sets limits to the exploitation of the class as a whole. The result of this conception and the actual use of coercion in the Soviet Union at the time under consideration was an acceleration of the disintegration of the real working class and a further twist in the downward spiral of labour productivity. By the winter of 1920–1 the application of compulsion to the workers and peasants had become absolutely counterproductive, and had become a factor in the general collapse of the economy facing the Bolsheviks.

NEP and the Market: A New Equilibrium

The most critical and decisive breakdown of the economy was that of the rupture between town and country. This manifested itself in the falling returns in grain collections for provisioning the towns and the Red Army. This decline was partly masked in 1920 by an increase in deliveries, but this was because requisitioning was by then taking place over a larger area of the country as a result of the defeat of the White Guard armies. But through the autumn of 1920 there was a series of peasant uprisings directed against the forced deliveries of grain.

As early as February 1920 Trotsky had put before the Central Committee of the Bolshevik Party a plan to end grain requisitioning and replace it with a fixed tax in kind; also to allow the peasants to sell their surpluses on the (to be revived) market. He pointed out that despite the increase in the quantity of grain collected 'the food reserves are in danger of drying up, and against this no improvement in the requisitioning machinery can help.'[59] However, these proposals were rejected at that time.

But throughout 1920 there were abundant signs that Trotsky's prediction would be fulfilled. By the spring of 1921 sufficient evidence was available to convince the overwhelming majority of the ruling party of the need for a change of policies in relation to agriculture. Following on from the Kronstadt sailors' revolt in that year, Lenin introduced a resolution at the Tenth Congress of the Party in March 1921, which in substance adopted Trotsky's earlier proposals.[60]

What at first sight appeared to be limited concessions to the peasantry opened the way for a fundamental revision of Soviet economic policies and structures. As Carr pointed out, it was impossible to restore market relations in agriculture without doing the same for industry. And this is what happened. A wave of de-nationalisation of small enterprises (employing 20 or less people), followed by the introduction of 'economic accounting' for the majority of industry, plus the cessation of direct supplies of food to factories, meant the return to wages payments for workers. This meant that profit and loss became the criteria upon which the majority of industry had to operate (the defence industry being the exception).

Despite the drought and ensuing famine of 1921 it was clear by 1922 that the policy had been successful in generating increased production both in industry and agriculture, even though large-scale, heavy industry was slower to recover than other sectors.

The New Economic Policy, or NEP, was obviously a reversal of the naturalisation of economics that had been a fact during the period of 'war communism', and which Bukharin had lauded in *The Economics*. With the return to market relations for the bulk of the economy there also arose the need for a stable currency; this was effected over the next few years with the introduction of a new, gold based rouble, alongside the paper Soviet rouble which was finally driven out of circulation. Thus there emerged in Soviet Russia what was to become known as a 'mixed economy'.

What was Bukharin's attitude towards this drastic reversal of policy? We know from an article he wrote entitled 'The New Course of Our Economic Policy' that he enthusiastically endorsed NEP as early as August 1921.[61] In this article there was a degree of modification of his views on 'war communism', since he was arguing in it that it was an emergency policy, rather than the high-road to socialism.

Our economic policies in the epoch of so-called 'war communism' ... could not be policies aimed at developing the productive forces. The urgent and indeed all-embracing task was the Red defence of the country. Everything was directed towards this: material resources, organisational strengths, in short all the skilled elements of management. With regard to the national economy in such a state of affairs, the principal slogan was not concern for its lasting restoration ... but the immediate securing of *produce, even at the cost of undermining the productive forces.* Not to 'produce', but to 'take'; to take in order to supply the Red Army ... and so on, in the shortest possible time.[62]

He pointed to the conflict that such a policy engendered in the countryside:

This had a very striking effect on agriculture. Our economic policy here amounted to almost solely ... the requisitioning system of food and distribution. Under this system, however, the individual producer, the peasant, lost all interest and the incentive to expand production... So there was a conflict here between the requirements for the development of the individual farm and those of our policy. But since Russia's agriculture is a peasant agriculture ... our economic policies objectively conflicted with the *development* of agriculture as a whole. The agricultural crisis was bound to intensify, as indeed it did. But since agriculture forms the basis of our industry, it was by and large also an intensification of the crisis in the *national economy in general.*[63]

Thus there was a frank recognition of the disaster facing Soviet society if such policies had been continued. Not surprisingly the question of equilibrium was posed by Bukharin:

This inevitably gave rise to the following: that equilibrium between the classes which was established during the civil war and which depended not on the 'normal' economic processes but on the mutual military interests of the proletariat and the peasantry ... But at the same time, it is clear that as soon as the war was over the purely economic contradictions were bound to be excessively aggravated. Standing in the queue were problems of the economy, of the development of the productive forces, which, with regard to agriculture, was conceivable only in a form of the growth of *petty-bourgeois* economy.[64]

Such an equilibrium could only have been a temporary one, being based upon the fear of a common enemy, rather than on a positive material joint interest. The realities of the necessity for an 'exchange of substances' between town and countryside immediately became pressing as soon as the external pressures on the alliance subsided. It was this longer-term exchange that Bukharin recognised as being the central contradiction in the then current situation. Now, contrary to what he had said in *The Economics*, he acknowledged that this exchange could only be effected via market relations, i.e. 'petty-bourgeois economy'.

Given that the long-term aim was the establishment of a communist society, Bukharin argued that it was necessary to develop large-scale, particularly heavy, industry:

> But as soon as we bring up this question ... we come up against a 'sore subject'. To consolidate heavy industry one needs 'funds' (funds of food-stuff, raw materials, additional equipment and so forth). And this is where we are in danger of finding ourselves in a vicious circle: for industry one has got to have products and to get products one has got to have industry ... Thus it is clear that *to develop heavy industry one must increase the supply of products at all costs and by all means. At all costs!* Because otherwise we shall not even have the most elementary preconditions for this development ... *By all means!* Because the additional quantity of products which must flow into our heavy industry has to be taken *from outside,* not from within the sphere of heavy industry itself, which is in the hands of the workers' state, but from elsewhere, from other external sources, whatever the price we have to pay.[65]

Bukharin thus posed the problem facing the Bolsheviks in its starkest form, a problem that was to be hotly debated for nearly a decade to come. The apocalyptic vision of a rapid transition to socialism was reduced to the more pressing and mundane problem of the extraction of the necessary food and raw materials for the barest survival of the towns and industry. The precise methods of extracting these necessary 'products' from this 'external' source was also to be one of the major *practical* and theoretical problems of the 1920s.

Up to this point Bukharin still regarded the peasantry as being 'external' to the working class, *and* a source of 'petty-bourgeois economy', a position he was later to modify. He had raised the question of the 'two souls' of the peasants in *The Economics*, but here he recognised that in the given situation then facing the Bolsheviks the 'petty-bourgeois' aspect would dominate. He argued that the 'increase in the supply of goods is the supreme law of the present economic situation', and suggested that one of the main sources for this supply must be the peasantry. However:

> *The peasant farm* is, as everyone knows, an individualistic, petty-bourgeois farm. But we have already seen above that we cannot do without an *intensification* of growth, the development of this petty-bourgeois farm. On the contrary its development is an essential condition for the growth of our heavy industry ... The extraction of an additional amount of products from this sphere pre-supposes its growth, which – temporarily, in the present phases of development – is none other than the growth of bourgeois relations. But this growth makes it possible to obtain an additional supply of goods.[66]

He admitted that – from a communist point of view – such a development had great dangers and what was involved was the 'competition of economic forms'.

> Indeed, strengthening the petty-bourgeois economy means none other than apportionment on the basis of commodity circulation of the buyer-up, the trade capitalist and owner. The capitalist tenant, the concessionaire and so forth will similarly have a firm base in the growing economically petty-bourgeois element.[67]

The political embarrassment that such admissions created for the Bolsheviks were smoothed over by presenting the necessity for NEP in terms of an analogy with the Brest Litovsk peace treaty with Germany in 1918, that is, as being a breathing space. In the case of the treaty it gave the opportunity for the Red Army to be created, which at a later date was able to go on to the offensive. In the same way NEP was presented as a breathing space for the creation of socialist industry with which later to mount an economic offensive against the petty-bourgeois elements in the national economy.

If NEP was presented as a retreat, however, giving ground to capitalist economy to gather strength for a later offensive, this suggested that 'war communism' was desirable, even if not immediately practicable. In this respect Bukharin displayed the same indecision – one might say double thinking – that was evident on the part of many Bolsheviks when faced with the necessity of NEP. They did not want to repudiate totally their previous policies, yet had to recognise the disaster of which they had been part. Later on Bukharin was to present NEP, not as a retreat, but as a *return* to the early policies of 1918.

In Russia we started not with War Communism but with the so-called New Economic Policy. This was followed by intervention, by an ... intensification of the class struggle, which assumed the form of civil war. This gave rise to War Communism. Then followed the return to NEP.[68]

Despite this somewhat shilly-shallying attitude, Bukharin was very clear in one respect: 'We can see the new course of our economic policies as a mighty *strategic* operation ... intended to last for a number of years.'[69] The strategic aim, for Bukharin, was the development of large-scale industry as a springboard to communism:

Once we have achieved this, we shall ... 'turn the rudder'. But this new turn of the rudder in the opposite direction will not signify a return to the previous situation, that is, to the appropriation of surpluses and so forth. For these methods, used to regulate consumption on the basis of a *drop* in the economic power of the town relative to the village, will be quite inappropriate to a state of affairs whose basis lies in *developing* the productive forces ... The 'turn of the rudder' will be the gradual economic liquidation of the large private enterprises and the economic subordination of the small producer to large scale industry. The small producer will be drawn into a socialised enterprise, not by means of non-economic coercion, but chiefly by the economic advantages which will provide him with a tractor, electric light bulbs, agricultural machinery and so on. He will be enmeshed for his own good in the electric wires which bring with them life-giving energy to make the farm fertile.[70]

Thus, in 1921, Bukharin was developing his theory of equilibrium both in the theoretical aspects and in its application to current questions. As we have seen, his view of the transition to socialism was one of the breakdown of the fundamental equilibrium of capitalism and the creation of a new equilibrium by the establishment of the dictatorship of the proletariat.

For Bukharin, the transition period encompassed two distinct phases. The first can be encapsulated in his term expanded negative reproduction. This took the form of the disintegration of social, political and economic equilibrium, with all the waste that accompanied such a process. And this process was not immediately halted by the accession to power of the Bolsheviks. On the contrary 'war communism' gave further impetus to the economic decline, yet at the same time provided the framework for a new social and political equilibrium.

This new social and political equilibrium had no solid economic foundation, however. Only NEP, with its circulation of commodities and the laws of the market – not merely the exchange of products – could provide this economic foundation. And in essence this was an equilibrium on a contradictory basis. At this point Bukharin did not suggest in any detail how the new equilibrium was to be achieved; but he was willing to move more cautiously and pragmatically.

Given this overall approach it was clear that the question of the so-called worker–peasant alliance was to be one of the main economic, social and political problems in the period that lay ahead. And, given the view held by Bukharin (and the majority of the Bolsheviks) that the peasants were, by definition, a hot-bed of 'petty-bourgeois anarchy', a sort of bubbling yeast out of which constantly emerged petty capitalists, such an alliance (equilibrium) had latent dangers of a renewed bout of violent class struggle.

In his article 'The New Course of Our Economic Policy' there had been a retreat from some of the more blatantly utopian ideas of *The Economics*; gone was the euphoria; it was now acknowledged that product exchanges and naturalisation of the economy were not an immediate prospect. Instead it was understood that there would be a long period of commodity circulation *and all that that implied*. This in turn implied that the transition period was now viewed, not as a relatively short, chaotic time, but as an epoch that would develop its own laws of equilibrium.

A further implication of the necessity of NEP was the need for the lessening of coercion, particularly in relation to the peasantry but also generally. But this was not taken to mean any loosening of the monopoly of political power by the Bolsheviks. Nevertheless, within the framework of NEP, Bukharin was seeking the means for establishing the necessary equilibrium of social and political, as well as the economic, factors.

The introduction of the 'mixed economy' did not imply any acceptance by Bukharin of the notion of 'market socialism'; on the contrary, he saw the market as a *means* to achieving socialism within the framework of the 'mixed economy' in which the state and state-planning dominated. And if the 'mixed economy' was seen only as a framework, then like the scaffolding surrounding a building, it would be dismantled when the task in hand had been completed. But for Bukharin the market had no place within the fully developed socialist economic system once that condition had been achieved. The long-term aim of the naturalisation of economic relations was still central to Bukharin's view of socialism. And since for him the market implied *commodity* production, and value as a mediating form in social economic relations, the idea of 'market socialism' would have been anathema. The path to socialism, for Bukharin, consisted of using the market, as a means of eliminating the market and the *gradual* naturalisation of human relations. How he worked out the details of this path emerged in his debate with the opposition, particularly Preobrazhensky, in the mid-1920s.

6

Unproductive Consumption and Expanded Negative Reproduction

War and Economic Decline

In his book *The Economics of the Transition Period* Bukharin discussed the effects of war and war production upon the economy, pointing to the illusory growth of the national product – measured in current prices – to which a war economy gave rise. As we have seen in a previous chapter, he argued that such an illusory growth could in fact mask a real decline in values and use-values. Bukharin pointed out that:

> Development of the productive forces is the basis for human development in general and so it is necessary to examine every fact of social life with this in mind. The position of the development of the productive forces is closely related to that of reproduction: the growth of the productive forces corresponds with expanded reproduction, when static they correspond with simple reproduction and their decline is expressed in the fact that an ever-diminishing share of periodically consumed products is replaced. In this last instance we have social regression.[1]

Since means of production and means of consumption *normally* re-enter the productive process, their consumption can be called productive consumption. That part of the total social product which does not re-enter the productive process, either directly or indirectly, can be considered unproductive consumption. Therefore:

> Military production has an altogether different significance: a gun is not transformed into an element of a new productive cycle: gun powder is shot into the air and does not appear in a different guise in the next cycle at all ... The economic effect of these elements *in actu* has a purely negative value ... If we take means of consumption which is supplied to the army, we observe the same phenomenon here. The means of consumption do not create labour power, since soldiers do not feature in the

production process ... [So] ... a considerable part of the means of consumption will not serve as means of production of labour power.[2]

Thus, Bukharin argued, if total unproductive consumption is greater than the total surplus product/value regression is set in motion. And this is the case when 'What we have ... is not expanded reproduction, but an ever-increasing *under-production*. This process may be called *expanded negative reproduction*.'[3]

The fact that paper 'values', the quantity of paper money and near money in circulation greatly increases only masks this decline in *real* production.

Although Bukharin was primarily concerned with a war situation, in which there was not only a direct diversion of a large part of the GNP to the production of means of destruction, but also a direct destruction of the forces of production, his formulation can also be applied to 'peace time' capitalism. The phase usually used to cover this situation is 'permanent arms economy'. It is not the purpose of this chapter to explore all the ramifications of the debate on the 'arms economy', rather I want to focus upon Bukharin's ideas in relation to the main question, that is, unproductive consumption and the conditions for equilibrium.

Marx on Unproductive Consumption

The question as to what is, or can be considered to be, productive and unproductive labour, and productive and unproductive consumption, has been the subject of hot debate, going back to Adam Smith and beyond. But whatever definition one accepts, let us agree that there are such categories, and for the purpose of this work I shall define productive labour as being: labour which is exchanged with capital and produces a surplus-value, a surplus-value moreover which is embodied in *material* commodities, the form of which is *capable* of being used as capital for the reproduction and extension of capital.[4] It will be seen that such a definition excludes the production of the means of destruction (armaments).[5]

In this respect we have to examine the question of luxury goods and their production. This is necessary since there appears to be some confusion about what Marx classified as luxury goods and the character of the labour embodied in them. Is the labour embodied in luxury goods productive or unproductive labour?

Marx's definition of luxury goods was fairly straightforward; they were 'all goods which are not necessaries and which are not commonly used by the labouring class.'[6] We should not collapse luxury goods production and their consumption, however, into unproductive consumption, since unproductive consumption covers a wider spectrum. There are many instances of necessary unproductive consumption, both in the absolute and historically determined sense. Similarly much social labour may be necessary but not productive. But it is not always possible to state *a priori* if labour is productive or unproductive, since it is the particular circumstances which determine this. In other words, it is not merely the circumstances of the immediate production process which determine if labour is productive, but the total social circumstances, including the use to which products are put, which determine *post hoc* whether the labour involved has been productive or not. The *material form* of the surplus-product has an important bearing upon this.

Bukharin's theory of expanded negative reproduction *is* one that takes both value and material aspects of commodities into account: 'It is exceedingly important to note that the analysis of ... enlarged reproduction given by Marx in his famous arithmetically formulated schemes in the second volume of *Capital* brings in both the value (economic) and the natural (technical) aspects of reproduction.'[7]

In Chapter XX of Vol. II of *Capital* Marx discussed the relationship between luxury goods production and consumption and the production of necessary means of consumption. In this discussion he used a model of simple reproduction to illustrate the relationship, dividing Department II into two sub-departments. Dept. IIa produces all necessary means of consumption, which are consumed by both workers and capitalists; whilst Dept. IIb produces only luxury goods which are consumed solely by the capitalists. It must be recalled that Marx was using a very abstract model, in which only workers and capitalists appear as economic *persona*. Therefore surplus-value is equated with profits, since he did not consider the division of the surplus-value into various sub-categories, i.e. rent, profit on money capital, industrial profit, etc. Moreover, since all unproductive consumption is considered to be capitalist personal consumption, the question of the unproductive consumption of the state does not arise in his discussion at that point.

Marx used a numerical model of simple reproduction, which we have seen in Chapter 3, and suggested that Dept. II be divided into a and b along the following lines:

Dept. I	$4000c + 1000v + 1000s$	$= 6000$
Dept. IIa	$1600c + 400v + 400v$	$= 2400$
Dept. IIb	$400c + 100v + 100v$	$= 600$

$$6000c + 1500 + 1500 = 9000$$

The assumption that Marx made, therefore, is that capitalist consumption is divided 3/5 for necessaries and 2/5 for luxury goods. Thus, s is divided into s_n and s_l. This gives a division of surplus-value along the following lines:

I	$600s_n + 400s_l$	$= 1000s_1$
IIa	$240s_n + 160s_l$	$= 400s_{2a}$
IIb	$60s_n + 40s_l$	$= 100s_{2b}$

From this the following equations may be derived:

$$c_1 + v_1 + s_1 = c_1 + c_{2a} + c_{2b}$$
$$c_{2a} + v_{2a} + s_{2a} = v_1 + v_{2a} + v_{2b} + s_{n1} + s_{n2a} + s_{n2b}$$
$$c_{2b} + v_{2b} + s_{2b} = s_{1l} + s_{2al} + s_{2bl}$$

and equilibrium demands:

$$v_1 + s_{n1} + s_{1l} = c_{2a} + c_{2b}$$

All of the above is relatively simple and clear. However, if one applies Marx's method to extended reproduction certain questions arise that need to be answered. Let us assume the following model: taking the same total value, we have rearranged it for extended reproduction.[8] For ease of exposition we have substituted Dept. III for IIb thus:

Dept. I	$4400c + 1100v + 1100s$	$= 6600$	$= w_1$
Dept. II	$1400c + 350v + 350s$	$= 2100$	$= w_2$
Dept. III	$200c + 50v + 50s$	$= 300$	$= w_3$

$$6000 + 1500 + 1500 = 9000 = W$$

In constructing the scheme we have assumed that the division of surplus-value between unproductive consumption and accumulation would be 50 per cent each; and also that the unproductively consumed part would be divided in the same proportions as Marx used.

In the above $p_m = 0.2$, $\alpha/S = \underline{b} = 0.5$ thus $(1 - \underline{b}).p_m = g' = 0.1$. We also find that $(w_1 - C)/C = g = 0.1$. (See Chapter 3 for definition of these equations.)

And this produces a theoretical division of the surplus-value of:

I	$440\beta_c + 110\beta_v + 330s_n + 220s_1$	$= 1100$	$= s_1$
II	$140\beta_c + 35\beta_v + 105s_n + 70s_n$	$= 350$	$= s_2$
III	$20\beta_c + 5\beta_v + 15s_n + 10s_1$	$= 50$	$= s_3$

And in this case we find:

$$v_1 + \beta_{v1} + s_{1n} + s_{1l} = c_2 + \beta_{c2} + c_3 + \beta_{c3}$$

And this defines the theoretical equilibrium conditions.

All the above holds on the assumption that Dept. III does produce a material product and the workers in that department do provide surplus labour and thus surplus-value. However, what we need to know is, to what extent can Dept. III be considered truly productive on a social scale?

Dept. II produces a total of 2,100 necessary means of consumption. From this total there is a call upon it of $v_1 + v_2 = 1450$ which is necessary to maintain production at the existing level. Secondly there is the product/value which goes to maintain the extra workers if production is to expand, i.e., $\beta_{v1} + \beta_{v2} = 145$. Next there is the capitalist consumption of necessaries, i.e., $s_{1n} + s_{2n} = 435$. The total of these three categories is 2030. We have total value for Dept. II of 2,100, therefore $2,100 - 2,030 = 70 = v_3 + \beta_{v3} + s_{3n}$, and which is also equal to S_{2l}.

Similarly in Dept. I we have a value of 6,600. The necessary productive consumption to maintain and expand production in Depts I and II is 6,380; and $6,600 - 6,380 = 220 = c_3 + \beta_{c3}$.

The result of this examination indicates that it would be possible for Depts I and II to decrease their respective production by approximately 3.3 per cent, and providing Dept. III was abolished they would still be able to grow at 10 per cent per cycle. Alternatively, if the resources which went to Dept. III were used for accumulation in Dept. I and Dept. II they would be able to increase their accumulation to 13 or 14 per cent per cycle. Therefore, in terms of the total social capital accumulation and social reproduction, Dept. III *has no function*. So, when looked at from the point of view of total social production, Dept. III does *not* produce surplus-value; on the contrary, it consumes it.

This view would actually seem to accord with Marx's own

expressed view that 'although all surplus-value takes the form of surplus product, surplus product as such does not represent surplus-value.'[9] He also considered that 'the production of surplus-value is the chief end and aim of capitalist production.'[10] And, given this overall consideration, 'surplus-value is convertible into capital solely because the surplus-product, whose value it is, already comprises the material elements of new capital.'[11] It follows from this that 'it is characteristic of all *unproductive labourers* that they are at my command ... only to the same extent as I exploit *productive labourers* ... however, my power to employ *productive labourers* by no means grows in the same proportion as I employ unproductive labourers, but on the contrary diminishes in the same proportion.'[12]

Certain conclusions may be drawn at this point. First, one cannot crudely equate surplus labour, surplus product and surplus-value. Secondly, given the condition of expanded reproduction, a part of the social surplus-value will be embodied in use-values whose material form makes them suitable for use as means of production, i.e., they appear exclusively in Dept. I. Lastly, if use-values which do embody surplus-value are used by unproductive workers they cannot be productive of further surplus-value, even though the material form makes them suitable as capital.

The usual approach to discussion on the role of armaments in modern Marxist literature has been to allocate a third department of production specifically for such production. For purposes of exposition there is nothing wrong with such use of the schemas. But it is often assumed that so doing is to be following in the footsteps of Marx, when he gave his example of luxury goods production, basing himself on the premise that the sub-department IIb produced only goods for capitalist consumption. A number of objections can be raised, however, against both Marx's method and the subsequent use made of the third department for arms production. As we have already seen, there are different results once one modifies Marx's original assumption of simple reproduction to that of extended reproduction. Obviously if the whole of the surplus-value is consumed unproductively it makes little difference *how* it is consumed, either as necessaries or as luxuries. And, from the capitalist's point of view, the workers in the luxury goods producing department appear to be as productive as those engaged in the production of necessary means of consumption or means of production.

But once one assumes that accumulation is taking place – and Marx asserts that this is the chief aim of capitalism – then the proportion of surplus-value which is unproductively consumed has quite a different significance. And in this case the workers engaged in the production of luxury goods should now be seen as a social cost.

This brings us to the question of how we should consider that portion of the surplus-value which is unproductively consumed. Marx assumed that this portion is capitalist *personal* consumption, but this is a highly simplifying assumption that does not hold once we move only marginally away from the very highest level of abstraction at which he was working. To suggest that all unproductive consumption is solely capitalist *personal* consumption is to go beyond the bounds of credibility. Out of the surplus-value which is unproductively consumed there will obviously be a portion which goes on personal consumption. And we may concede that in the modern era of capitalism the *volume* of such personal unproductive consumption has increased greatly, compared with, say, a hundred years ago. As to whether it has also increased proportionally is a matter that could only be determined empirically, although one could surmise that it has so increased. Nevertheless, with luxury goods we have a definite *species* of personal consumption: jewellery, large houses, certain kinds of motor car, luxury yachts, etc., as well as personal services. On the other hand, none of these items can be considered to be collective consumption, as are roads and street lighting, for example. And to complicate matters somewhat, historically many items that first appeared as luxury goods later became items of mass consumption and thus entered into the determination of the value of labour-power; these include motor cars, vacuum cleaners, washing machines. Therefore the dividing line between luxuries and necessaries is a shifting one, in time and place, even today. But the distinction between personal and collective consumption remains fairly clear.

In the modern era the state is the provider of the collective or general conditions of capital valorisation and accumulation, as opposed to particular conditions. When we consider the nature of many items that only the state uses (or hopefully does not use!) ICBMs, nuclear submarines, tanks etc., it is highly unlikely that they will ever become items of mass personal consumption as marketable commodities.

Therefore it is wrong to collapse arms production into the same category as Marx's luxury goods in Dept. IIb: in economic terms they are qualitatively different. And, as Bukharin pointed out, such products – armaments – are non-reproductive, and this combined with the fact that they are paid for out of surplus-value makes them non-productive of further surplus-value. Such collective 'consumption' must be viewed as a cost levied upon current production. But since capitalists' profits are seen as being constituted by accumulation and personal consumption, the sum of realised profit will be perceived as being smaller that the actual social surplus-value.

Taxes paid out of profits will be seen as a cost for the particular firm, and will not be included in net profit. Similarly, workers view their real money wage as being what they actually collect, i.e., their net wages. However, from the capitalists' point of view it is gross wages that are computed as costs. So what should we consider the difference between gross and net wages? Does this difference constitute a part of the variable capital or should it be considered as being part of the social surplus-value? If one divides all newly created value into $v + s$ it follows that if v only represents that portion which workers actually receive, then all monetary deductions from wages belong to surplus-value. But from the point of view of the capitalist profits will be less than S. These brief remarks by no means exhaust the discussion of such problems, but they do suggest that the problem posed by collective consumption, and particularly unproductive collective consumption, is much more complex than Marx's original propositions allowed for.

Therefore, in what now follows, since we shall be examining *social* reproduction, I only count as variable capital that which is actually apportioned to the workers, and surplus-value will constitute the whole of the *social* surplus-value.

Expanded Negative Reproduction: An Algebraic Model

We shall consider Bukharin's propositions in the light of the above considerations, and examine them at the most abstract level possible. Initially we shall do this using an algebraic model. In the first instance we shall consider total social production being constituted by the division into two main departments of production. As before, Dept. I produces all means of consumption and Dept. II produces all means of consumption. Therefore:

$$C + V + S = W$$
$$c_1 + v_1 + s_1 = w_1$$
$$c_2 + v_2 + s_2 = w_2$$
$$\therefore w_1 + w_2 = W$$

$C + V = K$, and $S/K = p_m$ = social rate of profit margin. α = sum of

unproductively consumed surplus-value or unproductive consumption.

$\therefore \alpha/S = \underline{b}$ and $(1 - \underline{b}).p_m = g'$ = rate of accumulation.

Let $(w_1 - C)/C = g$ = maximum rate of investment in constant capital, and

$g'.(C.m)/C.m = G$ = the rate of growth.[13]

Then, $c_1.g' = \beta_{c1}$, $v_1.g' = \beta_{v1}$, $c_2.g' = \beta_{c2}$, $v_2.g' = \beta_{v2}$, giving us:

$$c_1 + v_1 + \beta_{c1} + \beta_{v1} + \alpha_1 = c_1 + \beta_{c1} + c_2 + \beta_{c2}$$
$$c_2 + v_2 + \beta_{c2} + \beta_{v2} + \alpha_2 = v_1 + \beta_{v1} + v_2 + \beta_{v2} + \alpha_1 + \alpha_2$$

And by elimination we obtain:

$$c_2 + \beta_{c2} = v_1 + \beta_{v1}\, \alpha_1.$$

Thus far we are on familiar ground, but now let us separate S into four parts, $\beta_c + \beta_v$, α_p which is personal unproductive consumption and α_c which is collective unproductive consumption. Therefore in this case $\alpha_p + \alpha_c = \alpha$. Furthermore, we shall assume that α_c is used solely for the production of armaments.

In Production Period 1 (PP1), we have :

$$c_1 + v_1 + \beta_{c1} + \beta_{v1} + \alpha_{p1} + \alpha_{c1} = c_1 + \beta_{c1} + c_2 + \beta_{c2} + c_3$$
$$c_2 + v_2 + \beta_{c2} + \beta_{v2} + \alpha_{p2} + \alpha_{c2} = v_1 + \beta_{v1} + v_2 + \beta_{v2} + \alpha_{p1} + \alpha_{p2} + v_3$$

In the above we have assumed that $c_3 + v_3 = \alpha_{c1} + \alpha_{c2}$, and that $c_3 + v_3$ are the constant capital and variable capital used for the production of means of destruction.

But in this case,

$$\frac{w_1 - (c_1 + c_2 + c_3)}{c_1 + c_2} = g'$$

And this implies a lower rate of accumulation and, *cet. par.*, a lower rate of growth.

Whilst g' is positive growth will continue, but at a reduced rate. However, if g' becomes negative in the productive sectors of the economy then a decline will ensue, even though 'Dept. III' may continue to grow for a period. In other words, so long as $\underline{b} < 1$ growth will be positive and if $\underline{b} > 1$ then it becomes negative.

Looking at our algebraic model, if we now assume that in PP2 g' becomes negative, then in PP3 we would find that:

$$(c_1 - (c_1 \cdot g')) + (v_1 - (v_1 \cdot g')) + s_1 = w_1$$
$$(c_2 - (c_2 \cdot g')) + (v_2 - (v_2 \cdot g')) + s_2 = w_2$$
$$w_1 + w_2 = W$$

And using superscripts to denote production periods, we would find that $W^2 > W^3 > ... W^n$. But for a short time it would still be possible for $\alpha_c^2 < \alpha_c^3 < \alpha_c^n$; in other words, it would still be possible for arms production to be growing whilst the productive sectors of the economy were actually declining.

In the above I have assumed that we are dealing only in values, and that we are not considering how prices of production, average rate of profit, etc., are formed by the introduction of 'Dept. III', which as we know is unproductive of surplus-value. This being the case, we only indicate the means of production and means of consumption used up for the production of the means of destruction.

Expanded Negative Reproduction: A Numerical Model

Let us now consider a numerical model illustrating these points:

PP1

Dept. I	8800c	+ 2200v	+ 2200s	= 13,200	= w_1
Dept. II	3200c	+ 800v	+ 800s	= 4,800	= w_2

$$12000C + 3000V + 3000S = 18,000 = W$$
$$C + V = K, \ S/K = p_m = 0.2, \ (w_1 - C)/C = g = 0.1$$

Assuming that 50 per cent of the surplus-value is consumed unproductively, then $\alpha/S = \underline{b} = 0.5 \therefore (1 - \underline{b}) \cdot p_m = g' = 0.1$, and in this case $G = 0.1$ also. This means that, as constructed, the model can grow at 10 per cent per production cycle. This being the case the surplus-value is divided along the following lines:

I	$880\beta_{c1}$	+ $220\beta_{v1}$	+ $1100\alpha_1$	= $2200s_1$
II	$320\beta_{c2}$	+ $80\beta_{v2}$	+ $400\alpha_2$	= $800s_2$

1200	+ 300	+ 1500	= 3000S

Now let us modify our assumptions and introduce armament production, which is *additional* unproductive consumption. In this case α will be divided into $\alpha_p + \alpha_c$. Here α_p will remain as 0.5 of surplus-value, whilst α_c will be 0.2 of surplus-value. Using our model for PP1 above we find that, with the same p_m, now g' = 0.06 and in this case the surplus value will be divided so:

I $528\beta_c + 132\beta_v + 1100\alpha_p + 440\alpha_c$ = $2200s_1$
II $192\beta_c + 48\beta_v + 400\alpha_p + 160\alpha_c$ = $800s_2$

720 + 180 + 1500 + 600   = 3000S

Supply and demand will take the following form:

Supply		Demand in PP2	
	Dept. I		
13,200		$c_1 + \beta_{c1}$ =	9328
		$c_2 + \beta_{c2}$ =	3392
		c_3 =	480
			13,200
	Dept. II		
4,800		$v_1 + \beta_{v1}$ =	2332
		$v_2 + \beta_{v2}$ =	848
		v_3 =	120
		$\Sigma\alpha_p$ =	1500
			4,800

PP2
Dept. I   9328c + 2332v + 2332s = 13,992 = w_1
Dept. II 3392c + 848v + 848s = 5,088 = w_2

12,720C + 3180V + 3180S = 19,080 =   W

'Dept. III' value of armaments = 600

Let us now assume that α_c is increased to 0.4 of S, but α_p is maintained at 0.5, this gives us (1– <u>b</u>).p_m = g' = 0.02. From this we can derive the division of surplus value as follows:

I $186\beta_c + 47\beta_v + 1166\alpha_p + 933\alpha_c$ = $2332s_1$
II $58\beta_c + 17\beta_v + 424\alpha_p + 339\alpha_c$ = $848s_2$

254 + 63 + 1590 + 1272   = 3180S

Supply PP2   Demand PP3
            Dept. I
13,992 $c_1 + \beta_{c1}$ =   9514

                                    $c_2 + \beta_{c2}$ =   3460
                                    c_3 =   1018
                                                            ─────────
                                                             13,992
            Dept. II
5088 $v_1 + \beta_{v1}$ =   2379
                                    $v_2 + \beta_{v2}$ =   865
                                    v_3 =   254
                                    $\Sigma\alpha_p$ =   1590
                                                            ─────────
                                                              5088

Dept. I   9514c   + 2379v + 2379s = 14,272 = w_1
Dept. II 3460c   + 865v + 865s = 5,190 = w_2
                                            ─────────────────
          12,974C + 3244V + 3244S = 19,462 =   W

Dept. III   1272 'value' of armaments

Again we shall assume that α_c is increased by 0.2 of surplus-value, so that now $\alpha_c = 0.6$ and $\alpha_p = 0.5$. This gives us $(1 - \underline{b}).p_m = g' = -0.02$, giving us as the division of surplus-value:

I. $- 190\beta_c$ $+ - 48\beta_v$ $+ 1190\alpha_p$ $+ 1428\alpha_c$ = $2379s_1$
II. $- 69\beta_c$ $+ - 17\beta_v$ $+ 432\alpha_p$ $+ 519\alpha_c$ = $865s_2$
      ───
      $- 259$ $+ - 65$ $+ 1622$ $+ 1946$ = $3244S$

Supply   Demand in PP4
            Dept. I
14,272 c_1 =   9324
                                    c_2 =   3391
                                    c_3 =   157
                                                 ─────────
                                                   14,272
            Dept. II
5190 v_1 =   2331
                                    v_2 =   848
                                    v_3 =   389
                                    $\Sigma\alpha_p$ = 1622
                                                 ─────────
                                                    5190

PP4

| Dept. I | 9324c | + 2331v | + 2331s = 13,986 = | w_1 |
| Dept. II | 3391c | + 848v | + 848s = 5,087 = | w_2 |

$$12{,}715C + 3179V + 3179S = 19{,}073 = \qquad W$$

Dept. III 1946 'value' of armaments

Thus we can see the expanded negative reproduction appearing, as Bukharin posited. If we compare the progress of the schemas above with the results if g' had continued at 0.1 we should find that in PP4 W = 23,958 as opposed to the actual 19,073. Even if we were to include the value attributed to armaments in PP4 we would only arrive at a total of 21,019. But to do this would be double counting, since the value embodied in the arms production was actually produced in PP3.

What we have seen from this investigation is that the concept of proportionality is an essential component of Bukharin's theory of equilibrium, particularly when applied to the dynamics of the economy. This proportionality not only applies in the relationship between Dept. I and Dept. II, but also imposes limits upon unproductive consumption. Moreover it imposes limits upon the proportion of labour-power which can safely be devoted to unproductive labour.

Bukharin was one of the first, if not the first, to recognise that arms production, far from being productive of surplus-value, was in fact value and surplus-value consuming. Because of his firm grasp of the relationship between the *material* elements of reproduction he was not hoodwinked and thus saw all armaments as being essentially unproductive consumption *and* wasteful.

This concept of proportionality was to become one of the key issues in the debates in the late 1920s regarding the formulation of the Soviet First Five Year Plan, as we shall see.

7
The Laws of the Transition Period: Bukharin versus Preobrazhensky

The Dispute on Method

In 1926 E.A. Preobrazhensky, a close collaborator of Leon Trotsky and a one-time collaborator of Bukharin, published his book *The New Economics*. In this work he set out his basic theoretical ideas on the Soviet economy, as then structured in the period of NEP. This book had been preceded by the publication of one of its chapters, in 1924, in *The Communist Academy Herald*. The book was an elaboration of the idea in the original article along with a reply to critics, foremost of whom had been Bukharin. The dispute between the Central Committee majority, represented here by Bukharin, and the opposition, in this instance represented by Preobrazhensky, was conducted at two levels of polemic. The first level was of abstract theory and method; the second was centred upon current policy questions. The more abstract aspects of the discussion arose from, and in some cases came later than, the disputes around current policies, but the former provided the underpinning for the latter. Moreover, the two aspects of the debate were not always synchronised in the same people or at the same time. There were, of course, many participants in this discussion, but Bukharin and Preobrazhensky stand out not only for the number of contributions they made but also because of the quality of these interventions. Because of this I shall concentrate upon the debate between them and in particular on the abstract theoretical aspects, only touching upon the practical policy implications.

The most contentious ideas advanced by Preobrazhensky were those relating to his theory of 'primitive socialist accumulation'. But before he stated his 'law' on this subject in his book he proceeded to examine the methodological basis of his opponents and in the process stated his own premises. It was, therefore, this aspect that Bukharin dealt with when coming to criticise Preobrazhensky's book.

Preobrazhensky argued that:

In theoretical economics, abstraction begins with the very principle on which investigation proceeds, since this science begins with the basis. This is not to belittle the role of the superstructure and the importance of studying that side of men's relations in commodity economy; but investigation does not begin with the superstructure. In Marx's first draft of the plan for *Capital* there was a section on the State, but he proposed to approach this question from afar, after analysing capitalist economy in the strict sense of the word. Why is it not possible to begin with the basis in a *theoretical* analysis of Soviet economy.[1]

And he concluded:

I devote myself to the modest task of first abstracting from the actual economic policy of the State, which is the resultant of the *struggle* between two systems of economy, and the corresponding classes, so as to investigate in its pure form the movement towards the optimum of primitive socialist accumulation, to discover the operation of the conflicting tendencies, as far as possible in their pure state, and then try to understand why the resultant in real life proceeds along one particular line and not another.[2]

This, then, was Preobrazhensky's argument: that one must first abstract from state policies in examining the relations between the state sector of the Soviet economy and the private sector. In this sense he was predicating his examination upon the operation of a *self-regulating* system for both state and private economy. He recognised the law of value as that law which regulates the private commodity economy, and insisted that the law of primitive socialist accumulation is the one that regulates not only the internal workings of the state sector but also its relationship with the private sector. In so far as he argued for the separation of economics from politics for the purpose of analysis, in a *theoretical* examination of the Soviet economy he seemed to be following in the footsteps of Marx.

However, Bukharin keenly contested this claim, pointing out that:

It is not hard to see what comrade Preobrazhensky's mistake here is resting upon. It is resting upon the fact that he completely fails to see the *originality* in the correlation between basis and superstructure under the reign of the proletarian dictatorship. As is generally known, true Marxism lies in the fact that he examines models of production and their superstructure from the standpoint of their specific historical features (*model* features). But in *this* instance, comrade Preobrazhensky has *completely forgotten* about this fundamental methodological demand of Marxism.[3]

We can see that Bukharin had put his finger upon a central problem. Preobrazhensky was claiming to be an orthodox Marxist, and indeed claimed that his opponents were vulgarisers, but he was attempting to apply the method of historical materialism in an *un*-historical manner. Preobrazhensky not only forgot that it is necessary to examine each mode of production in its specific, if general, forms but also that the manner of investigation will be conditioned by these forms. The content and form of social and economic formations along with institutions cannot be properly investigated by projecting preconceived notions. Marx's abstractions were not of such an order, rather his abstractions were concrete historical ones.

Bukharin pressed home his attack, saying:

> Indeed, 'classical capitalism', the analysis of which in its abstract form was given by Marx, was a sort of socio-productive structure where the *economic subjects*, from the viewpoint of their economic functions, did not take part directly in the apparatus of state power. The state *was by no means* a constituent part of the productive relations, which economic theory has been called upon to study. The state *served* the processes of capitalist reproduction, exerted influence on it, as the corresponding political integument – *and only thus*, whilst the economic regularities took shape on the basis of the spontaneity of the entire process as a whole.[4]

Therefore, because capitalism as a system posited a separation of state and direct economic power – in its classical form – it was possible to examine the regularities of economic processes and development by abstracting the role of the state from this process.

This was not to deny, of course, that the state did intervene in the economy. Even the 'nightwatchman' state of nineteenth century England did this, but not as an active and *necessary persona*. It was quite possible for a capitalist to operate his business without consulting any state agency. The state might impinge upon such a business through taxation, import duties etc., but not in the actual *production* process and the creation of surplus-value. In the production of surplus-value the state played no direct role, merely intervening in its division. In this lay the historical peculiarity of the capitalist mode of production.

There are two salient features of this historical peculiarity: first, the historical uniqueness of the capitalist mode of production in the manner of its extraction of the surplus product from the direct producers. The money-form of value mystifies this extraction to a considerable extent; moreover it *seems* not to require the intervention of the state. Yet in reality the state sets the 'external' framework for this surplus extraction to operate within. This dichotomy of surplus extraction and extra-economic coercion in the capitalist mode of production, although giving rise to a variety of state forms, has tended to detract from the role of the state, ideology and all other aspects of the 'superstructure' within the *totality* of this mode of production.

Secondly, and equally important, the various modes of production predating capitalism were all methods of direct appropriation of the surplus product, even when this was transformed into money-forms of payment of rent (commutation of feudal labour service to money rents). Given this situation, the particular configuration of state, ideology, custom, kinship etc., can be seen as having a significance previously underrated in determining the precise nature of a mode of production. This is particularly important since it locates a mode of production as an essential totality, and is thus not dependent upon this or that outstanding feature to arrive at a determination.

Accepting the uniqueness of capitalism in the disjunction between the extraction of economic surplus and extra-economic coercion also suggests that in *post-capitalist* societies the correlation between base and superstructural *form* is highly significant, i.e. that 'pure' economics do not exist in such societies. This correlation must then be a major factor in determining the *totality* of such societies.

It was precisely along such lines that Bukharin advanced his objections to Preobrazhensky's attempt to remove the state and its policies from theoretical analysis, even at the high level of abstraction that had been suggested. In relation to the Soviet state-trusts Bukharin pointed out that:

> *our* trusts and syndicates *do take part* in the combined state apparatus, and their policy forms a most important part of state power. *The apparatus of our state economy forms a component*

part of the production relations of Soviet society, that is, it is itself wholly included in the 'basis'. It is this 'small' peculiarity to which comrade Preobrazhensky simply pays no heed ... But let us pose the question with all real Marxist sharpness. What is *typical* of Soviet economic as distinct from all previous structures? The fact that the working class also plays a leading role *in the production process*: that the old production hierarchy is *turned upside down*; that the old 'relation' of domination and slavery ... is absent. It receives concrete expression in the first instance in the proletarian control of industry, in general – in the proletarian leadership of the entire economic life of the country. The economic organs of the state apparatus are the apex of our specific basis.[5]

Bukharin, then, correctly defined the peculiarity of the Soviet economy in the above passage, in fact – even in the mid-1920s – the 'base' and 'superstructure' were inextricably interwoven, and to abstract the state in the manner suggested by Preobrazhensky was to attempt to examine Soviet society in an unhistorical fashion. Preobrazhensky was in fact trying to analyse Soviet economy without reference to the specific historical features of that formation. As Bukharin said:

To abstract oneself from them, means to abstract from ... the fundamental characteristic of the 'new economics [since] the fundamental, *decisive* relationship of production is the relationship of the working class leadership in production both towards every stratum of the proletariat taken separately and towards the technical intelligentsia ... It is possible and permissible to abstract yourself from whatever you like, but to abstract yourself from that which determines the content of an historical production model is something not permitted to the Marxist.[6]

To make such an abstraction is to remove oneself to so rarefied a plane that the object of one's interrogation becomes an eternal category and is therefore a pointless exercise. The specifics to which Bukharin referred were:

The state of the proletariat in its economic functions (economic policy) is a rational principle, the collective economic subject. Throw that away 'abstract yourself' from it and you *thereby* abstract yourself both from the plan and from the development of the spontaneous into cognised laws, and from the development of political economy into a science ... Comrade Preobrazhensky, however, contrives to perform such a conjuring trick: he categorically insists on the 'plan' and other good things, and at the same time even more categorically insists on abstracting from the functions of state power in the sphere of the economy. He has a plan, but a plan without subject; planning, but without any planning organs, the rational principle but without any definite place to accommodate that principle.[7]

Thus, at the *formal* level of the debate, on method, Bukharin roundly trounced Preobrazhensky and exposed his opponent's confused methodological analysis. In this respect Bukharin's grasp and use of historical materialism was superior to that of Preobrazhensky. However, as I shall indicate in my concluding chapter, there were faults in Bukharin's own work.

Economic Regulators

The next point of contention was the question of the economic regulator or regulators of the Soviet economy. In so far as Preobrazhensky claimed that there was a *law* of primitive socialist accumulation in the Soviet economy which operated along with the law of value, he denied that there could be one, single, regulator for the whole economy. He said:

The second methodological objection has been directed against the proposition developed in this book that economic equilibrium in the Soviet economy is established on the basis of conflict between two antagonistic laws, the law of value and the law of primitive socialist accumulation which means denial that there is a single regulator of the whole system.[8]

Bukharin rejected this method of posing the question, since he rejected the concept of a *law* of primitive socialist accumulation. But this does mean that he thought that the law of value was the regulator of the Soviet economy. Bukharin began his critique by quoting from a letter written by Marx to his friend Kugelmann on 11 July 1868, and since it is a keystone in Bukharin's case it is well worth reproducing the same extract here. This what Marx wrote:

Every child knows that a country which ceased to work, I will not

say for a year, but for a few weeks, would die. Every child knows
too, that the mass of products corresponding to the different
needs require different and quantitatively determined masses of
the total labour of society. That this necessity of distributing
social labour in definite proportions cannot be done away with
by the *particular* form of social production, but can only change
the form it assumes, is self-evident. No natural laws can be done
· away with. What can change, in changing circumstances, is the
form in which these laws operate. And the form in which this
proportional division of labour operates, in a state of society
where the interconnection of social labour is manifested in the
*private exchange of the individual products of labour, is precisely
exchange-value* of these products.[9]

Bukharin commented that 'the law of proportional labour
expenditure or, for short the "law of labour expenditure" is a
necessary condition of social equilibrium *in all and every
socio-historical structure.*'[10] A question might legitimately be raised
here: is not Bukharin (and Marx) guilty of suggesting 'eternal laws'
such as he had criticised in Preobrazhensky? One could answer this
by suggesting that here we are on the borderline between social
and physiological laws. Since the human species is distinguished
from other animals by – amongst other things – the capacity to plan
and execute the use of tools and produce its own means of life, it
follows that such activity involves labour. Therefore all activity that
is characteristic of people involves the expenditure of labour and
the need to apportion that labour to different tasks. Obviously,
both the concrete and social forms of this labour change through
time. And the human species cannot be considered to be eternal
either, as we know it did not always exist in its present form, nor
can we expect it to have an infinite existence. Bukharin was not
therefore proposing an eternal law, but indicating that the law of
labour expenditure was an historical feature of human interaction
with nature.

Bukharin maintained that 'it may take different "forms of
manifestation". In particular, in a commodity (both a capitalist
commodity and *any commodity*) society it wears the fetishistic
costume of the law of value. The law of value is a historically
relative law; it is a specific form "on the face of which is writ large"
that it "belongs to the kind of social structure where the productive
process masters ('hemeistert') men and not men the productive
process" (Marx)'.[11]

He was quick to point out, however, that one should not

therefore equate the law of value with the law of labour expenditure, since to do so would be to lose sight of the specific historical form and character of value relations. Nevertheless, whatever the particular historical form the law of labour expenditure takes, be it patriarchal, slave-owning, feudal, capitalist or communist it 'turns out to be the compulsory and universal regulator of economic life.'[12]

As we have seen, Bukharin maintained that the law of value is the capitalist form of the law of labour expenditure, at least in its prices of production guise. But, far from seeing the question in relation to the Soviet Union as being one of confrontation and *only* confrontation between the law of value and 'primitive socialist accumulation' he viewed the matter as being more complex than that. He assumed that 'the law of value cannot develop into anything other than the law of simple labour expenditure'.[13] And:

The development process of the law of value into the law of labour expenditure finds its expression in the fact that by way of a *plan*, 'prices' in their semi-fictitious function (i.e. no longer as prices determined by the 'barometric fluctuations of the market') consciously turn out differently from how they would spontaneously. [14]

Therefore:

When we speak of our economic growth *on the basis of market relations* (this is the 'meaning' of NEP from a certain angle), we thereby disprove the thesis of the opposition of socialist accumulation (even) to the law of value. Figuratively speaking, we also make the law of value serve our aims. The law of value 'helps' us and – strange as it may sound – thereby prepares its own downfall.[15]

What Bukharin was doing here was pointing to the unity, as well as the contradiction, within the commodity-socialist economy – as Preobrazhensky called it. Moreover, he saw Preobrazhensky as arguing for the violation of the material essence of the law of labour expenditure and not merely for violating the social form of the law of value. Bukharin stated this forcefully, as follows:

the proletarian plan, according to comrade Preobrazhensky consists in systematically disturbing the equilibrium of society, systematically breaking down the socially necessary ratio between the different branches of production, i.e. systematically fighting what is the most elementary conditions of society's existence. Well, I declare, a fine 'regulator'.[16]

This was Bukharin's main concern here: he posed the question of the relationship of planning to the law of value as being symbiotic, a gradual process whereby the law of value withers away, and the greater the conscious control of society exerted over economic processes, the faster this withering will be. He saw Preobrazhensky as viewing the problem only in terms of struggle and confrontation, which would have been disruptive of social equilibrium. Preobrazhensky says in his reply to his critics, in the foreword to the second edition of his book, that Bukharin is too general, and not specific enough, since he 'merely' talks about the law of labour expenditure and not the form it would take in the transition period. But the view of both sides in this debate hinged upon how they viewed the so-called law of primitive socialist accumulation. And it is to that aspect that we shall now turn.

Primitive Socalist Accumulation?

Preobrazhensky defined his law of primitive socialist accumulation as follows:

By socialist accumulation we mean the addition to the functioning means of production of a surplus product which has been created within the constituted socialist economy and which does not find its way into supplementary distribution among the agents of socialist production and the socialist state, but serves for expanded reproduction. *Primitive socialist* accumulation, on the other hand, means accumulation in the hands of the state of material resources mainly or partly from sources lying outside the complex of state economy. [17]

And:

By the law of primitive socialist accumulation we mean the entire sum of conscious and semi-spontaneous tendencies in the state economy which are directed towards the expansion and consolidation of the collective organisation of labour in Soviet economy and which are dictated to the Soviet state on the basis of necessity: (1) the determination of proportions in the distribution of productive forces, formed on the basis of struggle against the law of value inside and outside the country and having as their objective task the achievement of the optimum expanded socialist reproduction in the given conditions and of the maximum defensive capacity of the whole system in conflict with capitalist commodity production; (2) the determination of the proportions of accumulation of material resources for expanded reproduction, especially at the expense of private economy, in so far as the determined amounts of the accumulation are dictated compulsorily to the Soviet state under threat of economic disproportion, growth of private capital, weakening of the bond between the state economy and peasant production, derangement in years to come of the necessary proportions of expanded socialist reproduction and weakening of the whole system in its conflict with capitalist commodity production inside and outside the country.

The following are inevitably subordinated to the law of primitive socialist production: the amount of surplus product alienated from private economy; the level of wages in the state economy; prices policy; the regulation of internal and external trade; the tariff system; credit policy; the structure of the budget; the structure of import plans; and so on. [18]

It is interesting, in the light of the above, to note what Preobrazhensky said about the law of value: 'The law of value is the law of spontaneous equilibrium of commodity-capitalist society.' [19] We can see that he had two views of what constitutes a 'law', or perhaps we should say that he had two views as to how 'laws' manifest themselves. With his law of primitive socialist accumulation Preobrazhensky saw it essentially as being conditions which were imposed upon the Soviet economy; either the state sector will grow or it will succumb to the private sector, but the 'law' itself is only manifested by a series of conditions which were *conscious* acts upon the part of the Soviet state, since it involved plans and planning. All of which contrasts with his definition of the law of value, which was seen as a *spontaneous* phenomenon or mechanism, which acts 'behind the backs of the participants', where there are market controls, rather than being controlled.

We can see, therefore, that Preobrazhensky was propounding two essentially different concepts of social law. The law of primitive socialist accumulation arises from conscious decisions and actions. The decision to create a socialist economy and the consequences that flow from that cannot be placed upon the same level as the results of unconscious decisions and actions (at the macro level) which result in equilibrium for a commodity-capitalist economy, since the later is *post hoc*, whilst the former is the result of the initial decision to build a socialist economy. Clearly, we are dealing with two quite different social phenomena. Capitalist economy was not built as the result of an overall, collective, decision; no one nor one group sat down and said 'we shall now proceed to build capitalism.' Therefore its 'laws' of regulation and equilibrium only emerge as the result of a myriad of private actions, the results of which cannot be foreseen. Thus these 'laws' appear to be spontaneous and even 'natural laws'. On the other hand, Preobrazhensky's law of primitive socialist accumulation is merely the next logical step, or steps, based upon the premise of the conscious decision to build a socialist economy. In the circumstances, therefore, it was misleading and confusing to emphasise primitive socialist accumulation as a *law*.

The question of the validity of the conception of *primitive* socialist accumulation is obviously related to the above, but is a separate issue.

There were, of course, numerous forms and methods in which this 'law' expressed itself, but the most characteristic aspect was that of the transfer of resources to the socialist sector from the private commodity sector, and this is the process that – according to Preobrazhensky – *imposes* itself upon the socialist sector. State policies were seen as merely modifying the particular application of the law. In outlining his 'law' Preobrazhensky took as his starting point Marx's theory of primitive capitalist accumulation, and in particular the section of Vol. I of *Capital* dealing with this topic.

Bukharin rejected Preobrazhensky's whole conception of primitive socialist accumulation, and with good cause as we shall see. Bukharin asked: 'What is the historical-economic essence of so-called "primitive accumulation" according to Marx?' And answered with the following quotation from *Capital*:

The so-called primitive accumulation ... is nothing else than the historical process of divorcing the producer from the means of production. It appears as primitive, because it forms the prehistoric stage of capital and of the mode of production corresponding with it.[20]

Bukharin saw the separation of the producers from the means of production, that is the breakdown of peasant economy and the driving from the land of the peasants, as the main historical form of this primitive accumulation and further quotes Marx to this effect.[21] Bukhárin argued, moreover, that primitive accumulation belongs to the prehistory of capitalism and therefore does not belong to a consideration of its history proper nor of its modern functioning. As can be seen from the quotation from Marx, above, this was also the view of Marx himself. Bukharin pointed out that many features that characterise primitive accumulation carry on into the history of capitalism itself, yet they do not thereby mean that capitalism is forever stuck in that particular stage of development.

Is not the history of capitalism full of the destruction of the peasantry, colonial robberies, the constant expropriation of small-scale production parallel with the most brutal methods... But these are all moments of 'primitive accumulation'. In our opinion these considerations are profoundly erroneous. The main thing has been missed here, the fact that, according to Marx, 'so-called primitive accumulation' is 'not the result, but the starting point' of capitalist development.

It would be silly therefore to place, for example, contemporary imperialism, so long as it is directed against 'third persons' and is a tool for 'devouring' and 'expropriating' them, under the heading of 'primitive accumulation'. Either one of two things: either the period of primitive accumulation is taken just as 'pre-history'; in which case it has a *strict time-limit* ... or we see it as a process of ousting 'third persons' in general – in which case the *concept itself* has to be abolished, since in that case it does not express anything special, specific, etc.[22]

Bukharin was making clear the distinction between the period when means of production were gathered into the hands of certain groups, who then used them as capital and thereby began the process of the accumulation of capital, and *reproduction* of capitalist relations of production. This was compared with the situation where capitalist methods of production were used to further undermine pre-capitalist methods of production. The first phase must almost certainly involve the use of coercion and brutal methods; the second phase need not rely upon such methods, but can use the methods of the market by introducing cheap goods with which to destroy petty-commodity or peasant production. Marx himself used the example of the destruction of Indian cotton manufacturing in the late eighteenth and early nineteenth centuries by British capital using the 'battering rams of cheap prices'. Marx did not thereby characterise this as being primitive accumulation on the part of British capital, but rather as period of development of capital on the basis of the capitalist mode of production, even though this entailed the destruction of pre-capitalist forms.[23]

This was an extremely important distinction that Bukharin was making in his debate with Preobrazhensky, since it entailed the question of how the Soviet state should act in its relations with the peasant population. To telescope primitive accumulation and the destruction, or replacement, of petty-commodity production into one continuous process was for Bukharin not only unjustified theoretically, but also could, and did, lead to unacceptable policies being pursued in practice. We shall return to this point later.

Bukharin pointed out that:

Comrade Preobrazhensky has ... defined socialist accumulation as something where *not a single* 'Copek' is obtained from the non-socialist sphere! And *primitive* socialist accumulation he defines as something where at least only 'one Copek' comes from the non-socialist sphere ... If one took analogies seriously and from such a definition ... of 'so-called primitive capitalist accumulation', then *literally the whole of capitalism*, right up to its death *would end up in* the 'pre-history' of capitalism: for capitalism obtains surplus profits from 'third persons' throughout its entire existence; there is and will be no such stage in the life of capitalism when profits were not to come its way on the basis of exploitation of third persons.[24]

Having rejected the blurring of quite distinct phases in socio-economic history Bukharin then said:

What then could – very conditionally – be called the 'period of primitive socialist accumulation'? *Only* the act of 'expropriating the expropriators' with its concomitant measures could be called thus. If capitalist primitive accumulation was characterised as the separation of the producers from the means of production, then here we have their unification; the use of force, the characteristic of the process, as 'revolution', the 'suddenness and forcible nature' of the process, finally, the characteristic of the process as an historical pre-requisite and the 'starting point' for development not its 'result' – all these are elements of similarity. But, nevertheless, the term 'primitive socialist accumulation' is a '*childish game*'. Why? Well, because this 'childish game' conceals the peculiarities of our development, the facts are far fetched, many things stand *in a completely false perspective.* We have expropriation – it is the economic revolution against the only-just ex-ruling classes; during the period of primitive capitalist accumulation there is neither revolution nor fight against the old master, but the destruction of peasants; in that case there is the creation of a necessary class pole; in our case nothing similar. There, subsequent measures take the same course of further expropriation of 'third persons'; we have a problem of expropriation directed *against the bourgeoisie and landowners,* but the main further problem, which comrade Preobrazhensky discusses, is the problem of the *small-scale producers,* i.e. of *another* class; there, further development takes place from the point of view of destruction, exclusion or, if you like, 'devouring' – here, from the point of view of 'getting along together', 're-educating', 'assimilating' and so on. Given such a state of affairs, the parallels and analogies which comrade Preobrazhensky has constructed could not be anything other than a childish game of terminology.[25]

In the above passage Bukharin exposed the confusion within Preobrazhensky's conception of 'primitive socialist accumulation'. Preobrazhensky had a blanket term to cover two quite different situations: (a) the expropriation of the bourgeoisie and feudalists and the gathering of large-scale industrial production into the hands of the proletariat; and (b) the transformation of small-scale petty-commodity peasant production into socialist agricultural production. Bukharin's point was that the same *methods* cannot be used to carry through these two quite distinct tasks.

On the question of the transfer of surplus produce/value from peasant petty-commodity production to the state, Bukharin said: 'no one will try to deny that industry does and will receive into the fund for its accumulation surplus-value from the small producers.'[26] This then was *not* the substance of the disagreement between the two protagonists. Bukharin realised, just as well as Preobrazhensky, that there would have to be a transfer of resources to industry if industrialisation was to proceed. It was a fundamental difference as to the methods to be used to acquire the surplus, and the time-scale of the transformation of agriculture into large-scale units, that divided them.

Moreover, Bukharin pointed out, whilst Preobrazhensky claimed to be dealing with abstract theory, he was in reality dealing with current economic policies.

Comrade Preobrazhensky complains that I did not 'warn the reader with single word': his article, he says is a 'theoretical analysis of the fundamental regularities of our economy' and not at all an analysis of 'the economic policy of the state'. I confess I did not 'warn'. And I did not 'warn' for the simple reason that I radically differed and differ from comrade Preobrazhensky in my estimation of his article: he does lay claim to the above mentioned analysis, but in my opinion there is *absolutely* no analysis itself. Even now I am looking through the chapter on the 'law' again: the question of colonial robbery (p. 62), 'the alienation ... of the surplus product from all pre-socialist forms' (p. 62), 'the taxation of private capitalist profit' (p. 64), the question of state loans (pp. 64–65), currency emission (p. 65), railway tariffs (p. 70), the monopoly of the banking system and the credit policy (pp. 70–73), home and foreign trade (pp. 73–84), the 'prices policy' (sic pp. 84–89), and so on and so forth, with further argument on the theme that socialism is fighting against capitalism and in order to win it must accumulate at the expense of the private economy – and the more the better – this is the entire content of the work. Comrade Preobrazhensky preaches abstraction from politics but in point of fact, apart from politics, *there is absolutely nothing* in the work. Only his politics are *bad*, about which in due course I did 'warn'. *Theoretical* analysis ought to show what objective laws determine our policy, how the correlation between production and need changes, whether the dynamics of the proportion between branches of production advances, how the law of value is transformed into the law of labour expenditure, what new mechanisms of the law of labour expenditure will emerge in the transition period, where the limits of our policy are, etc. But the reader will *not* find this in comrade Preobrazhensky's work. A theoretical analysis of the economy, the question of objective regularities turning into norms – over our heads – is precisely absent from him. Whilst preaching abstraction from politics to the glory of theory, comrade Preobrazhensky has in reality 'abstracted himself' from theory to the glory of politics.[27]

This was the gravamen of Bukharin's complaint, that Preobrazhensky, whilst claiming to discuss abstract theory, was in fact discussing matters that could only relate to concrete current policies. None of the questions highlighted above by Bukharin can be abstracted from state policies in a Soviet type economy, even that of the mid-1920s, therefore once one had made a few generalisations about the need to transfer surplus from the private sector to the state sector of the economy, all else came down to precise policies which are *not* self-regulating but consciously decided upon. Bukharin was suggesting that one cannot construct a theory of transition *a priori* but must pragmatically steer towards a given objective, only then will the *theory* of transition emerge upon the basis of practical and concrete experience. This, incidentally, was something of a retreat by Bukharin from his stance of 1920, but by the time the present text was written he was being far more cautious; the exuberance of 'war communism' had run its course.

Bukharin mocked Preobrazhensky for his attempt to define a 'pure law' for the working of the state economy in such a transition period, by abstracting from its relations with the private sector, i.e. by examining the state sector in isolation. He made the point that:

If we were to dismiss 'third persons', then we would arrive at 'pure socialism', but at the same time all the categories and problems of the transition period would disappear. Try to dismiss the entire petty-bourgeois environment, then the problem of value disappears *altogether*, such forms as that of wages etc., will disappear. Nothing 'transitional' will remain even in this sphere of the 'state economy'.[28]

Moreover:

to disengage oneself from 'third persons' in an analysis of the transition period is inadmissible, this is to dismiss *all the specific* theoretical problems. The theoretical misunderstanding of this entails an incorrect line in the sphere of economic policy. Presenting the laws of development in the manner of two sticks in the hands of the two classes, bitterly beating each other, comrade Preobrazhensky loses sight of the *unity* of the system: although this unity is contradictory, it *is* a unity, with the mutual conditionality of the parts.[29]

So, by attempting to abstract state industry from its relations with the private sector, and particularly the peasant sector, Preobrazhensky abstracted from the particular and peculiar nature of the *transitional economy*. But where he did recognise the private sector he merely saw conflict and not the contradictory unity. Here we see Bukharin's concept of equilibrium coming into play. Bukharin recognised that NEP was not merely a compromise of 'principles' but also an acceptance of the balance of class forces in the Soviet economy and society generally. Having arrived at some form of equilibrium, Bukharin was concerned that this should not be equilibrium with 'negative indications', but one that would have mobile growth without cataclysmic consequences. Preobrazhensky attempted to define some optimum rate of primitive socialist accumulation for the state sector in an abstract manner. He suggested that there should be drawn up such an ideal optimum, and only then should the private sector be taken into account to see how the 'ideal' and the possible would diverge, but always attempting to push towards the ideal. But as we have seen, Bukharin argued that such a method was quite wrong, since it presupposed that the two sectors were wholly antagonistic, whereas they formed a contradictory unity, a living totality. Bukharin pointed out that: 'The law of *correlation* presupposes both members of this correlation. Taking one out (peasant economy), you thereby destroy the whole.'[30]

Two Methods – Two Perspectives

Let us attempt to summarise what the differences between Bukharin and Preobrazhensky were:

1. Methodological, with particular reference to the level of abstraction used. Preobrazhensky said that it was necessary provisionally to abstract the Soviet economy from particular state policies. That is, he wanted to disregard the particularities and establish general laws for 'socialist state economy', without taking into account the interaction between state and private economy. Bukharin rejected this since he argued that to do so would be to disregard the historical character of the dictatorship of the proletariat. And to do so would produce an unhistorical abstraction that had no concrete usefulness.

2. Regularity of the laws of transition. Preobrazhensky said that in the transition period there are two laws: (a) the law of socialist (sometimes primitive) accumulation; and (b) the law of value. These are expressed through planning and the market respectively. Bukharin again disagreed, arguing that there is basically only one law, that of proportional labour expenditure. The effects of the law of value will disappear when planning has been fully established. In the transition period planning will modify the law of value, but on the basis of the law of labour expenditure.

These two differing approaches related to how the peasants were assessed as a class: (a) as a petty-bourgeois formation and a breeding ground for capitalism; or (b) pre-capitalist petty-commodity producers who can either grow into capitalist producers *or* move towards socialist forms of production via co-operation.

Preobrazhensky took view (a), hence his constant theme of struggle between the state sector of the economy and peasants. Bukharin took view (b); here his theory of equilibrium becomes important in understanding his stance. Since he viewed Soviet society as a totality with a mobile equilibrium, he considered it necessary to *steer* the peasants towards co-operation and eventually to socialist forms via exchanges between the two sectors on the market. But this was to be a market that was not wholly free or spontaneous.

Preobrazhensky also wanted to use the market mechanism to extract surplus from the peasants so that state industry could accumulate and grow. Therefore a part of the dispute between the two theorists revolved around how the market mechanisms were to be used, and what pricing policies should be pursued for industrial and agricultural production.

In practical terms what was at stake was the need to close the price scissors, as Trotsky termed it, that is, the disparity between the high prices for industrially produced consumer goods and means of production, compared to the prevailing world market prices, and the prices being paid for agricultural produce. This price 'scissors' reflected the unequal exchange between 'town' and 'country'. The high prices of industrial consumer goods deterred the peasants from buying, and the low prices offered by the state for agricultural produce deterred them from selling or even sowing. The prices problem was of course a reflection of the low volume of industrial production and the low level of productivity in Soviet industry. Soviet agriculture was relatively backward, even though the volume of production had, overall, overtaken its pre-1914 figures by the mid-1920s.

In the case of industrially produced consumer goods it was a question of increasing supply by a proportionally greater extent than that of agricultural production, and for this it was necessary to invest. But to accumulate meant that it was necessary to obtain agricultural products at prices that would transfer the necessary surplus to the state sector.

Bukharin's basic approach was what could be termed increasing the surplus by accelerating the turnover of capital; which included a policy of lowering prices for industrially produced consumer goods. This would provide the incentive for the peasants to produce the necessary agricultural produce, particularly the grain with which to feed the towns and for export. Such a policy would be seen to benefit both town and country and hence lessen the tensions and contradictions within the system as a whole.

Preobrazhensky's approach implied an increase in the surplus labour within industry, i.e., increased productivity, but a price policy that would not fully reflect this increase, i.e., a monopolistic surplus-profit policy. This meant further discontent on the part of the workers *and* peasants, which would have meant a greater use of coercion by the state.[31]

In terms of equilibrium theory, Bukharin was concerned that the existing, and fragile, equilibrium should not be destroyed by untoward leaps which would threaten the Soviet regime. After the traumas of war, revolution and civil war he thought that it was necessary to have a prolonged period of social and political peace which would provide the correct climate for the economic growth that all desired. Within the limits of the one party dictatorship prevailing in the Soviet Union Bukharin could be considered to be a consensus politician, seeking growth through co-operation not conflict. This model would obviously allow for contradiction and divergence but would be one of mobile equilibrium with positive indications.

Preobrazhensky, on the other hand, seemed implicitly to work with a model predominantly of conflict. To use the language of the dialectic, Preobrazhensky saw thesis and antithesis, but one would prevail by annihilating the other. Bukharin's equilibrium theory specifically allowed for a synthesis arising from this contradictory unity. His proposed mechanisms we shall explore in the next chapter.

The Notes of An Economist: Optimum versus Maximum Investment

The First Five Year Plan

The Fifteenth Congress of the Bolshevik Party in December 1927 was notable for a number of reasons. Firstly, it had been postponed to allow the United Opposition of Trotsky, Zinoviev and Kamenev to be expelled from the Party before the Congress actually convened. Secondly, the Congress adopted a resolution initiating the First Five Year Plan (FFYP) of industrialisation and collectivisation of agriculture, both of which had long been advocated by the opposition. Thirdly, as Lewin noted,[1] despite the seemingly united Congress there were undercurrents of differences in interpretation as to the precise meaning of the resolutions adopted. These differences of interpretation were to become the basis for new divisions within the ruling Party majority.

The formal decision on industrialisation had already been made at the Fourteenth Party Congress in 1925; therefore the Fifteenth Congress could be claimed to be merely a continuation of previous policies. However, all serious historians have noted that the 1925 decisions had been merely a formality, more honoured in the breach than in their application. The 1927 Congress decisions reflected the changed situation, since by that date industry had reached its 1913 levels of output and there loomed ahead the need to expand industrial capacity plus the renewal of much worn-out industrial plant. The problem of replacement had been made particularly acute because of the lack of repair and replacement in earlier years, especially during the war and civil war. None the less, by 1927 there was a general recognition of the need to accelerate the rate of investment, particularly in industry and, above all, in the machine-producing sector.

However, the ambiguity – already noted – hidden in the resolutions of the Fifteenth Congress began to take more definite shape in the attempt to formulate the FFYP. It became manifest that within the ruling Party majority there was a fraction crystallising which was in favour of very high rates of industrial investment; this was associated with Stalin. Bukharin, on the other hand, based himself upon the formal wording of the resolutions of the Fifteenth Congress, which had actually formulated a more cautious and balanced growth rhythm.

The emerging strains in the Centre-Right Bloc in the party were already beginning to show in July 1928 when Bukharin wrote his now celebrated 'Notes of An Economist'. These 'Notes', whilst ostensibly aimed at the Trotskyist Opposition (which had officially been routed in 1927) were in reality directed against the 'super-industrialisers' amongst the ruling majority. This form of political 'discourse' has become painfully familiar in the years since then, but it was sufficiently new at the time to mislead many as to the true target of the strictures. One of those misled was Trotsky himself, who completely misread the real import of what Bukharin had written, as we shall see in the next chapter.

The 'Notes' appeared in *Pravda* on 1, 3 and 7 July 1928. The timing of another action by Bukharin should be noted: on 11 July he held a secret meeting with Kamenev to propose an alliance between the Left and Right groups against Stalin. In other words, the cautious phrases of the articles in *Pravda* hid a sharp political turn on Bukharin's part, but not a sharp turn in his views regarding economic policies. Implicit in this turn was an acknowledgement that the differences between the Left and the Right groups on *practical* policies were much narrower than the fractional struggle had previously admitted; a common phenomenon in left-wing politics.

The political turn was signalled publicly in an address given by Bukharin at a memorial meeting on the fifth anniversary of the death of Lenin on 21 January 1929. This speech was published in *Pravda* on 24 January under the title of 'Lenin's Political Testament', which must have rung some warning bells for many within the Party since Lenin's actual political testament had not been published at that time. That Bukharin was preparing for a struggle with Stalin at this point cannot be doubted and he was attempting to drum up international support among other parties of the Comintern. Rosa Levine-Meyer recounted to me how Bukharin met and discussed his plans with members of the German Communist Party in the late summer and autumn of 1928. Bukharin and his associates used Rosa and Ernst Meyer's hotel room in Moscow for meetings to discuss the mounting struggle inside the Bolshevik Party, meetings at which they ridiculed the ever higher figures being propounded for the drafts of the First Five Year Plan.[2]

In his address of 21 January Bukharin painted a broad picture of how he interpreted Lenin's vision of NEP and the transition to socialism. He reiterated the major points made in his 'Notes of An Economist' – of which more later – but also sketched out the *political* implications of his earlier essay. Again we are faced with having to read between the lines, but the allusions must have been clear to most of Bukharin's contemporaries. The main themes that Bukharin pursued were: (1) the need to cut down on the excessive unproductive consumption of the state bureaucracy; and (2) the need to draw the widest possible strata of the people into the planning process and into controlling the state. In other words, Bukharin was cautiously calling for curbs on Stalin's power, even if he was not referred to by name. How else do we explain Bukharin's reference to Lenin's urgent call for a reorganisation of the Commissariat of Workers and Peasants Inspection? Everyone knew that this body had been a key element in Stalin's rise to power and that any criticism of it was, by inference, a critique of Stalin.

Once more Bukharin dwelt upon what he considered to be the unique character of the Russian revolution: that it was a combination of workers revolution and peasant war, which implied the need for a *long-term* alliance between the two classes. Such an alliance, for Bukharin, implied that co-operation was the keystone of success, not confrontation, as implied by the drive towards forced collectivisation. On the question of co-operation with the peasantry Bukharin stated:

This does not mean that Lenin is here denying the class war, for the 'peaceful', 'cultural' work of 'organisation' is also *a special form* of class struggle. It means that the proletariat is leading the *entire* working nation behind it, that it is responsible for the development of *the whole of society*, that it is becoming a great collective organiser of the *entire national economy*, that the direction of development is *not* towards a widening of the gulf between the fundamental class (the working class and peasantry) and that things are not moving towards a 'third revolution', etc.[3]

Who was intent upon launching such a third revolution? Stalin. Of course during the previous factional struggles it had been Trotsky who had been accused of advocating policies which would have led to a split between the working class and peasantry, but now it was Stalin who was in Bukharin's sights. And as if to point up this change Bukharin declared, 'Our Red Army, which is to an enormous extent composed of peasants, is the greatest cultural machine for the re-education of the peasantry, which leaves it with a new mentality.'⁴ Taken in isolation such a remark would not be significant, but in a speech which had mentioned the two institutions with which Stalin and Trotsky had been most closely associated, this reference to the Red Army must be seen as nudge and wink towards Trotsky. By his lauding the progressive role of the Red Army Bukharin's audience would have grasped what he had in mind. Clearly Bukharin was signalling the need for a new political alignment, especially as he had repeated Lenin's warning against a split in the Party.

Rather than seeing the exploitation of the peasantry as the means to industrialisation Bukharin insisted that 'a qualitative increase in the productivity of national labour, and a determined fight against non-productive expenditure ... are the main sources of accumulation.'⁵ And 'for co-operation to lead to socialism, *civilised co-operation* is needed, for which it is necessary to trade *not in an Asiatic*, but in a European way.'⁶ And who represented the 'Asiatic' in this context? Again, Stalin. Thus Bukharin had come to recognise that the bureaucratic stratum which had coalesced around Stalin now posed an incomparably greater threat to his vision of the transition to socialism than the opposition of Trotsky ever did. However, it was in the 'Notes' that Bukharin gave a precise résumé of the differences on economic questions between himself and Stalin.

The Necessity for Balanced Growth

The first point of importance in what Bukharin said in the 'Notes' is that, despite the accelerated rate of industrial investment and growth presaged by the FFYP, he argued that there would be no fundamental change in the basic strategy of the New Economic Policy.

> Naturally, the transition *to the reconstruction period* does not entail a fundamental change in economic policy as was the case in 1921. It is however, of immense importance, so to speak, from another angle. For there is a tremendous difference between, let us say, *repairing a bridge and building* one. The latter process demands a knowledge of higher mathematics, the strength of materials and thousands of bits of wisdom. The same applies to the *whole* economy. The reconstruction period raises a number of complicated *technical* problems ... a number of extremely difficult tasks in the overall management of the economy.⁷

Bukharin was warning that there should not be such a fundamental revision of policies as would mean a return to the arbitrary and commandist methods of 'war communism'. This meant that, for Bukharin, industrialisation should proceed within the established framework. Accordingly, this meant that market relations, especially those between 'town and country' must be continued, even though in a modified form. Moreover, the reference to the technical abilities needed to build a bridge was directed as a warning *against* grandiose schemes which lacked a firm technical basis; and *for* the need for patient, long-term methods of work, rather than substituting the 'shock-troop' methods of 'war communism' for more prosaic means.

It was no accident, therefore, that Bukharin went on to point out the real advances already made by the Soviet economy, particularly in industry, during the preceding period. He mentioned oil, chemicals, engineering and electrical engineering, all of which had made solid progress. To emphasise the point, he said in relation to overall investment:

The systematic growth of *totally new* industrial construction is a further point of great interest. The share of means accorded to this construction work, calculated in percentages of the total allocation to industry, has increased steadily. In 1925–6 this share was 12 per cent, in 1926–7 21 per cent, in 1927–8 23 per cent. The specific weight of heavy industry is increasing rapidly ... as also the specific weight of the production of the means of production in our industrial sector.[8]

Then he made the point that 'all this shows how rapidly the industrialisation of the country is proceeding and how clear the simultaneous process of the *socialisation* of the whole economy is.'[9] Obviously, since the whole economy was engaged in this process there could not be, according to Bukharin, a *wholly* unbalanced growth, even though there would be certain imbalances as a result of growth taking place in different sectors at somewhat different rates.

He did admit, however, that the growth itself had induced 'peculiar crises', but not of the same character as those observed in the capitalist economies. He highlighted the differences by a series of juxtapositions: 'over-production' versus 'goods famine'; 'over-production of grain' versus 'under-production of grain', i.e., disproportion between production and consumption, but in the capitalist countries this took the form of over-production, in the Soviet Union of under-production, 'disproportion between various branches of production' etc. In other words, Bukharin was positing disequilibrium with positive indications for the Soviet economy, and negative indications for the capitalist economies.

> In a word, the past year, especially, has confronted us with the problem of *'our crises'*, which are the result of the initial stages of a transition economy in a country with a backward, petty-bourgeois population and surrounded by hostile forces.[10]

Thus while capitalism's crisis was seen as one of decline, he viewed the Soviet crisis as the result of growth. Given Bukharin's reference to disproportionality it was not surprising that he should refer to Marx's schemata of reproduction. In his book *Imperialism and the Accumulation of Capital* Bukharin had already dealt with such questions at some length. However, in his 'Notes' he came out solidly for disproportionality as being the fundamental cause of crisis in the capitalist economies.

> Marx, as you know, gave us a theory of *capitalist crisis*. These crises he showed to be caused by a general lack of planning (anarchy) of the capitalist methods of production, by the impossibility of attaining correct *proportions* between elements of the process of reproduction under capitalism, especially between production and consumption ... he showed the cause to be the incapability of capitalism to maintain an equilibrium among the various elements of production.[11]

We have already met this formulation when we examined Bukharin's theory of capitalist crisis. The reason why he introduced these ideas at this point in his discourse was to bring out the similarities *and* differences between Soviet problems and those pertaining to capitalism, since he went on to say:

> If our 'crises' apparently possess the character of capitalist crises 'turned inside out', and if effective demand of our masses has overtaken our production, then is not the 'goods famine' perhaps a general law of our development? Are we not perhaps condemned to periodical or non-periodical 'crises' on an *inverted* basis, on a *different* correlation between production and consumption? Are these critical differences not an iron law of our development?[12]

In posing the idea of such an 'iron law' Bukharin unwittingly predicted the actual course of events in the Soviet Union that has persisted up to the present time, that is, the continual shortfall of consumer goods production as compared to the growing population and the growth in monetary incomes. In posing such a possibility Bukharin was of course seeking to avoid it. He went on to reject the premise for such an 'iron law', since he argued that production would catch up with demand as industry developed, and any disproportions arising would derive from faulty planning. And the reason for this would be:

> The relative *lack of planning*, or the *relatively* planned character of the economy in the transition period originates in the existence of small undertakings, of market connections, that is, of anarchist elements of considerable strength. Therefore, the plan itself has a character of its own; it is not by any means a more or less 'complete' plan of a developed socialist state of society. The plan contains many elements of the prognosis of the *anarchical* factor (e.g. the estimate made of crops, of the amount of grain available as a commodity, the amount of commodities represented by peasant production generally, and consequently, the estimate of prices), and this prognosis becomes the starting point for this or that directive. Precisely for this reason it is impossible for us to have an ideal plan.[13]

This passage forcibly expressed Bukharin's concern that, given the conditions then prevailing, the 'plan' should not be regarded as being actually able to control all the elements that had to be taken into account. He also suggested that planning as then envisaged could not really be more than a series of approximations. To recognise that reality meant that such plans had to be rigorously controlled to take account of actual conditions. He continued:

> Precisely for this reason [the anarchic factor] there may be errors up to a certain point. But the fact that an error can be explained, even an unavoidable error, does not mean that it thereby ceases to be an error. That is the first point.[14]

In other words, the best laid plans will contain errors, and not to recognise them as such would only further compound them. 'The second [point] is that the grossest violation of fundamental proportions ... and the resultant erroneous calculations, are *by no means unavoidable*.'[15]

Again we see Bukharin arguing that a violation of fundamental equilibrium is avoidable, so long as proportionality is used as a guide around which the plan would oscillate. But any conscious attempt to disregard this proportionality would inflict unnecessary losses and suffering. Moreover, any disregard for the fundamental proportionalities of the economy leads to 'upsetting the political balance of the country'.[16]

It would seem, therefore, that Bukharin was attempting to set the drive for industrialisation within the wider socio-political framework of the worker–peasant alliance upon which NEP was founded, rather than within merely narrow 'economic' guidelines.

Increased Turnover Leads to Increased Accumulation

During the course of his argument Bukharin sketched out what he considered to be the three variants of the development of agriculture under capitalism, these were:

> Within the confines of capitalism three fundamental models of these relations can be distinguished: the *first* is that of the most backward semi-feudal agricultural economy with its pauper peasants, rack-rents, ruthless exploitation of the peasantry and the weak capacity of the home market. (Example: pre-revolutionary Russia.) The *second* type: considerably fewer relics of serfdom, the landowner has to a considerable extent already become a capitalist, the peasants are better off and the peasant market has a greater capacity, etc. The *third* model is the 'American' one, the almost complete absence of feudal relations, 'free' land, in the initial stages of development, no absolute ground rent, well-to-do farmers and a large home market for industry.
>
> And what do we see? It is not difficult to see that the ... power and extent of the growth of the productive forces, have reached their highest point in precisely the *United States*.[17]

This passage is interesting for several reasons. First, there is clear approval of the 'American' way as a means of development in agriculture *and* industry, that is, the provision of mutual markets for the respective products. As to whether this was an historically accurate account of American development is beside the point, since he was using it as a debating point. Secondly, the consumption of the producers forms a part of Bukharin's growth equation. Total consumption is not the relevant part of this equation; rather the consumption of *producers* is the key variable. Moreover, since in this context the producer-consumer is mainly the agricultural one, we can see that Bukharin followed his previous thoughts on the necessity for growth and equilibrium to be seen as an interlocking set of social, political and economic factors. Lastly, there is his first 'model' of agriculture, with its paupers, ruthless exploitation etc., of which he says pre-revolutionary Russia was an example. But this was not an exercise in historical analogy for Bukharin; it was a veiled reference to a possible future. In February 1929 he actually accused the majority of the Central Committee of creating a 'military-feudal exploitation of the peasantry'.[18] In other words the pauperisation and misery of the peasantry, which undoubted occurred, was attributed by Bukharin to the policies, particularly forced collectivisation, of the Soviet state.

The whole of Bukharin's arguments in this period, 1928–9, can be summed up as being directed towards the development of an optimum rate of investment and growth as opposed to maximum investment rates. He argued that attempts to impose a maximum investment rate would in fact lead to a *lower* overall rate of growth than would an optimum one.

The difference between maximum and optimum investment, and hence of growth rates, hinges upon the relationship between growth and consumption, and more particularly the relationship between the productivity of labour and the consumption of the producers. And, it could be argued, the lower the initial level of consumption by producers the greater will be the link between productivity and consumption. This presupposes that given a low level of development of the productive forces, and a correspondingly low level of consumption by producers, a significant rate of growth not only depends upon the rate of investment but also upon an increase in the consumption of the direct producers.

We can formalise some of the above propositions along the following lines: Let F = fixed capital, cc = circulating constant capital (raw materials, fuels, etc.), v = variable capital, s' = rate of surplus-value, T = expected life-span of F, and F/T = d = depreciation, d + cc = c (constant capital in normal Marxist usage), and finally w = product.

Given the above assumptions we find that:

$$\frac{c + (v.(1+s'))}{v.(1+s')} = \underline{u} \text{ productivity of labour}$$

$$\frac{F}{v.(1+s')} = \emptyset \text{ fixed capital-labour ratio}$$

Then $\underline{u}/\emptyset = \underline{m}$ = output coefficient of fixed capital.

And we find that $\underline{m}.F = w$

It will be seen that $\underline{m}$ is dependent upon a number of variables, any change in one or more will alter the value of w. And with a given $\underline{m}$, any change in F will also alter w.

It follows that (where subscripts denote production periods):

$$F_1.\underline{m}_1 = c_1 + v_1 + s_1 = w_1$$
And: $F_1 + \Delta F = F_2,\ cc_1 + \Delta cc = cc_2$

Giving us: $F_2.\underline{m} = c_2 + v_2 + s_2 = w_2$

Now, if $v_2 = v_1$ and s' remains constant, then $\underline{m}_2 < \underline{m}_1$.

This means that although w_2 will be greater than w_1, it would have been even greater had $\underline{m}_2 = \underline{m}_1$. However, to achieve $\underline{m}_2 = \underline{m}_1$ when $v_2 = v_1$ it would mean that: (1) s' rises: (2) less surplus-value is consumed unproductively; or (3) less surplus-value is devoted to accumulation in F and/or cc.

What the above suggests is that there is an optimum value for F and cc which lies between F_1 and F_2 and cc_1 and cc_2 which will allow v to rise and increase $\underline{m}$, thus producing a greater value for w. (See addendum to this chapter for a demonstration of this.)

Bukharin pointed to such problems and themes when he said:

Clearly the question of reserves is closely bound up with both the question of *productive* consumption (including capital construction) and the question of *personal* consumption (the personal consumption of the masses). It is a generally known fact that here our bow is at a very high tension. To increase this tension further and aggravate the goods famine even more is impossible.[19]

And:

Those who believe that the growth of planned economy brings with it the possibility (on the narrow basis of the dying out of the law of value) of acting just as one pleases, do not understand the ABC of economic science.[20]

To emphasis the point further he said:

> When a plan drawn up during a period of supply crisis fails to analyse thoroughly the question of the balance of supply and demand this of course is no 'external' defect, no 'formal' omission, but a profoundly internal fault. The acuteness of the goods famine must certainly be alleviated and not in some remote future but during the next few years.[21]

Bukharin specifically warned against tying up too many resources in long-term capital projects, and argued for a balanced approach which would actually yield a greater product:

> With respect to the correlation between the development of *heavy and light industry* we must again proceed from the optimum combination of both factors. Whilst regarding as correct the shift of the centre of gravity to the production of the means of production, we must at the same time remember the danger involved in tying up too much state capital in major construction work, which cannot be realised on the market for many years. On the other hand it must be remembered that a more rapid turnover of light industry (production of essential articles) permits its capital also to be used to build up heavy industry, whilst developing light industry at the same time.[22]

Here we see Bukharin repeating his argument for a speeding up of the circulation of commodities, which he said would provide a greater surplus out of which investment of all types could be increased. He perceived very well the dangers involved in an attempt to concentrate too many resources upon major capital projects.

> The over-straining in capital expenditure: (1) will not be accompanied by *actual* construction to a corresponding extent; (2) will lead in time to the curtailment of work already under way; (3) will react unfavourably on other branches of production; (4) will exacerbate the goods famine in every direction; and (5) will finally retard the speed of development.[23]

The whole of the 'Notes' was thus devoted to arguing that optimum investment would produce a greater product than would maximum investment; and that, maximum investment would actually retard the rate of overall growth. But what was the actual result of the FFYP?

Plan and Reality

First there is the question of the fulfilment of the plan; we find that in percentage terms very few of the eventual increased target figures were met, i.e., coal 72.3, crude oil 107.1, electricity 49.1, pig iron 43.3, steel 24.4, rolled steel 19.3, cement 36.3, cotton goods –3.0, woollen goods 3.3, shoes 26.1, paper 32.2, matches 1.6, soap 36.9.[24] Of course the low percentage achievement does in part reflect the very high targets that were set as the plan was revised upwards during the course of the period, and it was carried out under the slogan of 'the five year plan in four years'. In fact there were several drafts of the plan, each more ambitious in terms of targets set than the previous one. As Medvedev noted, the 'plan' became almost like a 'think of a number game':

> Stalin and Molotov suddenly at a meeting of the Council of Commissars ... proposed that the control figures of the plan be increased twofold ... in June 1930, Stalin suddenly announced sharp increases in the goals – for pig iron, from 10 million to 17 million tons by the last year of the plan; for tractors, from 55,000 to 170,000; for other agricultural machinery and trucks, an increase of more than 100 per cent.[25]

And for the workers there was an actual decline in real wages during the FFYP, and only in 1940 did they recover their 1928 level.[26]

Jasny maintained that 'Instead of actually rising by 55 per cent in the five years from 1927/28 to 1932/33, as provided in the approved version of the Five Year Plan, total farm output declined by 14 per cent between 1928 and 1933.'[27]

And Conquest said that 'Grain exports during the early thirties were higher than at any time since the revolution, running around 5 million tons a year in 1930–31 and $1\frac{3}{4}$ million tons during the famine period of 1932–33. In 1929–30 it had been less than 200,000 tons.'[28] Alongside this must be set Conquest's estimate of 5 to 6 million deaths during the famine.[29] And he maintained:

> Collectivisation destroyed about 25 per cent of the production capacity of Soviet agriculture. The Five Year Plan postulated a grain output ... of over 100 million tons. It did not reach 70

million, and the original target was not achieved before the outbreak of war.[30]

Jasny produced the following table for industrial production:

	Targets	Fulfilment
Total industry	136	113
Producer Goods	204	190
Consumer Goods	103	63[31]

No doubt there would be disagreement as to precise figures, both in absolute and percentage terms for Soviet economic growth during this period; and the above small selection is only meant to be indicative. The fulfilment or non-fulfilment of inflated 'plans' does not, of course, detract from the very real increases in industrial production that took place during the FFYP. But there can be little or no dispute about the appalling state of agriculture as a result of forced collectivisation and the fact that millions of farm animals were slaughtered by the peasants rather than allow them to be collectivised, nor can the starvation and deaths be disputed. However, since we are supposed to be dealing with *planned* growth, there surely must be *some* connection between targets and fulfilment. Let us admit that since the FFYP was the very first exercise of its kind in history, it would not be surprising if there were discrepancies, failures of some kind. It is not our purpose here, however, to re-examine the details of the success or otherwise of the FFYP as a whole. What is being done is to argue that the failures were of the order to suggest that Bukharin had been correct in his prediction *before* the event, not after it.

What emerges from an examination of the FFYP is that it set a pattern for the Soviet economy that persists up to the present day. The reason for the actual results is not hard to determine; as Mandel pointed out:

The mistake committed by the Stalinist planners during the First Five Year Plan ... is a confusion between *maximum* and *optimum* rate of accumulation. Or rather: these planners started from a wrong assumption that the maximum rate of accumulation is also the optimum rate.[32] [And] the mistake has its roots in the absurd assumption that the productivity of labour is independent of the consumption of the producer.[33]

The result, according to Mandel, was that:

There were in 1928 3.1 million workers and employees (technicians and engineers with university degrees not included) in Soviet industry. In order to achieve the First Five-Year Plan, figures worked out at that moment estimated that the manpower necessary for attaining the production goals at 4.1 million workers and employees (i.e. an increase of 1 million or 33%). In fact, in 1932–33, *without* all the goals of the FFYP having been achieved, 6.7 million workers and employees were working in Soviet factories, an increase of more than 110% over that of 1928, and of 65% over the planned number of workers! What should have been produced by 4 million workers needed 6.7 million to be manufactured, i.e. *per capita* productivity *was more than 50% below the planned level.* The maximum rate of accumulation was ... far from maximising the social product.[34]

And, as Lewin pointed out, there was a deterioration in the quality of goods produced plus considerable waste of materials.[35] And along with this there was a considerable increase in unproductive costs.[36]

This pattern still subsists: one of priorities for heavy industrial investment; discrepancies between targets and fulfilment; a continual lagging behind of the production of consumer goods as compared with the production of the means of production; low productivity rates, low investment priorities for agriculture. One might almost be driven to conclude that there are in fact two 'plans', the public one which always seems to go awry and a secret one that the economy actually works to.

In retrospect Bukharin's 'Notes of An Economist' stand out as a clearsighted warning against the headlong rush to industrialisation – without due regard to proportionality – that was embarked upon with the FFYP. Moreover, the strictures against maximum investment rates were vindicated, as we have seen above. Nor were his warnings a fluke; his ability to provide such foresight was based upon his theory of equilibrium. Bukharin understood better than most that Stalin's mania – as it was shown to be – for breakneck industrialisation was to bring many years of misery and suffering to all the Soviet peoples. And most of this catastrophe was avoidable; there was no inevitability, only wilful arrogance and a disregard of humanity. The most bizarre manifestation of this disregard was to be the purges that swept across Soviet society in the middle 1930s.

Addendum to Chapter 8

Let us assume a reproduction schema along the following lines:

F   cc   v
10 + 19 + 4
$T = 10$, therefore $F/T = d = 1$

Therefore $d + cc = c = 20$, and if we assume that $s' = 1$, then:

$$\frac{c + (v.(1+s'))}{v.(1+s')} = \underline{u} = 3.5$$

$$\frac{F}{v.(1+s')} = \emptyset = 1.25$$

Therefore, $\underline{u}/\emptyset = \underline{m} = 2.8$
And $F.\underline{m} = w_1 = 28$

Now let us assume that all surplus, i.e. $w - (c+v) = s = 4$, is invested in F +cc in the same proportion as above, we then have:

F   cc   v
11.4 + 21.6 + 4

Assuming that T remains constant, then $d = 1.4$. Therefore $d + c = c = 22.74$, and if s' remains constant then:

$\underline{u} = 3.8425$, $\emptyset = 1.425$, and $\underline{m} = 2.6944912$
Thus $F.\underline{m} = w_2 = 30.74$.

Clearly, as one would expect, w_2 is greater than w_1. But what would have happened if we had divided the surplus between F, cc and v, instead of only between F and cc?

Assuming the same proportion between the three elements as in the first production period, we should find that in production period two we have:

F   cc   v
11.22 + 21.3 + 4.48

And, assuming that T remains constant, we now find that $d = 1.22$, therefore c = 22.422. This being the case, then:

$\underline{u}$ = 3.5024553, ø = 1.2522321, thus $\underline{m}$ = 2.79696797, and:

F.$\underline{m}$ = w' = 31.382

It would seem therefore that, as Bukharin suggested, the maximum rate of investment does not provide the maximum social product. Obviously, here we have not allowed for any unproductive consumption, but this is merely a simplifying assumption, since it would not have basically altered the simple proposition regarding the relationship between the productivity of labour and the consumption of the producers.

All the above assumes that s' remains constant; however, it is quite feasible that with an increase in v, which also allows for an increase in consumption per capita, there would also be an increase in s'. In other words, if the same number of workers obtain 4.48 instead of 4, then there would be the possibility of an increase in productivity arising from an increase in the real wage, because it would have been possible to increase the intensity of labour. If there *were* the possibility of an increase in s' then that too would allow for a further increase in w. Therefore, a balanced or proportional growth theorem does not necessarily lead to a return to scale. On the contrary, it was Bukharin's thesis that with a steady growth in consumption by the producers, overall growth would be exponential.

Conclusions

Marxism and Equilibrium Theory: Bukharin Vindicated

I began this study by posing some questions regarding Bukharin's theory of equilibrium and I gave some answers at the end of Chapter 2. There I argued that on the basic question of the compatibility of Bukharin's theory and Marx's ideas there were no significant divergences, and therefore Bukharin must be considered to be a Marxist in every sense of the word. The critics of Bukharin who suggested that there was some incompatibility between *Bukharin's* equilibrium theory and Marxism have, in my opinion, been shown to have been in error themselves. Moreover, the mistaken views of Bukharin's critics often flowed from an inadequate appreciation of his main work on this topic, *Historical Materialism*, and the structure of his arguments therein. Furthermore I feel that there has been a tendency on the part of some later critics to accept uncritically the 'general consensus' about Bukharin without an independent evaluation. That Bukharin often formulated his ideas in the language of absolutes, as Richard Day suggests,[1] cannot be denied. And as I suggested earlier, Bukharin often gave ammunition to his critics by some of his formulations, but the actual content of his writings is far less 'absolute' than Day would have us believe.

In examining Bukharin's use and application of his theory of equilibrium in his work in the 1920s I feel that I have demonstrated that this work was not only consistent with Marxism, but can also be seen as an extension and a rounding out of many parts of the basic ideas propounded by Marx and Engels.

At the same time, a compatibility of equilibrium theory and Marxism does not in itself tell us if the equilibrium theory is useful as a method of analysis. As I have indicated, Bukharin's theory of equilibrium is much more than a set of economic postulates, since in his *Historical Materialism* he seeks to establish general historical laws of development for society. Despite the fact that the book was written over 60 years ago it still remains the most comprehensive attempt by a Marxist to set out these general laws of development in a systematic manner.

Contrary to what the majority of Bukharin's critics assert, I have demonstrated that the *strength* of his theory of social development lies precisely in his establishing the close links between society and nature; and his insistence on the necessity for an equilibrium to subsist in the exchanges between society and nature. In this he emphasises the material basis of development in a concrete manner. Bukharin's approach finds its echo in the present day in the concerns of the 'Green Movement' and its emphasis on the need for a balanced ecology. In the same way Bukharin locates technology as being *social* technology, which must have a proper proportionality if it is to function in a satisfactory manner in the exchanges between society and nature. Far from being a 'technological determinist' he posits the reciprocal nature of the relationship between society and the types of technology that are developed and used. Therefore each particular combination of mode of production and technology will, for Bukharin, produce a particular configuration of society, in terms of politics, economics, social relations, art, literature, etc. And this configuration is *not* predetermined.

What emerges from an examination of Bukharin's basic theory, and the manner in which he attempted to apply it, is the high degree of flexibility and adaptability of which he was capable. This adaptability has given rise to a particular criticism of Bukharin: that he was erratic in his politics. Erlich says: 'He was undoubtedly the best educated economist not only of his group, but the whole party as well, with a truly astounding facility for the rationalization, in terms of theory, of any political viewpoints he happened to embrace, and for pushing them towards the furthest logical consequences.'[2] Erlich has completely misjudged Bukharin regarding his 'astounding facility', since he merely observed, inaccurately, the changes in Bukharin's policy prescriptions without reference to his basic theory and the circumstances which led him to make such changes in his prescriptions. This flexibility had its basis in an inner core of intellectual strength arising from a coherent theoretical viewpoint. On the other hand, Trotsky's seemingly iron will and intransigence, on closer inspection, seem to have been a cover for inner doubts and uncertainties at certain points in his life.[3] Nor was the penchant for pushing arguments to their furthest logical consequence a defect, if it be one, solely of Bukharin. As Lewin noted, regarding the debates in Russia in the mid-1920s, 'themes of ideological character, seemingly matters of principle hotly debated with dogmatic intransigence, turned out to be of no great consequence when translated into practical policy proposals.'[4]

The reason for this paradox I will deal with later. However, this much is clear: Bukharin was not some sort of 'rent a theory' politician, as Erlich suggested, but an independent thinker who was prepared to pursue critically his own lines of thought, sometimes regardless of the consequences.

There were, after 1917, only two apparent major changes in Bukharin's stance. The first was in 1921 when he endorsed the introduction of NEP, which as I have already pointed out was a near unanimous decision forced upon the Bolsheviks by the parlous conditions arising from the civil war and 'war communism'. But Bukharin's reaction to this was not one of mere pragmatic adjustment; rather he began to articulate the premises for the new equilibrium which he saw arising in the post-civil-war society of Soviet Russia. The changes and shifts that were evidenced during the 1920s were only such as Bukharin thought could be absorbed within the new equilibrium. Moreover his most 'voluntarist' writing, *The Economics of the Transition Period* and his most 'evolutionist' work, *Historical Materialism,* were written consecutively and both were animated by, and were an exposition of, his theory of equilibrium.

The second apparent shift was in the year 1927, when the period of 'recovery' had come to a close and the phase of 'reconstruction' had opened. In effect this meant that all the existing plant and machinery had been brought back into operation and the pre-war level of industrial production had been obtained. This meant that far more emphasis had to be placed upon the construction of new industrial capacity, and an increased volume of investment was the order of the day. But the change was not as sudden as might be supposed, since the basis for it had been laid in the formal decisions of the Fourteenth Congress of the Party in 1925, which Bukharin was fully in accord with. And the evidence is that new industrial construction was already a steadily rising proportion of total investment by 1927.[5]

Therefore the second shift in Bukharin's stance was, again, more apparent than real. As Lewin noted, many of the disagreements of the mid-1920s between Bukharin and the opposition, when stripped of their polemical excesses, were a matter of nuance and timing. *Both* sides in the debate were for industrialisation and planning; the disagreements were about timing and methods. Moreover, when the First Five Year Plan was finally put into operation, along with frenzied construction and *forced* collectivisation, the disagreements which this engendered produced quite a different configuration of opinions and alignments within the Bolshevik Party than the previous factional fights might have indicated. The apparent shift by Bukharin in 1927 can be traced to two quite different sets of ideas which some commentators and his Party opponents confused. The first is that Bukharin argued for a 'snail's pace' tempo in the march towards socialism. The second relates to the tempo of industrialisation. Even during those times when Bukharin was placing more emphasis upon the 'snail's pace' he was also pointing to, applauding and encouraging the *rapid* growth of industrial production.

If socialism is conceived as being a highly industrialised classless society, then in Soviet conditions this presupposed the complete transformation of the peasantry via co-operation and eventually collectivisation, but the material basis for this was to be the long-term development of industry. The transformation of agriculture would be, in Bukharin's opinion, a matter of *decades*. But this process would entail a relatively rapid tempo of industrialisation. In other words, within the perspective of a stable equilibrium with positive indications, the proportions within that equilibrium would be subject to constant change, but in a controlled manner. Therefore, whatever shift took place in 1927 was one, for Bukharin, of a change of 'gear' rather than a fundamental change in direction away from NEP.

Trotsky Also Advocated Balanced Growth

In this respect, what is important here is that Bukharin did have a *theory* of equilibrium. It can easily be shown that Bukharin was not alone during the 1920s in using the concept of equilibrium; it is possible to find it mentioned in a number of contributions to debates, particularly by Trotsky and Preobrazhensky. However, Bukharin was the only one who set out in a systematic manner his *theory* of equilibrium, and this was central to his approach to the problems he addressed. The others merely used the concept of equilibrium without articulating the precise meaning of the term. Preobrazhensky's use of the concept of equilibrium was a narrower one than that used by Bukharin, being mainly focused on economics.[6] Trotsky also used the concept, but in a somewhat wider framework.[7] And, as time went on, Trotsky's use of the concept of equilibrium came more and more to match Bukharin's theoretical framework. In my opinion the convergence between sections of the Left Opposition and the Right Opposition in the

Bolshevik Party after 1928, as noted by Deutscher and Lewin, is in some degree attributable to the fact that Trotsky absorbed much of Bukharin's theory of equilibrium without an acknowledgement, or perhaps without even being conscious of the process of absorption.[8]

This was not a one-way process, however: Bukharin too adopted (too late) a number of arguments from the armoury of the Left after 1928 regarding questions of inner-Party democracy and allied demands about mass participation in government. This latter point was quite clear in his remarks on *Lenin's Political Testament,* as was mentioned in the previous chapter. On the other hand, it is noteworthy that Preobrazhensky capitulated to Stalin when the forced pace of industrialisation was adopted in the process of the fight against Bukharin and his allies.

Trotsky remained profoundly sceptical of Stalin's 'left turn' and remained in opposition in exile. Thus it is ironical that Trotsky dismissed Bukharin's 'Notes of An Economist' with these words: 'The article is a product not only of theoretical weakness, but also complete political impotence.'[9] Politically impotent Bukharin may have been, but it was largely self-imposed since he and his allies chose not to fight Stalin openly, preferring to hide the split in the Party majority. Trotsky's political impotence, on the other hand, had been thrust upon him by opponents, who had effectively removed him from the scene in 1927 by way of exile first to Alma Ata and then in 1929 to Turkey. The irony of Trotsky's remarks resides in the fact that Bukharin's article argued for an optimum investment rate, proportionality between heavy and light industry, between production and consumption, etc., all of which Trotsky was to espouse in the following years when faced with Stalin's policies. In so far as there was this convergence between Left and Right after 1928 Stalin was not so wrong when he later talked of a Left/Right bloc, even though, of course, this Bloc did not take the form of even a political alliance let alone the criminal conspiracy he alleged. Stalin was certainly aware of the connection, not only in practical terms of the possibility of the Left and Right working together, but also on the theoretical level. In his speech of 27 December 1929 he specifically attacked equilibrium theory as having 'nothing in common with Marxism'.[10]

The Party Factions of the 1920s

This brings us to the paradox of the bitter factional fights in the mid-1920s over what in retrospect can be seen as matters of nuance and timing. What was being argued about were two different time scales. Trotsky in particular was concerned about the relatively long-term perspective of development, whilst the (shifting) majority of the Central Committee, of which Bukharin was the pre-eminent theorist, were engrossed in short-term problems. This is of course a simplification, since Bukharin did have a long-term view of development, but in many respects this was propounded in an 'algebraic' manner without always filling in the details. None the less, such a supposition seems borne out by the new configuration of forces which the Stalinist forced pace of industrialisation and brutal collectivisation of agriculture brought about.

Bukharin's inadequate appreciation of the role of fixed capital in his theory of capitalist crisis, as we noted earlier, led him to underestimate the need for investment in industry, such as Trotsky had advocated. On the other hand, Trotsky, by his advocacy of the 'dictatorship of industry', conjured up in Bukharin's mind all the worst excesses of the period of 'war communism', which *would* have meant a clash with the whole peasantry, not merely the Kulaks, resulting in a breakdown of the fragile equilibrium of NEP Russia. That Trotsky did not actually mean such a clash to occur can be seen by a study of his writings, especially his critical notes on Preobrazhensky's use of the idea of 'primitive socialist accumulation', but he never did voice these doubts in public.[11] Thus, despite what Trotsky wrote or said in the mid-1920s, the signals he was transmitting to his opponents – especially Bukharin – by his personality, language and the company he kept, were to some degree false ones. And much the same can be said of Bukharin, since he lined up with Stalin and waged a campaign of vilification against the Left Opposition which still reeks to anyone who reads it. Yet the excesses of Bukharin, which were mainly verbal, were the product of fear; fear of unleashing further periods of turmoil, confusion and suffering which he *felt* the Left's programme implied.

The turn by Stalin towards a forced pace of industrialisation led to a decisive split in the ranks of the Trotskyist Opposition. Preobrazhensky, who was considered to be the leading economist amongst them, capitulated to Stalin. A large number, if not the majority, of the Left Opposition deserted Trotsky between 1928 and 1930 to line up with the Stalinists against the Right Opposition. This indeed would seem to have been the logic of the particular positions adopted up to 1927. Trotsky, on the other hand, found himself criticising the Stalinists more and more from the 'right' and in the process there was revealed – in retrospect – a fundamental agreement on a whole range of issues with Bukharin, something Trotsky was never to acknowledge in his life time, nor incidently by his followers since his death.[12]

The main weakness of all factions in the Bolshevik Party during the 1920s was that they equated state industry with socialist industry, and the rule of the Bolshevik Party with the rule of the working class. In other words, all factions had a very 'statist' conception of socialism, and a narrow view of proletarian democracy. Both Left and Right factions had the conscious aim of not merely industrialising Soviet Russia but of building a socialist society. But this was attempted upon the incredibly meagre material basis of the remnants of the Tsarist Empire. The working class, in whose name the Party allegedly ruled, had practically disintegrated by 1921 and had to be reconstituted in the process of recovery and reconstruction. Therefore the dictatorship of the proletariat, which all factions claimed to subsist in Russia, was nothing but a fiction to cover the authoritarian rule of a Party that had increasingly lost its roots in the working class and had become embedded in the administrative apparatus of the state and industry.

Yet this fiction had an enormous ideological hold over all the participants in the debate around the issue of industrialisation. Had they acknowledged the reality of Soviet society they would have had to face up to the fact that they had made the 'wrong' revolution. Therefore, at one level, the whole debate about 'socialism in one country' was a diversion, important as it was theoretically. Indeed, Trotsky, whilst firmly fixed in popular mythology as being the foremost antagonist of Stalin's theory of 'socialism in one country', actually considered joining forces with Stalin and Bukharin against Zinoviev and Kamenev in 1925; and it was Zinoviev who launched the first attack upon Stalin's theory.[13] We also find that Trotsky was capable of considering a 'bloc' with Bukharin in 1928, despite his contempt for the 'Notes of An Economist' and the fact that the opposition had considered Bukharin and his immediate allies to be the 'main danger'. Moreover, Bukharin was considered by Trotsky to be the main ideologue of 'socialism in one country'.[14]

In essence, then, the debate about 'socialism in one country' was about how to square the circle of backwardness. Trotsky sought to escape from the dilemma of a 'dictatorship of the proletariat', in which the proletariat played no part, by means of 'permanent revolution'; something that he had himself by his own admission consigned to the archives of history in the early 1920s.[15] Bukharin, basing himself upon his own understanding of the real and existing equilibrium in Soviet Russia, saw socialism as a distant prospect to be reached by evolutionary, gradualist means over a long time-span, i.e., he postponed the problem. Trotsky did not disagree with the substance of this time-scale for the actual realisation of socialism. What neither of these protagonists envisaged was 'socialism' being built at breakneck speed, in a few short years, via the horrors of forced collectivisation coupled with a brutally maximised rate of investment in *heavy* industry. In other words, neither the Left nor the Right had any vision of or penchant for the subsistence rations and millions of dead that the First Five Year Plan produced.

Stalin, on the other hand, along with many former Left Oppositionists, 'solved' the question as to whether socialism could be built in one country by the installation of a bloody totalitarian regime presiding over an atomised and terrorised populace and then declaring *that* to be socialism. In the process Stalin completely destroyed the equilibrium of NEP Russia socially, politically and economically, to produce an entirely new form of society with its own lopsided proportions and equilibrium. The reality of such a society was, and is, far removed from socialism as the founding fathers – Marx and Engels – would have understood it. Moreover, it has produced a society that is unable to be autarkically self-sufficient, either in terms of technology or in food supplies.

How then can we judge Bukharin's theory of equilibrium? In terms of a tool of social analysis it has stood the test of time, and provides an extremely useful and valid method. Above all it provides an account of the *stability* of societies, as well as suggesting mechanisms that can lead to change. It is this insight into the conditions of stability that distinguishes Bukharin and his theory from the voluntarist element in much of what passes for Marxism. Moreover Bukharin's theory is able to explain both change and stability as being aspects of a continuous process. His conception of equilibrium with positive indications explains how a society may indeed be subject to change, with growth and decay combined, but at the same time maintain a basic stability in its social, political and economic processes. And, for those intent upon changes on a major scale – as Bukharin was – it is a salutary reminder of the forces making for stability.

Bukharin's theory also provides us with insights into the possibility that, given a major disruption of social equilibrium, there may actually be regression or that the resulting new equilibrium may be quite different to that envisaged by those actively seeking change. This certainly seems to have been the case as far as the Russian revolution was concerned; the overthrow of Tsarist absolutism and the expropriation of private property by the new state did not lead to the socialist millennium, but rather to the creation of another repressive and equally exploitative regime. If Bukharin did not acknowledge this reality it is not the fault of his theory; he, just like the other Bolsheviks – especially Trotsky – could not admit that they were people who had 'arrived before their time'. Engels had warned about the results of such a situation in his writings on *The Peasant War in Germany*[16], but for the Bolsheviks it was a fate too horrible to contemplate.

Certainly Bukharin used his theory to guide him in the 1920s, but never to question the whole enterprise that had been embarked upon in October 1917. He attempted to chart a course of development using a faulty set of indicators: and even the best 'navigational' theory will come to grief in such circumstances. The theory remains a testament to his own intellectual audacity and perception. His personal and political capitulation to Stalin should not be used as criteria when judging equilibrium theory.

The historical judgement upon Bukharin as a *political* leader must be one that points to his deficiencies. In this respect Trotsky stands head and shoulders above Bukharin. Trotsky, for all *his* failings, has left a far greater imprint upon the sands of history; his ideas still animate – in however bowdlerised a form – many groups of political activists. There are no such comparable 'Bukharinist' groups. Yet Bukharin's theories *do* live on, and often in the self-same Trotskyist groups that reject his inheritance! As I have pointed out, Trotsky and his followers absorbed a great deal of Bukharin's theory of equilibrium, so that in a curious manner Bukharin's ideas do still remain active, if unacknowledged. And, who knows, it may well be that with his rehabilitation in the Soviet Union we may yet see Bukharin restored to some of his former eminence in that country too.

Therefore, in judging Bukharin's theory of equilibrium we have to separate out the politician from the theorist. Of course there can be no absolute division, but it can be done sufficiently to arrive at a more balanced view than hitherto. As I said in the introduction to this work, it is not my intention to create a new Bukharin myth in place of the old one. What I have done is to present to the reader a more comprehensive account, and a more truthful one. For too long Bukharin has been presented to the world as a totally flawed Marxist, or on the other hand as some kind of saintly martyr. I hope that I have restored the balance. The flaws remain – no cosmetic can hide them – but they are minor aspects of the man as a theorist.

Appendix: Bukharin and the Acceleration of Capital

As we have seen, one of the themes of Bukharin's writings in the mid-1920s was what he referred to as the increased turnover of commodities. This idea had been dealt with by Marx in Vol. II of *Capital*, under the heading of 'acceleration of capital'. I shall deal with Bukharin's ideas and also Preobrazhensky's, utilising some of the theorems developed earlier.

Let $F + Cc + V + S$ = life-span of F, fixed capital
$d + cc + v + s = w_m$ = value in money of one 'year's' product
$d + cc + v = k$ = cost
w_v = volume of production in one 'year'
T = time in 'years' of the turnover of fixed capital
T' = turnover time of product, t' = production time and t^* = circulation time. Therefore, $t' + t^* = T' = 1$, and $T' < T$.

$$\frac{S}{F + Cc + V} = P' \qquad = \text{rate of profit on all capital employed during } T$$

$$\frac{s}{k} = p' \qquad = \text{rate of profit on capital employed during } T'$$

$$\frac{s}{k} = r \qquad = \text{rate of profit on capital advanced during } T'$$

It may appear that p' and r are identical, but as will be shown below the capital advanced and capital employed are not necessarily the same.

Therefore: $\dfrac{w_m - k}{k} = p'$ and $p'/T' = r$

Further, $w_m/w_v = p_c = $ 'price' per unit of product

Let us now assume that w_m is reduced x per cent, then $w_m - x\% = w_{m2}$, and $w_{m2}/w_v = p_{c2}$ and $p_{c2} < p_c$

And, since this implies a price reduction for all w_v, we shall assume that t^* is now reduced. If t' remains constant this means that T'_2 is now less than T'. Now, if k remains constant, then

$$\dfrac{w_{m2} - k}{k} = p'_2 \text{ and } p'_2 < p'$$

But, $p'_2/T'_2 = r_2$ and $r_2 > r$.

Because of the reduction in turnover time there are now two values for k; let k = total cost *employed* in one 'year' and k' = total costs advanced in one 'year'.

To find the value of k' we say $T'/T_2 = \lambda$. Therefore $k/\lambda = k'$, and $k' < k$. From this we find $\dfrac{w_{m2} - k'}{k'} = r_2$, and $r_2 > r$

Since there is now a difference between capital (costs) employed and advanced, i.e., $k - k'$, there are now two options:

(1) the capital released may be used to increase total production of the particular commodity, or
(2) it may be used on another project.

Let us assume that the first option is taken. If total capital, k, is now advanced, total capital employed will be $k.\lambda = k_2$. At the same time $p'_2 < p'$, but $k_2.p'_2 > k.p'$. Hence, the rate of profit on capital advanced is greater and the mass of profit has been increased also, whilst the rate of profit on capital employed has fallen.

There now arise some further questions, such as, how does the above affect the volume of production? Our original assumption left w_v constant, but if the capital employed is now increased this implies an increase in w_v, since out of the costs of production cc represents cost of raw materials, fuels etc., d = depreciation and v the value of labour power, it follows that there is a relationship between cc and w_v.

Assuming no change in the productivity of labour, this means that for any value of cc there will be produced a given volume of w_v. Let us say that $cc/w_v = \mu$, then obviously $cc/\mu = w_v$. It follows that out of k_2 the actual increase of w_v will depend upon the value of cc.

Now, if the amount of d remains constant, then the proportion of k_2 going to cc and v can be greater than with k. This would assume that whilst $T'_2 < T'$, T remains constant. However, if the proportion of $d/k_2 = d/k$ then less will be available for cc and v. It is clear therefore that if $d/k_2 < d/k$ then $cc/\mu = w_{v3}$. But if $d/k2 = d/k$ and $cc/\mu = w_{v2}$ then $w_{v2} < w_{v3}$.

However, $w_v < w_{v2} < w_{v3}$, so whichever of the two options is chosen the volume of production would have increased. The two options both have their own advantage. With $w_{m2} < w_m$ we found that $w_{m2}/w_v = p_{c2} < p_c$ but with $d/k_2 < d/k$ we find that $w_{m2}/w_{v3} = p_{c3} < p_{c2} < p_c$ i.e, there will be a greater proportional decrease in 'price' per unit of volume.

Under our original assumptions we would find that $d.T = F$, but with $d/k_2 = d/k$ we find that $d.T = F.\lambda > F$. Thus, where $d/k_2 = d/k$ there will an increased volume of production, and at lower 'prices' than there were in our original assumptions. And, because of accelerated depreciation of F over time T an increment of capital will be added to the original F to the value of $(F.\lambda)-F = \Delta F$. So, depreciation allowances will become a source of extra accumulation over and above increased surplus-value brought about by an acceleration of capital.

Where we have $d/k_2 < d/k$, volume w_{v3} will be greater and the 'price' per unit of volume will be lower, hence there can be a greater consumption of use-values.

Both results assume an unchanged productivity of labour. But, as we saw in Chapter 8, it is possible that with lower prices and increased consumption the productivity of producers may increase. (This, of course, assumes that the supply curve of labour does not become regressive.) *If* productivity of labour does increase then it is possible that v could remain constant in money terms but there would be an increase in real wages. Thus a greater proportion of k could then be devoted to cc, and with a given μ it would further increase the volume of production to w_{vn}. It has the possibility of exponential growth envisaged by Bukharin, since under such conditions the value of F would be declining, whilst its volume would be increasing.

Let us examine a simple numerical model:

$4400F + 39,600Cc + 11,000V + 11,000S$
  $440d + 3960cc + 1100v + 1100s = 6600 \ w_m$
  $d + cc + v = k = 5500$
  $T = 10, \ t' = 1, \ t^* = 11,$ therefore $t' + t^* = 12$ months
  Therefore $\dfrac{t' + t^* = T' = 1}{12}$

And: $\dfrac{S}{F + Cc + V} = P' = 0.2$

$s/k = p' = 0.2, \ p'/T' = r \ 0.2$

The assumption made here is, turnover time T' is one year. This means that over this one year period k will equal 5500 and this is the capital employed and advanced in that time.

Let us say $k + s = w_m = 6600$, and $w_v = 6600$, then $w_m/w_v = p_c = 1$
Let us now assume that there is a price reduction of 3 per cent, i.e $w_m - 3\% = w_{m2} = 6402$, but w_v remains constant at 6600.

This gives us: $w_{m2}/w_v = p_{c2} = 0.97$.

Now, given this reduction in price let us also assume that the circulation time, t^*, is reduced to 8, therefore $(t' + t^*)/12 = T'2 = 0.75$. Since at this point k remains constant, $\dfrac{w_{m2} - k = p'_2 = 0.164}{k}$

Therefore $p'_2 < p'$, but $p'_2/T'_2 = r_2 = 0.218666$, therefore $r_2 > r$

So, the rate of profit on capital employed has fallen, but the capital advanced now has a rate of profit higher than before. Now, $T'/T'_2 = \lambda = 1.333333$, therefore $k/\lambda = k' = 4125 =$ capital advanced and 5500 capital employed.

If we assume that all the original capital is advanced in one 'year', we find that $k.\lambda = k2 = 7333.3331$. This means that even at the reduced rate of profit p' the total amount of profit (the mass) will be 1202.666.

Now, $cc/w_v = \mu = 0.6$. If $d/k_2 = d/k$, then if $k_2 = 7333.3331$ this will give $d = 586.66664$ and $cc = 5280$; this will produce $cc/\mu = w_{v2} = 8800$.

But, if $d/k_2 < d/k$, say $d = 440$, then if the original ratio of cc to v remains constant, i.e. 3.6:1, we shall find that cc = 5395. Therefore, in this case $cc/\mu = w_{v3} = 8992$ (approximately).

We know that $w_m/w_v = p_c = 1$, but $w_{m2}/w_{v2} = p_{c2} = 0.97$ and $w_{m2}/w_{v3} = p_{c3} = 0.9492882$. Thus we find that:
$p_{c3} < p_{c2} < p_c$ and $w_{v3} > w_{v2} > w_v$.

Looking at Preobrazhensky's ideas, let us assume that it is possible to reduce cc + v by, say, 5 per cent, but d remains constant and the volume of production also remains constant. This means that $k_2 < k$, but with w_m and w_v constant then:
$$\frac{w_m - k_2}{k_2} = p'_2 \text{ and } p'_2 > p'$$
And, since the above assumes that T' also remains constant:
$p'_2/T' = r_2$ and $r_2 > r$.
Given these assumptions we shall find that $\mu_2 < \mu$. It follows that $w_m - k_2 = s_2$ and $v_2 < v$, then $s_2/v_2 > s/v$. On this assumption $w_m/w_v = p_c = 1$.

Now, if the saving in value is used to expand production, i.e., invested in extra cc and v, we find that $k_3 = k$, but $cc_3/\mu_2 = w_{v3}$ and $k_3.(1+p'_2) = w_{m3}$, but in this case $w_{m3}/w_{v3} = p_{c3} < 1$. The reason for the decline in price is that both μ and d/k_3 have fallen. This presents two options, either w_{v3} is sold at p_{c3} which would indicate a slight fall in the price per unit of volume, or w_{v3} is sold at $p_c = 1$ in which case not only has there been an increase in the rate of surplus-value, but there will be a transfer of value – in the form of monopoly profit – from the purchasers.

Looking at our numerical model above, if the initial cost of cc and v were reduced by 5 per cent and μ were to fall from 0.6 to 0.57 then we would have:
$440d + 3762cc + 1045v = 5247 = k_2$. Therefore, $wm - k_2 = s_2 = 1353$. And $s_2/k_2 = p'_2 = 0.2578616$. This means that $cc/\mu_2 = w_{v2}$ and $k.(1+p'_2) = w_{m2} = w_m$. Since p' = 0.2, $p'_2 > p'$ and given that T' remains constant $p'_2/T' = r_2$ and $r_2 > r$.

Now on the assumption that the savings in costs of cc and v are used to increase production by setting more labour-power and circulating means of production in motion we have:
$440d + (3762cc + 198\Delta cc) + (1045v + 55\Delta v) = 5500 = k_3$ and $\mu_2 = 0.57$,

therefore $(cc+\Delta cc)/\mu_2 = w_{v3} = 6947$ and $k_3.(1+p'_2) = w_{m3} = 6918$. Therefore, $w_{m3}/w_{v3} = p_{c3} = 0.99558255$.

But if prices are maintained at unity, then $w_{m4} > w_{m3}$.

Comparing the two approaches, Bukharin's leads to a greater volume of output per 'year' and over time T, and at lower 'prices'. Preobrazhensky's approach would increase the volume of output but by a lesser amount than Bukharin's method. However, it would also lead to a greater mass of surplus-value over the same time-span. But this increase rests upon the assumption that it would be possible to increase the volume of cc whilst decreasing its value and increasing the volume of labour supplied while at the same time decreasing the value of labour-power. Given that cc was to a large extent the product of peasant agriculture, although decreasing as industrialisation took off, Preobrazhensky's approach implied a double squeeze on the peasants, since it rested upon procurement prices, or delivery prices, being pushed down whilst at the same time obtaining a monopoly price for the products of industry. So while there was a projected increase in products it was at the expense of producers and the real benefits – brought about by higher investment rates – lay almost wholly in the future. Bukharin's proposition offered both short-term and long-term benefits for producers and consumers in town *and* country alike.

Notes and References

Chapter 1

1. *Historical Materialism: A System of Sociology*, hereafter HM.
2. There are 30 editions listed in *Nikolai I. Bukharin – A Bibliography*.
3. Lukacs' review of *Historical Materialism* first appeared in *Archiv fur die Geschichte des Sozialismus under der Arbeiter bewegung*, Vol. XI, 1925. An English translation, by Ben Brewster, was published in *New Left Review*, No. 39, September–October 1966. All references to Lukacs' critique of Bukharin are taken from the English text, and hereafter will be referred to as Lukacs.
4. 'Letter to the Congress' dated 25 December 1922, first published in the Soviet Union in *Communist*, No. 9, 1956. Official English translation by Foreign Language Publishing House, Moscow, nd. However, unofficial versions of this letter have been available since Max Eastman published all of it in the *New York Times*, 18 October 1926. The official text may also be found in Lenin's *Collected Works*, 4th edition, Moscow, Progress Publishers, 1960–70, Vol. 33, pp. 593–7, 603–4. There are some minor, but significant differences between the official and unofficial texts. In the unofficial text we read 'Bukharin is not only the most valuable and biggest theoretician of the party'; *see The Suppressed Testament of Lenin*, by Leon Trotsky, London, 1954. This rendering is based upon the Eastman text and is also used as a supplement to *The Real Situation in Russia*, by Trotsky, New York, 1928. It will be seen that in the unofficial text Bukharin is characterised as '*the* most valuable', whilst in the official text it is rendered as '*a* most valuable'. In his testament Lenin did not attempt to solve the problem of how the (a?) most valuable theoretician of a Marxist party could be considered to lack an education in, and an understanding of, dialectics!
5. *See* Stephen F. Cohen, *Bukharin and the Bolshevik Revolution*.
6. Ibid., p. 110.
7. Ibid., p. 122.
8. Introduction to HM, p. 7a.
9. Lukacs, pp. 33–4.
10. HM, p. 11.
11. Ibid., p. 12.
12. Ibid., p. 12.

13. Karl Marx, *Capital*, Vol. III (1962) p. 797.
14. Karl Marx, *A Contribution to the Critique of Political Economy* (1977) p. 206.
15. Ibid., p. 206.
16. HM, p. 13.
17. Ibid., pp. 13–14.
18. Ibid., p. 14.
19. Ibid., p. 14.
20. HM, p. 15.
21. Ibid., p. 14.
22. Karl Marx, *Preface and Introduction to A Contribution to the Critique of Political Economy* (1976) pp. 1–2.
23. Ibid., p. 3.
24. This is not to say, of course, that one should ignore Marx's published works on political economy before 1859. However, the 1859 text does represent a qualitative change, the basis for which may be seen in the *Grundrisse*.
25. Karl Marx and Frederick Engels, *The German Ideology*, 1964, For a shorter and more readable version see the text edited by C.J. Arthur (1970).
26. F. Engels, *Ludwig Feuerbach and the End of Classical German Philosophy*, 1965, p. 5.
27. HM, p. 20.
28. *See* Marx Preface and Introduction (1976) p. 31 for modern translation.
29. HM, p. 20.
30. Marx-Engels *Selected Correspondence*, 1965, p.123.
31. HM, p. 48.
32. Ibid., p. 30.
33. Ibid., p. 31.
34. Ibid., p. 48.
35. Ibid., p. 48
36. HM, p. 51.
37. Ibid., p. 51.
38. HM, p. 67.
39. HM, p.68.
40. Ibid., pp. 69–70.
41. Ibid., pp. 72–73.
42. Ibid., pp. 73–74.
43. Ibid., pp. 74–75.
44. Ibid., pp. 76–77.
45. Ibid., p. 78.
46. Ibid., p. 79.
47. Ibid., p. 104.
48. Karl Marx, 'Economic and Philosophical Manuscripts of 1848' in *Marx–Engels Collected Works*, Vol. 3, pp. 275–6.

49. Karl Marx, *Capital*, Vol. I, 1974, pp. 173–4.
50. HM, p. 121.
51. Lukacs, p. 29. Lukacs substantially repeats this criticism in the preface to a new edition of *History and Class Consciousness*, 1971, p. xxxiii.
52. HM, pp. 132–3.
53. Ibid., pp. 134–5.
54. Ibid., p. 135.
55. Ibid., pp. 136–7.
56. Ibid., p. 138.
57. Ibid., p. 138.
58. Ibid., p. 141.
59. Ibid., p. 148.
60. I will deal with this aspect more fully in the next chapter.
61. HM, p. 144.
62. Ibid., p. 144.
63. Ibid., p. 145.
64. Ibid., pp. 145–6.
65. Ibid., p. 146.
66. Ibid., p .134.
67. Ibid., p. 150.
68. Ibid., p. 158.
69. Ibid., p. 157.
70. Ibid., p. 157.
71. Ibid., p. 157.
72. HM, pp. 157–8.
73. Bukharin, 'The Economics of the Transition Period' in *The Politics and Economics of the Transition Period*, 1979, pp. 58–9.
74. Ibid., p. 59.
75. Ibid., p. 59.
76. HM, pp. 239–40.
77. Ibid., p. 241.
78. Ibid., p. 242.
79. Ibid., p. 243.
80. Ibid., p. 245.
81. Ibid., pp. 248–9.

Chapter 2

1. *See* Michael Haynes, *Nikolai Bukharin and the Transition from Capitalism to Socialism*, p. 48, fn 38.
2. *Antonio Gramsci Life of a Revolutionary*, by Giuseppe Fiori, p. 286, quoted from the inside cover of notebook 18.
3. Gustav A. Wetter, *Dialectical Materialism: A Historical and Systematic Survey of Philosophy in the Soviet Union*, 1958. Hereafter Wetter.

4. Ibid., p. 138.
5. Ibid., p. 140.
6. Ibid., p. 145.
7. HM, p. 189.
8. Ibid., pp. 188–9.
9. Ibid., p. 189.
10. Ibid., p. 20.
11. Ibid., p. 31.
12. Wetter, *Dialectical Materialism*, p. 146.
13. Ibid., p. 146.
14. Ibid., p. 146.
15. HM, p. 75.
16. Wetter, *Dialectical Materialism*, p. 146.
17. HM, p. 64.
18. Ibid., p. 79
19. Wetter, *Dialectical Materialism*, p. 148.
20. F. Engels, *Dialectics of Nature*, 1976, p. 246.
21. Lukacs, p. 28.
22. Ibid., p. 28.
23. Ibid., p. 29.
24. K. Marx, *Capital*, Vol. I, 1915, p. 25.
25. HM, p. 75.
26. Lukacs, p. 29.
27. Ibid., p. 29.
28. K. Marx, *Wage-Labour and Capital*, with an introduction by F. Engels, Lawrence & Wishart, London, 1941, p. 28. *See also Marx–Engels CW*, Vol. 9, p. 211.
29. Lukacs, p. 29.
30. HM, p. 134.
31. Ibid., pp. 135–6.
32. Ibid., p. 136.
33. Lukacs, op. cit. p. 29.
34. Marx, *Capital*, Vol. I, 1974, p. 457.
35. HM, p. 143.
36. Lukacs, p. 29.
37. HM, p. 74.
38. Bernice Shoul demonstrated this her article 'Karl Marx and Say's Law', in *The Quarterly Journal of Economics*, Vol. LXXI, November 1957, pp. 611–29.

Chapter 3

1. Bukharin, *The Politics and Economics of the Transition Period*, p. 149.
2. HM, p. 118.
3. Marx, *A Contribution to the Critique of Political Economy*, p. 190.
4. Marx, *Capital*, Vol. II, 1967, p. 396.

5. Ibid., pp. 397–8.
6. Marx obviously drew inspiration from Quesnay's *Tableau Economique; see* his letter to Engels, dated 6 July 1863, in *Marx–Engels Selected Correspondence*, p. 142.
7. Roman Rosdolsky deals with this neglect in *The Making of Marx's 'Capital'; see* Chapter 3.
8. HM, p. 118.
9. Ibid., p. 119.
10. Ibid., p. 119.
11. Ibid., p. 119.
12. *Die Akkumulation des Kapitals, Ein Beitrag zur okonomishen Erklarung des Imperialismus*, 1913; English edition 1951.
13. *Die Akkumulation des Kapitals oder was die Epigonen aus der Marxschen Theorie gemacht haben, Eine Antikritik*, 1921; English edition 1972.
14. 'Der Imperialismus Und Die Akkumulation Des Kapitals' in *Unter Dem Banner Des Marxismus*, No. 8/9, 1924, Nos. 1/2, 3, 1925; English edition 1972.
15. I have greatly simplified the arguments of Luxemburg here, and would refer the reader to her own text, especially the *Anti-Critique*, and my own introduction to that work which includes a survey of the English language contributions to the debate on Luxemburg's ideas.
16. For the full scope of Bukharin's critique of Luxemburg the reader should consult *Imperialism and the Accumulation of Capital*. In this work I am solely concerned with Bukharin's algebraic formulations.
17. *Imperialism and the Accumulation of Capital*, 1972, p. 154.
18. Ibid., pp. 155–6.
19. For some subsequent developments in this field, *see* Lange (1969), Sweezy (1962), Morishima (1973), Koshimura (1975).
20. The possibility that equilibrium *may* be maintained does not, of course, guarantee such equilibrium. What we have here is a necessary condition, but not a sufficient one.
21. Sweezy, *The Theory of Capitalist Development*, p. 164 fn.
22. Rosdolsky, *The Making of Marx's 'Capital'*, pp. 449–50.
23. Bukharin, *Imperialism and the Accumulation of Capital*, 1972, p. 160; hereafter IAC.
24. We may see why Bukharin's secondary equations do not hold from the following:
Let us look at a numerical model of extended reproduction:
Production Period 1 (PP1)
Dept. I 4400c +1100v + 1100s = 6600
Dept. II 1600c + 400v + 400s = 2400
And setting g' = 0.1 the division of surplus value would be as follows:

I. $440\beta_{c1} + 110\beta_{v1} + 550\alpha_1 = 1100 = s_1$
II. $160\beta_{c2} + 40\beta_{v2} + 200\alpha_2 = 400 = s_2$

PP2

Dept. I $4840c + 1210v + 1210s = 7260$
Dept. II $1760c + 440v + 440s = 2640$
and again assuming $g' = 0.1$

I. $484\beta_{c1} + 121\beta_{v1} + 605\alpha_1 = 1210 = s_1$
II. $176\beta_{c2} + 44\beta_{v2} + 220\alpha_2 = 440 = s_2$

Do Bukharin's secondary equations hold ?
Looking at PP1 we find

$c2 = 1600$, $\beta v1 + \alpha 1 = 1650$, clearly $1600 \neq 1650$, and $\beta c2 = 160$, $\beta v1 = 110$, and again $160 \neq 110$.

And the same applies for PP2. Clearly Bukharin's secondary equations, in the form that he presented them, do not hold.

25. Luxemburg, *The Accumulation of Capital*, 1951, Chapter XXV.
26. I have written in more detail on this point, *see* 'A Note on Luxemburg and the Accumulation of Capital', in *Critique*, No. 14, 1981, pp. 105–8.

Chapter 4

1. Makoto Itoh, *Value and Crisis*, 1980; Sweezy, *The Theory of Capitalist Development*, 1962; Mandel, *Marxist Economic Theory*, 1968; Day, *The 'Crisis' and the 'Crash'*, 1981.
2. Bukharin, *The Politics and Economics of the Transition Period*, 1979; hereafter PETP, p. 149.
3. Ibid., p. 150.
4. Ibid., pp. 122–3.
5. Bukharin, *Imperialism and World Economy*, 1972, p. 104.
6. PETP, p. 151.
7. Ibid., pp. 150–1.
8. Bukharin, IAC, p. 221.
9. Bukharin, 'The Notes of An Economist', p. 5.
10. IAC, p. 222.
11. Ibid., pp. 223–4.
12. Ibid., p. 124.
13. Ibid., p. 225.
14. Hilferding, *Finance Capital*, 1981, p. 261.
15. IAC, pp. 227–8.
17. Ibid., p. 232.

Chapter 5

1. *See* 'The Economics of the Transition Period' in PETP.
2. Parvus was one of these, in his work *Der Staat, die Industrie und der Socializmus, see also* August Bebel in *The Society of the Future*.
3. Rosmer, *Lenin's Moscow*, p. 43.
4. For details *see* Nove, *An Economic History of the USSR*, Dobb, *Soviet*

Economic Development Since 1917; Trotsky, *1905*; Carr, *A History of Soviet Russia, 1917–22*, Vol. II.

5. For Lenin's attitude, *see* Carr, ibid.
6. *See* Cohen, *Bukharin and the Bolshevik Revolution*, Chapter 3; also Daniels, *The Conscience of the Revolution*, Chapter 3; both works have detailed accounts of Bukharin's activities in this period. For the details of the Left-Communists' proposals *see The Theses of the Left Communists (1918)*.
7. Carr, *A History of Soviet Russia*, Vol. II, pp. 176–7, *see also First Decrees of Soviet Power*.
8. Ibid., p. 129.
9. Ibid., p. 144.
10. Serge, *Memoirs of a Revolutionary 1910–1941*, p. 117.
11. PETP, p. 58.
12. Ibid., pp. 59–60.
13. Ibid., p. 60.
14. Ibid., pp. 60–1.
15. Ibid., p. 61.
16. Ibid., p. 61
17. PETP, pp. 62–3.
18. Ibid., p. 66.
19. Ibid., p. 88.
20. Ibid., p. 55.
21. Ibid., p. 80.
22. Ibid., pp. 80–1.
23. Ibid., p. 81.
24. Ibid., p. 82.
25. Davies, *White Eagle-Red Star*, p. 142.
26. Carr, *A History of Soviet Russia*, Vol. II, p. 197.
27. Deutscher, *The Prophet Unarmed*, p. 4.
28. Deutscher, *The Prophet Armed*, p. 488.
29. PETP, pp. 82–3.
30. Ibid., pp. 83–4.
31. Ibid., p. 90.
32. Ibid., p. 112.
33. Ibid., p. 113.
34. Ibid., p. 115.
35. Ibid., p. 115.
36. Ibid., p. 115.
37. Ibid., p. 115.
38. Ibid., p. 115.
39. PETP, p. 116.
40. Ibid., p. 116.
41. Ibid., p. 116.
42. Ibid., p. 116.
43. PETP, pp. 117–18.

44. Ibid., p. 118.
45. Ibid., p. 57.
46. Ibid., p. 146.
47. Ibid., pp. 147-8.
48. Ibid., pp. 150-1.
49. Ibid., p. 154.
50. Ibid., p. 155.
51. Ibid., p. 155.
52. Ibid., p. 155.
53. PETP, p. 156.
54. Ibid., pp. 158-9.
55. Ibid., p. 159.
56. Ibid., p. 159
57. PETP p. 163.
58. Ibid., pp. 163-4.
59. Quoted by Deutscher in *The Prophet Armed*, pp. 496-7.
60. Carr, *A History of Soviet Russia*, Vol. II, Chapters 18 and 19.
61. Published in the Petrograd *Pravda*, quotations taken from unpublished English translation by Oliver Field.
62. Ibid.
63. Ibid.
64. Ibid.
65. Ibid.
66. Ibid.
67. Ibid.
68. *Inprecor*, No. 56, 27 August 1928.
69. Bukharin, *The New Course of Our Economic Policies*.
70. Ibid.

Chapter 6

1. PETP, p. 80.
2. Ibid., pp. 81-2.
3. Ibid., p. 82.
4. I have dealt with the question of unproductive labour at some length in an essay 'Marx, Productive and Unproductive Labour', in *Studies in Political Economy* (Canada) No. 12, Fall 1983.
5. I have published two essays on the problems associated with attributing a surplus-value creating role to armaments production; *see* Bibliography for details.
6. Marx, *Theories of Surplus-Value*, Pt. III, p. 43.
7. Bukharin, *Marxism and Modern Thought*, pp. 57-8.
8. This rearranged model was arrived at by the following method: assuming W = 9000 and assuming the same organic composition of capital, i.e., 4:1, plus s/v = 1; then we have 6000c + 1500v + 1500s = W, let c + v = k, then s/k = p'.
Now let us assume that only 50 per cent of s is consumed

unproductively, and α = unproductive consumption, then $\alpha/s = \underline{b}$ and
$(1- \underline{b}).p' = g' = 0.1$.
Then, $(C/W).(1+g') = \underline{x}$ and $W.\underline{x} = w_1$ and $W\text{-}w_1 = w_2$.

9. Marx, *Theories of Surplus-Value*, Pt. III, p. 370.
10. Marx, *Capital* (1974), p. 220.
11. Ibid., pp. 544–5.
12. Marx, *Theories of Surplus-Value*, Pt. I., pp. 405–6.
13. *See* Chapter 3 of the present work for the determination of $\underline{m}$.

Chapter 7

1. Preobrazhensky, *The New Economics* (1965), p. 60; hereafter NE.
2. Ibid., p. 62.
3. Bukharin, 'On the Question of the Regularities of the Transition Period', *Pravda*, Nos. 148, 150, 154, July 1926. I use an unpublished English translation by Oliver Field; hereafter QRTP.
4. Ibid.
5. Ibid.
6. Ibid.
7. Ibid.
8. NE, p. 8.
9. Marx, *Letters to Kugelmann*, pp. 73–4.
10. QRTP.
11. Ibid.
12. Ibid.
13. Ibid.
14. Ibid.
15. Ibid.
16. Ibid.
17. NE, p. 84.
18. Ibid., p. 146.
19. Ibid., p. 147.
20. Marx, *Capital*, Vol. I (1974), p. 668.
21. Ibid., p. 668.
22. QRTP.
23. The reference by Bukharin to 'third persons' relates to his polemic against Rosa Luxemburg's theory of capitalist accumulation.
24. QRTP.
25. Ibid.
26. Ibid.
27. Ibid.
28. Ibid.
29. Ibid.
30. Ibid.
31. I have given a more formal exposition of these two approaches in the Appendix at the end of this volume.

Chapter 8

1. *See* Lewin, *Russian Peasants and Soviet Power* (1968), Chapter 8.
2. *See* Rosa Levine-Meyer, *Inside German Communism*, pp. 214–18 for her account.
3. Bukharin, 'The Political Testament of Lenin'.
4. Ibid.
5. Ibid.
6. Ibid.
7. Bukharin, 'The Notes of An Economist'; hereafter NAE. Again I use an unpublished translation by Oliver Field.
8. Ibid.
9. Ibid.
10. Ibid.
11. Ibid.
12. Ibid.
13. Ibid.
14. Ibid.
15. Ibid.
16. Ibid.
17. Ibid. ·
18. *See* Lewin, *Political Undercurrents in the Soviet Economic Debates* (1975), p. 66.
19. NAE.
20. Ibid.
21. Ibid.
22. Ibid.
23. Ibid.
24. Cliff, *Stalinist Russia* (1964), p. 35.
25. Medvedev, *Let History Judge* (1976), p. 103.
26. Ibid., p. 107.
27. Jasny, *Soviet Economists of the Twenties* (1972), p. 45.
28. Conquest, *The Great Terror*, p. 45.
29. Ibid., p. 46.
30. Ibid. p. 47.
31. Jasny, *Soviet Economists*, p. 51.
32. Mandel, writing under the *nom de plume* of E. Germain in *Fourth International*, Paris, No. 4, Autumn 1958, p. 15.
33. Ibid., p. 16.
34. Ibid., p. 17.
35. Lewin, *Russian Peasants*, p. 397.
36. Lewin, *Political Undercurrents*, p. 63.

Chapter 9

1. Day, Introduction to *N.I. Bukharin: Selected Writings on the State and the Transition to Socialism* (1982).

2. Erlich, *The Soviet Industrialization Debate*, p. 9.
3. On Trotsky's doubts and uncertainties, *see* Day, *Leon Trotsky and the Politics of Isolation*, Chapter 4; and Deutscher, *The Prophet Unarmed*. Deutscher in particular recounts Trotsky's recurrent bouts of illness during the mid-1920s which seem to have had vague symptoms and thus were not amenable to precise diagnosis and treatment. These bouts seem to have coincided with political crises that Trotsky faced. *See* Chapter 2 for details of this.
4. Lewin, *Political Undercurrents*, p. 33.
5. See R.W. Davies Introduction to Christian Rakovsky's 'The Five Year Plan in Crisis', in *Critique*, No. 13, 1981.
6. This is illustrated in Preobrazhensky's 'Economic Equilibrium in the System of the USSR' in *The Crisis of Soviet Industrialization*.
7. *See* Trotsky, *The First Five Years of the Communist International*, Vols I and II. His speeches to the Comintern are studded with references to and analyses of equilibrium. *See also* his 'Towards Capitalism or Socialism' in *The Challenge of the Left Opposition 1923-25*.
8. From late 1928 onwards Trotsky developed a critique of the industrialisation drive and the forced collectivisation which clearly coincided with Bukharin's criticisms. *See* his numerous articles in *Political Writings*, for 1929, 1930, and 1930-1. For example we may cite: 'In June [1925] I wrote to Dzershinsky and Pyatakov, warning that this hurry-scurry was leading in a fatal way to a financial and industrial crisis. Neither ... understood, they even accused me ... of speaking up "against industrialization". I pointed out to them that the overall material base of industrialization, given a correct policy, could be considerably increased; but on the *given* material base industrialization should not be pushed ahead with the help of unreal credits.' And 'I have given this example in order to show that our industrialization program was never an abstract "general line" of bureaucrats but flowed from an appraisal of the living and active equilibrium between economic factors and class relations.' And 'in my opinion we are heading for a disturbance of the total economic equilibrium and consequently of the social equilibrium', *Writings 1929*, pp. 401-2.
9. Trotsky, *Challenge of the Left Opposition 1928-9*, p. 273.
10. Stalin, *Collected Works*, Vol. 12, p. 149.
11. Trotsky, 'Notes on Economic Questions' in *The Challenge of the Left Opposition 1926-27*.
12. There is a considerable element of 'Bukharinism' to be found in the writings of Ernest Mandel, who is one of the foremost international exponents of Trotskyism in modern times. *See* his *Marxist Economic Theory* where he puts forward ideas on negative expanded reproduction and optimum versus maximum rates of investment in the Soviet Union.

188 Bukharin's Theory of Equilibrium

13. For evidence of this, *see* Day, *Leon Trotsky and the Politics of Isolation*, pp. 117–18.
14. *See* Deutscher, *The Prophet Unarmed*, for the evidence of the mooted Trotsky–Bukharin 'bloc'.
15. Trotsky, *Challenge*, p. 145.
16. *See* pp. 138–9 where Engels warns of the fate of leaders who assume power before the social, economic and historical conditions are ripe for them to do so; e.g. 'The worst thing that can befall a leader of an extreme party is to be compelled to take over a government in an epoch when the movement is not yet ripe for the domination of the class which he represents.'

Bibliography

Section A: Writings of Nikolai I. Bukharin
[In order of writing by Bukharin]

Imperialism and World Economy, Merlin Press, London, 1972.

The Economic Theory of the Leisure Class, International Publishers, New York, 1927.

The ABC of Communism: A Popular Explanation of the Programme of the Communist Party of Russia (with E. Preobrazhensky), Communist Party of Great Britain, London, 1926.

The Politics and Economics of the Transition Period, edited and with an introduction by K.J. Tarbuck, Routledge & Kegan Paul, London, 1979.

Historical Materialism: A System of Sociology, with a new introduction by Alfred G. Meyer, University of Michigan Press, Ann Arbor, 1969.

The New Course of Our Economic Policy, Petrograd, 1921.

Imperialism and the Accumulation of Capital; *see* under Tarbuck.

'A New Revelation About Soviet Economics, or How the Worker–Peasant Bloc Can Be Destroyed (On the Question of the Economic Basis of Trotskyism), *Pravda*, No. 283, 12 December 1924.

'Concerning the Theories of Permanent Revolution', *Inprecor*, 7 February 1925.

'A Criticism of the Economic Platform of the Opposition', *Bolshevik*, No. 1, 1925.

Lenin as a Marxist, CPGB, London, 1925.

'The New Economic Policy in the Village', *Inprecor*, 30 May, 1925.

'On the Question of the Regularities of the Transition Period', *Pravda*, Nos 148, 150, 154, July 1926.

'The Party and the Opposition Bloc', *The Communist Review*, London, October, November, December 1926.

'Ten Years of Victorious Proletarian Revolution', *Inprecor*, Nos 3, 10, 1927.

'Notes of An Economist', *Pravda*, Nos 148, 150, 154, July 1928.

'The Problems of the New Economic Policy and War Communism', *Inprecor*, 27 August 1928.

'Lenin's Political Testament', *Pravda*, No. 19, January 1929.

'Organised Mismanagement in Modern Society', *Essential Works of Socialism*, Irving Howe, Bantam Books, New York, 1971.

'Marx's Teaching and its Historical Importance', *Marxism and Modern Thought*, Routledge, London, 1935.

Selected Writings on the State and the Transition to Socialism, translated, edited and introduced by Richard B. Day, with forewords by Stephen F. Cohen and Ken Coates, Spokesman Books, Nottingham, 1982.

Section B: Other Works

Abramovich, Raphael R., *The Soviet Revolution 1917–1939*, International Universities Press, New York, 1962.

Arthur, C.J. (ed.) *The German Ideology*, by K. Marx and F. Engels, Lawrence & Wishart, London, 1970.

Carr, E.H., 'The Legend of Bukharin', *Times Literary Supplement*, 20 September 1974; *A History of Soviet Russia: The Bolshevik Revolution 1917–1923*, 3 Vols, Pelican Books, Harmondsworth, 1966; *The Interregnum 1923–1924*, Pelican, 1966; *Socialism in One Country 1924–1926*, 3 Vols, Pelican, 1970.

Carr, E.H. and Davies, R.W., *Foundations of A Planned Economy 1926–1929*, Vol. 1, Macmillan, London, 1969.

Carr, E.H., *Foundations of A Planned Economy 1926–1929*, Vol. 2, Macmillan, London, 1971.

Coates, Ken, *The Case of Nikolai Bukharin*, Spokesman Books, Nottingham, 1978.

Cohen, Stephen F., *Bukharin and the Bolshevik Revolution: A Political Biography 1888–1938*, Alfred K. Knopf, New York, 1973.

Conquest, Robert, *The Great Terror – Stalin's Purge of the Thirties*, Pelican, London, 1971.

Cliff, Tony, *Russia: A Marxist Analysis*, International Socialism, London, 1964.

Crisp, Olga, *Studies In the Russian Economy Before 1914*, Macmillan, London, 1976.

Dallemagne, J-L., 'Justice for Bukharin', *Critique*, Glasgow, No. 4, Spring 1975.

Daniels, Robert V., *The Conscience of the Revolution – Communist Opposition in Soviet Russia*, Harvard University Press, Mass., 1960.

Davies, Norman, *White Eagle–Red Star: The Polish–Soviet War 1919–20*, Macdonald, London, 1972.

Day, Richard B., 'Historical Method in the Political Writings of Lenin and Bukharin', *Canadian Journal of Political Science*, Vol. IX, No. 2, June 1976, pp. 244–60; 'Trotsky and Preobrazhensky: The Troubled

Unity of the Left Opposition', *Studies in Comparative Communism*, Vol. X, Spring/Summer, 1977; *Leon Trotsky and the Politics of Economic Isolation*, Cambridge University Press, London, 1973; *The 'Crisis' and the 'Crash': Soviet Studies of the West (1917–1939)*, New Left Books, London, 1981.

Deutscher, Isaac, *The Prophet Armed: Trotsky 1879–1921*, Oxford University Press, London, 1954; *The Prophet Unarmed: Trotsky 1921–1929*, OUP, 1959.

Dobb, Maurice, *Soviet Economic Development Since 1917*, International Publishers, New York, 1966.

Dunayevskaya, Raya, *Marxism and Freedom*, Pluto Press, London 1971; *Philosophy and Revolution*, Dell Publishing, New York, 1973.

Engels, Frederick, *Ludwig Feuerbach and the End of Classical German Philosophy*, Progress Publishers, Moscow, 1969; *Dialectics of Nature*, Progress, Moscow, 1976; *The Peasant War in Germany*, FLPH, Moscow, 1956.

Erdos, Peter, *Contributions to the Theory of Capitalist Money, Business Fluctuations and Crises*, Akademiai Kiado, Budapest, 1971.

Erlich, Alexander, *The Soviet Industrialization Debate 1924–1928*, Harvard University Press, Mass., 1960.

Filtzer, Donald, 'Preobrazhensky and the Problem of the Soviet Transition', in *Critique*, No. 9, Spring/Summer 1978.

Fiori, Giuseppe, *Antonio Gramsci: Life of a Revolutionary*, New Left Books, London 1970.

First Decrees of Soviet Power, Lawrence & Wishart, London, 1970.

Gramsci, Antonio, *Selections from the Prison Notebooks*, edited and translated by Quintin Hoare and Geoffrey Nowell Smith, Lawrence & Wishart, London, 1971.

Haynes, Michael, *Nikolai Bukharin and the Transition from Capitalism to Socialism*, Croom Helm, London 1985.

Heitman, Sidney, 'Between Lenin and Stalin: Nikolai Bukharin' in *Revisionism: Essay in the History of Marxist Ideas*, ed. Leopold Labedz, Praeger, New York, 1962; 'Nikolai Ivanovich Bukharin' in *Problems of Communism*, November–December 1967; *Nikolai I. Bukharin – A Bibliography*, The Hoover Institute on War, Revolution and Peace, Stanford University Press, 1969.

Hilferding, Rudolf, *Finance Capital*, edited with an introduction by Tom Bottomore, Routledge & Kegan Paul, London, 1981.

Itoh, Makoto, *Value and Crisis*, Pluto Press, London 1980.

Jasny, Naum, *Soviet Economists of the Twenties – Names to be Remembered*, Cambridge University Press, London, 1972.

Kaser, Michael, 'Stalin and Russia's Great Leap Forward', the *Financial*

Times, 25 September 1969.

Katkov, George, *The Trial of Bukharin*, Batsford, London, 1969.

Kay, Geoffrey, *Development and Underdevelopment*, Macmillan, London, 1975.

Kemp, Tom, *Historical Patterns of Industrialisation*, Longman, London, 1978.

Knei-Paz, Baruch, *The Social and Political Thought of Leon Trotsky*, Clarendon Press, Oxford, 1978.

Kondratieff, N.D., 'The Long Cycles', *The Review of Economic Statistics*, November, 1935.

Korsch, Karl, *Marxism and Philosophy*, New Left Books, London 1970.

Koshimura, Shinzaburo, *Theory of Capital Reproduction and Accumulation*, ed. Jesse G. Schwartz, DRG Publishing, Kitchener, Ontario, 1975.

Lange, Oskar, *Theory of Reproduction and Accumulation*, Pergamon Press, Oxford, 1969.

Leibman, Marcel, 'Bukharinism, Revolution and Social Development', *Socialist Register 1975*, Merlin, London, 1975.

Lenin, V.I., 'Letter to the Congress' in *Collected Works, 4th edition*, Vol. 33, Progress Publishers, Moscow, 1960–1970, pp. 593–7.

Levine-Meyer, Rosa, *Inside German Communism – Memoirs of Party Life in the Weimer Republic*, edited and introduced by David Zane Mairowitz, Pluto Press, London, 1977.

Lewin, Moshe, *Russian Peasants and Soviet Power*, Allen & Unwin, London, 1968; *Lenin's Last Struggle*, Faber, London, 1969; *Political Undercurrents in Soviet Economic Debates*, Pluto Press, London, 1975.

Lukacs, Georg, 'Technology and Social Relations', *New Left Review*, No. 39 September–October, 1966; *History and Class Consciousness*, Merlin, London, 1968.

Luxemburg, Rosa, *The Accumulation of Capital*, with an introduction by Joan Robinson, Routledge & Kegan Paul, London, 1951; 'The Accumulation of Capital or What the Epigones Have Made of Marx's Theory – An Anti-Critique', *Imperialism and the Accumulation of Capital, see* under Tarbuck.

Mandel, Ernest, 'The Industrialisation of Backward Countries' under the *nom de plume* E. Germain, *Fourth International*, Paris, No. 4, Autumn 1958; *Marxist Economic Theory*, Merlin, London, 1968; *Late Capitalism*, New Left Books, London, 1975.

Marx, Karl, *Letters to Kugelmann*, Martin Lawrence, London, nd; *Grundrisse*, Allen Lane, London, 1975; *A Contribution to the Critique of Political Economy*, Progress, Moscow, 1977.

Preface and Introduction to *A Contribution to the Critique of Political Economy*, Foreign Languages Press, Peking, 1976; *Capital*, Vol. I, Progress, Moscow, 1965, 1970, 1974; *Capital*, Vol. I, Penguin, Harmondsworth, 1976; *Capital*, Vol. II, Progress, Moscow, 1967; *Capital*, Vol. II, Kerr, Chicago, 1915; *Capital*, Vol. III, Progress, Moscow, 1962; *Theories of Surplus-Value*, Vols I, II & III, Progress, Moscow, 1975.

Marx, Karl and Engels, Frederick, *The German Ideology*, Progress, Moscow, 1969; *Marx–Engels Selected Correspondence*, Progress Publishers, Moscow, 1965; *Marx–Engels Collected Works*, Lawrence & Wishart, London 1975 onwards.

Medvedev, Roy A., *Let History Judge*, Spokesman Books, Nottingham, 1976; *Nikolai Bukharin: The Last Years*, Norton, New York, 1980.

Morishima, M., *Marx's Economics: A Dual Theory of Value and Growth*, Cambridge University Press, Cambridge, 1973.

McKay, John F., *Pioneers for Profit: Foreign Entrepreneurship and Russian Industrialisation 1885–1913*, University of Chicago Press, 1972.

McNeal, Robert H., *Bride of the Revolution*, University of Michigan Press, Ann Arbor.

Narkiewicz, Olga A., *The Making of the Soviet State Apparatus*, Manchester University Press, 1970.

Nicolaevsky, Boris, *Letters of An Old Bolshevik*, ed. J.D. Zagoria, Praeger, New York, 1965.

Novack, George, *Polemics in Marxist Philosophy*, Monad Press, New York, 1978.

Nove, Alec, *An Economic History of the USSR*, Penguin Books, Harmondsworth, 1972.

Parvus (A.I. Helphand) *Der Staat, die Industrie und der Socializmus*, Dresden, 1910.

Pethybridge, Roger, *The Social Prelude to Stalinism*, Macmillan, London, 1974.

Preobrazhensky, E., *The New Economics*, with an introduction by Alec Nove, Oxford University Press, 1965; *The Crisis of Soviet Industrialisation: Selected Essays*, edited with an introduction by Donald A. Filtzer, Macmillan, London, 1980.

Rosdolsky, Roman, *The Making of Marx's 'Capital'*, Pluto Press, London, 1977.

Rosmer, Alfred, *Lenin's Moscow*, Pluto Press, London, 1972.

Serge, Victor, *Year One of the Russian Revolution*, translated and edited by Peter Sedgwick, Allen Lane, London, 1972; *Memoirs of a Revolutionary 1901–1941*, translated and edited by Peter Sedgwick,

Oxford University Press, 1967.

Seton-Watson, Hugh, *The Russian Empire 1801–1917*, OUP, London, 1967.

Shachtman, Max, *The Bureaucratic Revolution*, The Donal Press, New York, 1962.

Shoul, Bernice, 'Karl Marx and Say's Law', *Quarterly Journal of Economics*, Vol. LXXI, November 1957.

Smith, Keith, 'Economic Theory and the Closure of the Soviet Industrialization Debate', in *Economy and Society*, Vol. 8, No. 4.

Spulber, Nicolas, ed., *Foundations of Soviet Strategy for Economic Growth: Selected Essays 1924–1930*, Indiana University Press, Bloomington, 1964.

Stalin, J.V., *Collected Works*, Foreign Languages Publishing House, Moscow, 1955.

Sweezy, Paul M., *The Theory of Capitalist Development*, Dobson, London, 1962.

Szamuely, Lazzlo, *First Models of Socialist Economic Systems*, Akademiai Kiado, Budapest, 1974.

Tarbuck, Kenneth J., 'Rosa Luxemburg and the Economics of Militarism', *The Subtle Anatomy of Capitalism*, ed. Jesse G. Schwartz, Goodyear, California, 1977; 'Ernest Mandel and the Permanent Arms Economy: A Critique', *Intervention*, No. 3, Summer 1979; 'A Note on Luxemburg and the Accumulation of Capital', *Critique*, No. 14, 1981; 'Marx, Productive and Unpro-ductive Labour', *Studies in Political Economy*, Canada, No. 12, 1983; (Ed. and introduction to) *Imperialism and the Accumulation of Capital*, by Rosa Luxemburg and N.I. Bukharin, Allen Lane, London, 1972.

'Theses of the Left Communists' (1918), *Critique*, Glasgow, 1977.

Timpanaro, Sebastian, *On Materialism*, New Left Books, London, 1976.

Trotsky, L.D., *1905*, Allen Lane, London, 1971; *The First Five Years of the Communist International*, New Park, London, Vol. I, 1973, Vol. II, 1953; *The Real Situation in Russia*, Harcourt & Brace, New York, 1926; *The Suppressed Testament of Lenin*, New Park, London, 1954; *The Challenge of the Left Opposition 1923–25*, Pathfinder, New York, 1975; *The Challenge of the Left Opposition 1926–27*, Pathfinder 1980; *The Challenge of the Left Opposition 1928–29*, Pathfinder, 1981; *Political Writings*, 1929, 1930, 1930–1, Pathfinder, New York, 1973–5.

Wetter, Gustav, *Dialectical Materialism: A Historical and Systematic Survey of Philosophy in the Soviet Union*, Routledge & Kegan Paul, London, 1958.

Name Index

Bauer, Otto, 58
Bogdanov, A., 37
Brezhnev, L., ix

Cohen, Stephen F., 7, 35
Conquest, Robert, 156

Darwin, 14, 15
Day, Richard B., 73, 161
Deutscher, Isaac, 94, 165
Dunayevskaya, Raya, 35

Eastman, Max, 177 fn. 4
Engels, Frederick, 4, 13, 15, 42, 46,
    50, 55, 161, 168–9, 188 fn. 16
Erlich, Alexander, 162

Field, Oliver, 3

Gorbachev, Mikhail, viii
Gramsci, Antonio, 34, 35

Harrod, Sir Roy, 69–70
Haynes, Michael, 179 fn. 1
Hegel, 17–18, 39, 44–5
Hilferding, Rudolf, 76

Itoh, Makoto, 72

Jasny, Naum, 156, 157

Kamenev, L. B., 145–6, 167
Kautsky, Karl, 58
Khrushchev, N., viii
Kirov, Sergei, vii
Korsch, Karl, 35

Lassalle, Ferdinand, 14
Lenin, V.I., vii, 6, 7, 11, 23, 35, 38–9,
    40, 42, 50, 84–7, 146–7, 177 fn. 4
Levine-Meyer, Rosa, 146
Lewin, Moshe, 145, 158, 162–3, 165

Liebman, Marcel, 35
Lukacs, Georg, 6, 7, 23–7, 34, 36, 43–
    9, 177 fn. 3, 179, fn. 51
Luxemburg, Rosa, 58–9, 61, 67–8, 77,
    93, 185, fn. 23

Mandel, Ernest, 73, 157, 187 fn. 12
Marx, Karl, 4, 9, 10, 12, 13–15, 19, 20,
    22–3, 29, 38–9, 44–6, 48, 50, 52–6,
    58–9, 62–3, 65, 71–2, 75, 77, 114–
    120, 127–8, 131–2, 136–7, 150,
    161, 168
Medvedev, Roy, 156
Mehring, Franz, 43
Meyer, Alfred G., 7
Meyer, Ernst, 146
Molotov, V., 156

Parvus, 182 fn. 2
Plekhanov, Georg, 43
Preobrazhensky, E., 4, 112, 126–44,
    164–5, 166, 175–6, 187 fn. 6

Quesnay, 181 fn. 6

Rosdolsky, Roman, 65–6
Rosmer, Alfred, 84–5

Serge, Victor, 88
Shoul, Bernice, 180 fn. 38
Smith, Adam, 114
Stalin (Stalinist), viii, ix, 4, 5, 146–8,
    156, 158, 165–8
Sweezy, Paul M., 65–6, 73

Trotsky, L. D., vii, 5, 84, 105–6, 126,
    145–6, 148, 164–9, 177 fn. 4, 187

Van Halban, 51, 53

Wetter, Gustav, 36–42

Zinoviev, Grigori, 145, 167

Subject Index.

accumulation, theoretical rate of, 64, 67–71
aggregates, 24, 31, 34, 89
anarchy: of capitalist production, 74, 76–7, 89, 90, 91; of peasant production, 98, 151

causality, 14–16, 36
class struggle, 14, 75, 147
Communist International, 6
contradiction, 2, 17–20, 22, 29, 30, 33, 40, 44, 52, 70, 74
crisis, 72–83, 92, 149, 150, 155

dialectics, 6–7, 16–18, 31, 34–6, 38–9, 41, 43–6, 50, 51
disproportionality, 72, 74–7, 83, 150
division of labour, 25–8, 47–8, 90, 100

equilibrium defined: stable 18; unstable 19
essentialism, 9–11

fatalism, 15–16
First Five Year Plan (FFYP), 25, 125, 145, 148, 156–8, 163

Glasnost, viii

historical abstraction, 9–13, 15, 50, 130

ideas, production of, 29
imperialism, 61, 89, 92
industrialisation, 1, 4, 152, 166, 187 fn. 8
inevitability of socialism, 16

Kronstadt rebellion, 85, 106

Left Social-Revolutionaries, 86

market socialism, 4–5, 98, 112
mixed economy, viii, 111

morality, rules of, 29
Moscow Trials, vii

motion, origin of, 17–18, 36, 39, 40–2

naturalisation of economics, 5, 99, 111
necessary conditions, 15, 51, 53
New Economic Policy (NEP), viii, 2, 88, 105–12, 133, 148, 152, 164, 168

optimum growth, 153–5, 159–60, 165

Perestroika, viii
primitive socialist accumulation, 127, 131, 134–42, 166
proletarian science, 9, 11
proportional labour expenditure (law of), 132–3, 140–2
proportionality (proportional growth), 2, 46, 56, 58, 63, 65, 77, 80, 125, 152, 165

regularity (in nature and society), 13–16, 38, 51
reproduction: negative, 93–5, 110, 113–25
reproduction: simple, 19, 54–5, 57–8, 65–6, 93, 113; extended, 19, 54–5, 57–8, 65–6, 113
reproduction schemes, 19, 20, 52–3, 56, 58–9, 60–4, 67, 115–17, 122–5
revolution (necessary conditions for), 32

slavery (slave labour), 25–6
socialism in one country, 167

technology, 7, 23–7, 43, 46–50, 162

unproductive consumption, 60–1, 64, 67–8, 78, 114–20, 147, 148 fn. 4

value, 55–6, 60, 66, 75, 101–2, 114, 127, 131–5, 139

War Communism, 85, 88, 93, 98, 106, 109, 110, 163
Worker-Peasant Alliance, 2, 11